Tom Murton, a professional penologist, was Assistant Professor of Criminology at Southern Illinois University, prior to taking on the task of reforming the Arkansas Prison System. Before that he had served in Alaska as Superintendent of an Army stockade and five other institutions. When Alaska was granted statehood, he became acting Chief of Corrections, in which post he was responsible for developing the institutional programs of the new system.

Joe Hyams got his education from Harvard and New York University, and from being the West Coast Bureau Chief for the New York *Herald Tribune* from 1952 to 1964. In his post as Bureau Chief he covered every major news story in the West Coast area. He left the newspaper to become a full-time freelance writer; *A Field of Buttercups*, the biography of Polish educator Janusz Korczak, who died with two hundred orphans in Treblinka, is his most recent book prior to working with Tom Murton on *Accomplices to the Crime*.

Accomplices to the Crime

by Tom Murton, *Superintendent from February, 1967, to March, 1968, in the Arkansas Prison System*

and Joe Hyams

Grove Press, Inc., New York

*Copyright © 1969
by Thomas O. Murton and
Joe Hyams*
All Rights Reserved
First Evergreen Black Cat Edition 1970

First Printing
Manufactured in the
United States of America
Library of Congress Catalog
Card Number: 68-58147

No part of this book may be reproduced, for any reason, by any means, including any method of photographic reproduction, without the permission of the publisher.

For the inmates of the Arkansas State Penitentiary, both living and dead.

The captain asked the preacher, "Preacher, you think you can pick me three hundred pounds of cotton?"

The preacher said, "Captain, if the Lord's willing, I will get it for you."

But the preacher didn't get it, so that night the captain gave him ten hot ones across the back and asked, "Now preacher, you think you can pick me three hundred pounds of cotton tomorrow?"

And the preacher said, "Captain, I'm going to get it for you if the Lord is willing."

But he didn't get it on that day, so they whipped him again.

The next day when the captain asked the preacher if he could get three hundred pounds of cotton, the preacher said, "If the damn stuff's in the field I'll get it."

The preacher had learned his lesson. The Lord had forsaken His children in the Arkansas pen.

—*Parable from the Arkansas State Penitentiary*

Contents

PREFACE/*xiii*

Going In/1
Oh, Captain!/5
Reformers/17
Arkie-ology/22
Weevils and Beans/34
The Tucker Time Tunnel/41
The Real Heroes/49
The Freeworld Missionaries/62
The Convict Posse/69
The Condemned Prisoners/77
The Swinging Preacher/83
Sex and Isolation/90
Profit-Making—Modern Slavery; Modern Medicine/97
Committees, Consultants, and Commodes/112
Uptight/127
Rockefeller's Contribution/133
The Eleventh Hour/146
How Many Prisoners?/159
The Four and One-Half Pound Menace/170
Arkansas' "Model Prison System"/182
The "Paupers' Graveyard"/188
The Wipe Out/196

EPILOGUE:
  Politics/207
  Murton's Failings: Fictions and Facts/216
  The Spiral of Reform/223

Preface

A casual reader might say about this book, "Well, that was Arkansas. It could never happen here." The more callous ones will simply say: "At least it was done to convicts, and not decent people."

Some of the newsmen sent to Arkansas to write of the prison atrocities posed this provocative question: "How could this happen in twentieth century, civilized America?"

Prisons, mental hospitals, and other institutions are a thermometer that measures the sickness of the larger society. The treatment society affords its outcasts reveals the way in which its members view one another—and themselves. In a civilized country, is a man only his success? Or do we still value the life in a man who has stolen, murdered, or been unjustly convicted? Each member of our society must decide what treatment *he* wants our outcasts to receive: whether they should be destroyed, or given a chance to reconstruct their lives.

This is the story of my year as prison superintendent in the Arkansas State Penitentiary System. It deals with prisoners, penologists, and politicians. But it is not just a prison story: it is a universal story, unlimited by geography, time, or occupation. In varying degrees of sophistication, your institution, your power structure, and your town, are visiting humiliation and degradation on men—dehumanizing humans. We maintain the posture of respectability by engaging the services of "the professional"; the case worker, the organizational chart, the investigative report, the recommendations for change, and the staff meeting, all attest to the validity of the claim that we are being properly "cared for." But we, the inmates of our culture, recognize the claim for what it really is—pure mythology.

This travesty is possible only because we do not challenge the system. We, by default, contribute to its perpetuation. No significant innovation, discovery, or creation in the history of mankind has been a product of conformity. Yet the majority of the population justifies its inaction with clichés like, "You can't fight City Hall," or, "What can one person do?" These beliefs are merely the constructs of cowardice. You *can* fight City Hall (although you may not "win"), and one individual *can* bring about significant change.

To engage in such an effort, one must first re-examine his concepts of "success" and "failure." One definition of "success" might be the full use of one's intellect, training, and resources to correct an intolerable wrong. "Failure," then, would be not making a total commitment of one's talents toward this end.

To sustain oneself in this lonely venture, the true reformer, as opposed to the official reformer, must subordinate his professional success to his primary mission—doing what needs to be done for the benefit of his fellow men.

There is little danger for the expert who sits, detached from the real world, and expounds on what should be done. But then, he does not have much impact on the system, either. Real change is brought about by those who have both the vision and the power to effect it—hence, the most effective reformer is the person within the power structure. But he must move quickly, for the body politic will waste little time rejecting this foreign organism. Integrity is not a very marketable commodity, and the career crusader is not self-sustaining, because the occupation itself is self-defeating. The true reformer must accept each challenge with the knowledge that ultimately he will be consumed in the process.

The cynic quickly steps forward to pose the question: "Is it worth it?"

And by his answer, each man not only determines his destiny, but also declares his view of man.

—*Tom Murton*

Accomplices
to the
Crime

Going In

There was a .38-caliber revolver under the seat of my Ford van that evening in early February, 1967. I had just come from state police headquarters in Little Rock, Arkansas, where I had been sworn in as a major in the Arkansas State Police, so that I could legally carry a revolver. The rank would also allow me to immediately assume charge of the Tucker Prison Farm and the state police detachment, if the prison board should fire me as superintendent.

The gun gave me little comfort, though. I was bone tired after having driven nonstop in a thin rain for eleven hours from Illinois, where I had left my family. And I was apprehensive about what lay ahead of me.

If I had to use the gun, my trip would be in vain, and my confidence in my ability to take over Tucker without violence would be shattered.

Tucker had been without a superintendent for weeks, and the prison was in a state of siege, ready to explode. One superintendent had lasted only ninety days before he had been fired. After him came "Pink" Booher, my immediate predecessor; he had been on the job only thirty days when the state police discovered him sitting in his office, a Thompson submachine gun on his lap, challenging the inmates to "cross the line." Booher was fired by the new governor, Winthrop Rockefeller, for his own safety as well as that of the inmates.

Now the inmates were almost completely in charge of the prison, and the state police had been brought in to maintain order.

The situation was ludicrous, and frightening. Arkansas still uses the system of having inmates, called trusties, carry arms and serve as the prison guard force. Most of the seventy-six trusties, who would be my "staff," were serving long sentences for armed robbery or murder.

When Governor Rockefeller had visited the prison in mid-January, two weeks after taking office, his car had been stopped and the state troopers escorting him were forced to turn over their guns to the convict-guards.

Now I was being brought in, heralded as the man who would purge the system of corruption, brutality, and exploitation that was as old as the State of Arkansas itself. I was only too well aware that the trusties were opposed to me: any reform of the prison operation would affect their power and relatively easy lives.

The trusties were being kept in control only by the presence of unarmed state troopers, who were at the prison on an emergency basis under the command of Captain R.E. Brown. It was Brown who had escorted me the thirty-five miles from Little Rock through the dreary, flat countryside to Tucker.

Although Captain Brown's car was in the lead and we were expected, as we drove toward the guard shack on the edge of the prison farm an inmate signaled us to stop. A spotlight pierced the drizzle of rain, outlining a man wearing a khaki shirt and trousers with a .38 strapped on his hip.

I reached under the car seat, unholstered my own gun, and slipped it into the waistband of my trousers.

We were stopped, but then we were allowed to pass without difficulty, and I breathed easier as I followed Captain Brown along the macadam road past the infirmary, which was bathed in lights, to the huge two-story, ante-bellum mansion known as the Big House. Designed for gracious living and entertaining with a slave staff, the white-columned Big House was a silent testimonial to the not very distant days when the prison superintendent had been a fat-cat political appointee.

The Big House was lit up too. Thirteen state troopers were quartered there. There were troopers sleeping on cots downstairs in the living and dining rooms, and in all of the seven bedrooms. The one or two troopers who

Going In

were awake greeted me with the kind of reservation one uses with someone he doesn't expect to see again. I am certain that in their eyes I was as temporary as my predecessors.

I thanked Captain Brown for his services, told him he was to continue in command until I was ready to take over, and then sought out an empty bed. I was stopped in the hallway by the coldest eyes I have ever seen staring at me: a huge, audacious rat challenged my progress and withdrew only when I made threatening sounds.

I finally found a cot in the bedroom assigned to me by Captain Brown and crawled into it, only to lie awake listening to the rats, which seemed to be having bowling practice in the eaves. I heard the footsteps of troopers pounding back and forth across the corridors as they came on and off duty. I would not have been able to sleep anyway, because my mind was too busy with the job at hand. It was a job I had deliberately sought out, well aware that it would be the toughest I had ever encountered.

My story, which was to reach its grim climax eleven months later in January, 1968, when I discovered on Cummins Prison Farm the skeletons of three prisoners who had been murdered there, must begin with the Arkansas State Penitentiary System itself—an isolated remnant of an ancient philosophy of retribution, corruption, exploitation, sadism, and brutality.

As far back as 1897, the legislature authorized the acquisition of land to make the penitentiary a self-supporting enterprise. The initial acreage for what is now known as Cummins Prison Farm was acquired in 1902.

In 1916, more land was purchased for another farm, known as Tucker Prison Farm. Additional parcels of land were bought from time to time, until the prison holdings exceeded 21,000 acres.

At first, the prison development was very much like that in other states. Road gangs, forestry camps, prison farms, and similar facilities have long been used to relieve the crowded conditions of the parent prison, and at the same time provide useful goods or services for the state.

What happened next, however, is probably unique to Arkansas. In the 1920's, the electric chair and the prisoners on death row were moved from the main prison building in Little Rock to Tucker Prison Farm. Then the rest of the prisoners were transferred from the prison to either Tucker or Cummins, and the main prison was torn down to make room for state police headquarters.

The isolated prison farms evolved as a closed, dark, self-perpetuating system. From time to time, rumors would leak out of the atrocities on the prison farms.

But in Arkansas, people think a convict is sub-human, a moral pauper incapable of telling the truth, and that concept prepared the public to discount these reports of atrocities as unbelievable. They were unbelievable, but they were also true.

Oh, Captain!

For years, inmates of Tucker and Cummins had been smuggling letters out to newspapers telling of brutalities and extortion. The letters were mainly viewed with skepticism, but Larry Fugate of the *Pine Bluff Commercial* saved the letters and, in time, decided they formed a pattern that went beyond the usual complaints of convicts.

He took the letters to Orval Faubus, the governor then, who sent the Criminal Investigation Division (CID) of the state police to Tucker to investigate. That was in August, 1966.

The police, ostensibly checking on reports of excessive drinking and whiskey peddling, uncovered instead a horrifying pattern of extortion, whipping, and torture.

Arkansas was the only state in the United States where whipping was authorized by law and still practiced. Whippings were conducted without hearings and at the whim of The Man—the superintendent—who generally wielded the strap himself until he was tired. The CID investigators found that the strap—more than five feet long, five inches wide, three-eighths of an inch thick, with an eighteen-inch wooden handle—was just one tool in the arsenal for providing corporal punishment.

The following is a transcript of the beating of an inmate by then-superintendent Jim Bruton:[1]

---

[1] Transcript of a tape recording secretly made by an inmate of Tucker Prison Farm in 1966.

Accomplices to the Crime

Inmate: You can get any job you want as long as you can pay. Hey!

Bruton: Who are you talking to you ole crazy son of a bitch?

Inmate: [Unintelligible.]

Bruton: Reckon you can get along with me?

Inmate: Yessir.

Bruton: Get them pants off. Get down there. I took care of you 'cause you've got a lot of time. Pull your pants off.

Second Inmate: Pull the legs off. He'll knock the shirt off.

[WHAM!]

Inmate: Oh Captain!

[WHAM!]

Inmate: Oh Captain!

[WHAM!]

Inmate: Oh Captain!

Bruton: Get down . . . Now I forgot how many licks that is, one or two?

Inmate: Three.

Bruton: Three?

Inmate: Yessir.

[WHAM!]

Inmate: Oh Captain!

Bruton: Lay down there. We may have to hold you.

[WHAM!]

Inmate: Oh Captain!

Bruton: How many's that, four?

Inmate: Four.

[WHAM!]

Inmate: Oh Captain! five.

[WHAM!]

Inmate: Oh Captain, six!

[WHAM!]

Inmate: Oh Captain. That's seven.

[WHAM!]

Inmate: Oh Captain! That's eight.

[WHAM!]

Inmate: Oh Captain! That's nine.

[WHAM!]

Inmate: Oh Captain! That's ten.

Bruton: Get up from there.

Inmate: Yessir.

Bruton: You ole son of a bitch you're fixin' to get killed—God damn—that's the way you done.
Inmate: Yessir.
Bruton: Put that son of a bitch in the Longline in the morning. And you won't pay for nothin'; just do like I told you.
Inmate: Yessir.
Bruton: Don't never lie about what the captain said again for I'm gonna hit you when you do.
Inmate: Yessir.
Bruton: Why, you smoke-bred son of a bitch!
[Clang of the barracks door.]

There were other, more vicious, instruments than the strap.

Again and again the investigators heard of inmates being "rung up" on the Tucker "telephone," and of several "long distance calls." The euphemism was satanic.

The telephone, designed by prison superintendent Jim Bruton, consisted of an electric generator taken from a crank-type telephone and wired in sequence with two dry-cell batteries. An undressed inmate was strapped to the treatment table at Tucker Hospital while electrodes were attached to his big toe and to his penis. The crank was then turned, sending an electrical charge into his body. In "long distance calls" several charges were inflicted—of a duration designed to stop just short of the inmate's fainting. Sometimes the "telephone" operator's skill was defective, and the sustained current not only caused the inmate to lose consciousness but resulted in irreparable damage to his testicles. Some men were literally driven out of their minds.

The Tucker telephone was used not only to punish inmates but to extract information from them. One of the two telephones known to be on the farm was found hidden in a hat box on the top shelf of a linen closet in the Big House, where Jim Bruton was living then.

Bruton, who had been running Tucker for twelve years before the investigation, was a former state representative, and former deputy sheriff of Conway County, which had a political machine recognized by the public as the most powerful in Arkansas. During the investigation, Bruton asked CID investigator Duke Atkinson if he would like to have his job. In outlining the job's potential, Bruton gave a good indication of how he had operated the prison farm.

He said that the job paid $8,000 a year, and included a new car each year, a fourteen-room house, a complete expense account, and all your food. He assured Atkinson that the $8,000 salary was the smallest part of the compensation, because business people in the farm-supply trade and in the clothing business, and other interested parties, offered a lot of gifts.

Bruton said it was only smart to accept the gifts, and for Atkinson to be sure to do so without worrying about the rules, because the superintendent could do anything he wanted.

According to Atkinson's report, Bruton told him that if he accepted the position to "run the God damned place" he should let the prisoners know who was boss. If a prisoner got out of line, he should "hit him with anything you can get your hands on" because that's the only thing prisoners respect.

Bruton said that gambling, selling jobs, and drinking were as old as the penitentiary, and while it could be slowed down it would continue regardless of what was done to stop it. He said that people must learn to turn their backs on some things.

Bruton also gave the investigator a piece of advice that he himself should have heeded. He said that Atkinson should be smart enough to keep his mouth shut and not let anyone know his business.

Atkinson also inspected the inmates who worked on the Longline (field work crew) as they were brought into the kitchen to be fed. They all appeared to him to be at least forty pounds underweight. Their clothing was worn out and dirty. Several inmates were wearing trousers ripped up the inseam and outseam to the hips. Their shoes were in total disrepair, and often several sizes too large for them. Most had holes in the soles and across the tops. On being questioned, the inmates said that they had not been issued shoes and had to either wear rubber boots, go barefoot, or buy their own shoes, if they could. The inmates also said that two pairs of socks were issued twice a year, and that they had never been given underwear.

In the barracks, Atkinson found that the mattresses were rotten, and they smelled foul. Cotton was spilling out of most of them. The sheets were dirty and appeared to have been used for two or three weeks without change. More than half the beds did not have pillows; any pillows around were dirty and discolored.

The showers were leaking. There were only one wash basin, one urinal, and six commodes for each barracks of one hundred men. The commodes were stopped up or would not flush, the urinals were stopped up, and there were feces on the floor of the shower room. The entire barracks area was filthy and littered, and it stank.

The barracks were searched for weapons. The initial shakedown revealed an arsenal of sixty-one knives, five pairs of fighting knuckles, two palm weights, five blackjacks and clubs, three straight razors, and one hatchet.

During a search of the main prison building, investigators discovered and photographed the Tucker telephone, teeter board, straps, blackjacks, knives, whiskey bottles, keys to open all cell doors, gambling equipment in the form of playing cards and loaded dice, narcotics, and recording equipment. The superintendent's new office had already been bugged by one of the inmates; the inmate played back tapes of payoffs and deals for the investigator.

The CID investigators eventually interviewed more than a third of the Tucker prison population of three hundred inmates, using a code for names to protect the convicts. The following paragraphs are from statements the CID took from some of the inmates:

• FL-17 [code name of an inmate] stated that Superintendent Bruton's son, Ronnie, had come into the Black Angus cattle business rather suddenly when Tucker Prison Farm changed their cattle from Black Angus to Charolaise breed. Many newborn Angus calves were never put on the prison count. The mortality rate was adjusted to a greater loss of livestock than was actually lost by death and disease.

• FL-22 said an inmate used a prison tractor repeatedly

Accomplices to the Crime

to get back and forth to a liquor store in Tucker while he was out checking the skunk traps. The money to purchase the whiskey was furnished by inmate Winston Talley. It was common knowledge that Mr. Bruton got a good portion of the profits from money-lending deals and would sit down at the desk located in the hallway and call inmates out that owed money to Talley and collect the money himself. [The investigators noted: "This information was repeatedly confirmed by other inmates."]

• When LL-22, who is sixteen years old, arrived at Tucker he was placed in the Longline. The rider asked him for $2 a week or he would have him whipped. When the rider learned he did not have money, he took his watch in place of money, and for a few weeks the short hair [new inmate] had it pretty easy. Then, he was given five lashes with the strap for eating a pickle [cucumber]. Asked by the rider if the whipping hurt, he said no, and was taken back and given seven more lashes on the bare buttocks. He claimed he could have avoided the whippings and his problems at the prison if he'd become the punk [homosexual partner] of the rider.

• In August, 1965, the floorwalker [barracks security guard] tried to force LL-26 to give him money he had received from his family. When he refused he was taken into the shower, beaten, and "stomped" on the head with a pair of cowboy boots. His head required twelve stitches, and he was unable to eat because he could not open his mouth.

• LL-28 said he was brought in from the cotton fields and given fourteen lashes for being behind in his picking. On another occasion, he left some pickles [cucumbers] on a vine and was brought into the building and given ten lashes, then made to stand on the teeter board [a two-foot-long board with a block underneath as a fulcrum] for two hours, and then given ten more lashes.

• LL-31 said that in 1965, while picking "pickles," he was shot in the left arm by a Longline rider. He was brought to the prison hospital, where the inmate doctor treated him without giving him a shot. He passed out from the pain. He was hospitalized only two days before being sent back to work. Mr. Bruton told him that the rider

Oh, Captain!

should have killed him, and if he ever shot a gun again he had better have a dead convict to show for shooting a state shell.

• LL-1 said that in June, 1963, he got into a fight with a Longline rider and was hit on the foot with a hoe. He had been hospitalized for three days when Mr. Bruton came to see him and asked what happened. Mr. Bruton then had him put on a table in the prison hospital, belted down with one strap across his chest and one across his legs. Then the inmate doctor wired him up on the Tucker telephone with one wire to his penis and another to his big toe. The telephone was cranked five or six times.

• LL-2 said the floorwalker charged from $1 to $5 to give the inmates a good bed, and said that if an inmate would pay the kitchen rider he could have better food. On visiting Sundays it was the custom of families to bring food or clothing to inmates, but after the families left the trusties would take it for themselves.

• LL-13 said that although he was in poor health and assigned to work in the garden squad, he was put in the field hauling hay and picking strawberries, which he could not do. He refused to give money to the Longline rider and was whipped. Although he was examined by a doctor and told to lift nothing heavier than three pounds and do as little walking as possible, he was made to haul hay and feed.

• Soon after the arrival of LL-16 at Tucker on July 16, 1966, Mr. Bruton advised him to write to his mother. He wrote: "Dear Mom, I am at Tucker. Please help me." The following night Mr. Bruton and a warden came to the building and gave him five licks with the strap. Because he did not say "Oh, Captain!" with each lick, he was given six more.

• LL-34 said that in April, 1966, he was whipped for not picking enough "pickles," and Mr. Bruton ordered his head peeled [shaved] and he was given ten more lashes on the bare buttocks. He refused to cry out "Oh, Captain!" and was locked up for another hour, then given twenty more lashes by Mr. Bruton.

• LL-38 said that inmates had to pay $2 a week to the

laundry workers to have their clothes cleaned. He also claimed that the yardmen, or building tenders, stole personal items from the barracks while the inmates were gone.

• LL-44 was rung up on the Tucker telephone three times, each time for being in a brawl.

• In April, 1965, LL-44 was planning to escape with another man. One morning, Mr. Bruton came to the Longline and called him and his partner out. The two were brought to a building where they were questioned about their planned escape and a riot in the mess hall, which they knew nothing about. Mr. Bruton beat the inmates about the head with his cane and told a warden to get a statement from them any way he could.

• LL-33 said that he was stripped of all clothes. The warden then stuck needles under his fingernails and toenails. His penis and testicles were pulled with wire pliers and he was kicked in the groin. Two other inmates then ground cigarettes on his stomach and legs, and one of them stuck him in the ribs with a knife. The *coup de grâce* came from an inmate who squeezed his knuckles with a pair of nutcrackers. He said the warden and two inmates worked on him all afternoon and the next day. He was then put out in the field to work but he was unable to, so they put him in the hospital in isolation until his scars [wounds] healed. [The CID investigators produced witnesses for the torture session described.]

• LL-53 came to Tucker in October, 1964, and was told that unless he became the punk of the rider he would be whipped. He refused. Two days later the rider ran his horse over him, knocking him to the ground. The rider then dismounted and beat him with a rubber hose and stomped him until one tooth was knocked out. He received this type of treatment for two or three weeks and was finally sent to the hospital, where the inmate doctor told him he could not stay unless he paid $20. He had only $10 and was allowed to stay one day.

• LL-81 said that [in] March, 1964, Mr. Bruton told him he would be a free man on payment of $200. He was allowed to call his uncle, who brought a check for $200,

Oh, Captain!

which was cashed; and he was told he would be free the following Saturday. He is still in the penitentiary.

• LL-90 said that in June, 1966, his mother and stepfather paid Mr. Bruton $450 to get him a job in the prison hospital. During a visit to the farm, he told his mother and stepfather about some ill treatment he was receiving there. Mr. Bruton ordered him whipped on the bare buttocks until blood was running down his legs.

• LL-92 said that Mr. Bruton called him into his office and told him if he could get his wife to spend some time with him, he would get him a good job. [He made a deal with the superintendent and the next day he was put on the Little Rock crew breaking up rocks.]

Some time later, however, he was caught attempting to smuggle a letter out of the prison. Mr. Bruton ordered him into the building and, as he started up the steps, knocked him down five times. When he got up the steps and inside the building, Mr. Bruton gave him twenty-seven lashes and put him into the line [the Longline].

• In September, 1965, LL-92 was told that for $100 he could get a job in the laundry. On the next visiting day his mother gave the inmate $60 and put $40 on the books. Two days later Mr. Bruton put him into the laundry.

• LL-98 said that since he has been at Tucker he has been beaten with a baseball bat, a trace chain, a rope with knots tied in it, a hoe handle, a shovel, a rubber hose with lead in one end, and a tractor fan belt.

• LL-100 said he was forced to have oral and anal intercourse with inmates, or be beaten. Mr. Bruton would not let him answer sick call when he was sick and once placed a tomato on his head and stomped it into his eyes.

• LL-42 said he saw Mr. Bruton make an inmate with a bad heart run five miles and when the man got into the prison yard he fell dead. He also said he saw a colored inmate beaten so bad that he died in hospital.

• LL-10 told an investigator that one of the members of the parole board was running a "little Tucker" near Hughes, Arkansas, on a farm he owns. According to the inmate, the parole board member would parole convicts out and work them on his farm where, if they protested, they were beaten and sent back to prison.

• LL-95, who is in death row, said that on many occasions Mr. Bruton cursed the other inmates on the row and told them if they revealed anything to investigators they would be killed.

The CID report, stamped "Very Confidential," was given to Governor Faubus. The governor removed Bruton and three of his wardens in September, 1966, and charged them with meting out excessive punishment to Tucker convicts, with extortion, torture, and misuse of prison property. It is a comment on the Arkansas courts that, two years after he was indicted, the charges against Bruton were dismissed as being "unconstitutional." See p. 15 for an inmate's sworn statement regarding Bruton's brutality; the handwritten note on Owen's letter says, "Sir, I wrote mr Rockefeller over one year ago telling him some a little like this letter to you—So I didn't see this in the paper—and im not just telling you some lies—I tried when I wrote mr Rockefeller to help stop some of that Junk—and also help myself—Ask mr Rockefeller about the letter which I wrote him—Edward W. Owen."

The press did not see the CID report until January 15, 1967, when it was given out by a former aide to Governor Faubus who said he wanted to minimize whatever political gain the new governor, Winthrop Rockefeller, might seek by releasing it himself.

People reacted to the report, written in dry, precise, and unemotional language, with either horror or disbelief. The official reaction was predictable: State representative Lloyd Sadler said, "Ninety-five per cent of the complaints of convicts are lies. . . . I don't believe none of that stuff."[1] He had been chairman of the penitentiary board for fourteen years prior to his retirement in 1964.

Knox Nelson, a state senator, and head of a committee to study the prison, said, "Arkansas has the best prison system in the United States."[2]

---

[1] *Arkansas Gazette*, Little Rock, Ark., January 17, 1967, p. 1. Prison superintendent Jim Bruton was Sadler's nephew.
[2] As reported to the author by *Pine Bluff Commercial* reporter Tucker Steinmetz, on or about February 18, 1967.

RECEIVED
FEB 9 1968
SUPERINTENDENT'S OFFICE
ARKANSAS STATE PENITENTIARY

Station A West, E 4/4
Nashville, Tennessee
February 7, 1968

Mr. Thomas O. Murton, Warden
Arkansas State Penitentiary
Tucker Prison Farm, Ark.

Dear Sir:

During the past several months I have followed your endeavors through the news media. Your position of fairness has impressed me to the extent that I felt perhaps it might be mutually beneficial if I related the following facts as to some of the activities which prevailed at the time of my escape from that institution in November of 1965.

No doubt you are familiar with the previous superintendent's (Jim Bruton) implementation of the "Tucker Phone" for use in torturing prisoner's. On one occasion he ordered me "rung-up" for not picking all the cucumbers that was on a row I was harvesting. His order was carried out by an inmate (Earl Wind) who at that time was the "long line rider". I was carried to the hospital by a Captain Fletcher for the purpose of having this torture done.

When I became eligible for parole I "purchased" my release from Mr. Bruton but of course the parole wasn't granted. This was another contributing factor to my escape. Mr. Bruton also promised to have any and all detainers removed or "lost" but this was not the case either.

On a previous escape which was also motivated by the inhuman torture which I received while in that institution I was held down by inmates (Richard Davis for one) and Jim Bruton stomped my hands and feet; kicked my ribs in and kicked me in the groin. After that I wasn't allowed to smoke, talk to anyone, receive or send any mail, or be served coffee. I was notified that I would be tried and in the meantime I was again subjected to another beating.

Prior to going to court Mr. Bruton informed me that if I would keep my mouth shut in court and plead guilty that I wouldn't be beat anymore nor would I have to do any work on my return to the prison.

I was later placed in a small cell in the hospital unit and sometimes they "forgot" to feed me for two or three days. While in this cell in the hospital I was frequently seen by the inmate doctor Bill Morgan. Each time he saw me he would make reference to three prisoners he had "put to sleep" at Cummings and if given the go-a-head, he wouldn't hesitate to afford me the same treatment. He even went so far as to tell me that in each case Dr. Rollins had listed the cause of death as heart failure on the death certificates. It was from this cell that my last escape occured.

Be assured that if ever an indictment is found against Mr. Bruton I will readily testify to what I have related thus far.

Very truly yours,

Edward W. Owen.

Edward W. Owen, TSP#61944

Subscribed and sworn to before me this the 7 day of Feb, 1968.

My commission expires the 24 day of Jan , 1970 .

NOTARY PUBLIC

The report was studied by the Arkansas penitentiary board, and Jeff D. Wood, the chairman: "The way we look at it, it was just information gathered from inmates and you can get any kind of story if you listen to a prisoner."[1]

Newly elected Governor Rockefeller said, in January, that he didn't know why former Governor Faubus hadn't released the report. Faubus had obviously been aware of it in September, 1966, because he had fired superintendent Bruton and three wardens then, and had them charged with excessive brutality.

Faubus replied that he had seen the report only the day before he had left office, that he had intended to make it public but had overlooked it in the rush of clearing out. He also said that the purpose of a penitentiary was to punish, not rehabilitate. Ironically, during each of his campaigns for governor, Faubus had banned use of the whip—until after the election.

Governor Rockefeller said he had had the report in mind when, in his inaugural address, he'd described the state prison system as the worst in the nation.

At the time I was an assistant professor of criminology at an Illinois university. I had served previously in Alaska, as superintendent of an army stockade and five other institutions. As acting chief of corrections following statehood, I was responsible for developing the institutional programs of the new system. I also had served as a chief probation and parole officer and as Deputy U.S. Marshal. In Illinois, we were conducting seminars for twenty-two midwestern states under an Office of Law Enforcement Assistance Act grant administered by the Department of Justice, and I had recently returned from Arkansas, where I had gone to see why the state had not selected an officer to attend our spring session. I had visited the Arkansas prisons and found out why there was no training officer in Arkansas who could attend our program. It would have been necessary to obtain permission for him to come from the parole board—because in Arkansas, all the guards were prisoners!

---

[1] *Arkansas Gazette*, Little Rock, Ark., January 16, 1967, p. 2A.

Reformers

Three weeks after publication of the CID report I went to see Governor Winthrop Rockefeller at his penthouse suite in the National Old Line Building in Little Rock.

I knew very little about his background other than that he was from one of America's best-known and richest families, and had spent much of his time and fortune over the past thirteen years attempting to improve the quality of life in Arkansas. Almost alone, he had renovated the state's political structure. His electoral victory was an historic event: he had become Arkansas' first Republican governor since 1874; and reform of the state penitentiary had been one of his major campaign promises.

I was favorably impressed by the governor. He was bigger and huskier (six foot three, 210 pounds) than I had expected, and he had a disarming smile with imperfect teeth mottled by the two packs of unfiltered Picayune cigarettes he smokes a day. His only distracting trait was a nervous tic which caused his head to bob and weave for a few moments just before he started any statement. His ruddy complexion, which I then took as a sign of health and body tone, I realized later was probably the result of excessive drinking habits.

But he spoke with animation, in an affable and direct manner, which set me instantly at ease. "Arkansas prisons stink," he said at one point in our conversation.

I was quick to agree. I had read the state police report, and spent the previous day at Tucker Prison Farm seeing the eighteenth century methods used there. A visit to Tucker was like going through a time tunnel. I was convinced the inmates were uptight and ready to riot.

"In my opinion the prison can blow up in a matter of hours," I told the governor.

"We need a consultant," he said.

"You need a consultant like Custer needed television," I said. "You need somebody who will do what needs to be done. I would like to offer my services as superintendent of Tucker. You have a vacancy and you need to hire somebody. I'd like to go to Tucker and demonstrate to the people of Arkansas that you can run a prison without torture and brutality."

The governor looked to his aide for his reaction. The aide nodded agreement, as I had expected he would. Tom Eisele, who was in his forties, already had a reputation as a crusading attorney committed to reform. He had spent much of his time since graduating from the University of Arkansas fighting battles of principle.

I had met with another of Rockefeller's aides, John Haley, two days before. Haley had made headlines in 1957 during the Little Rock integration crisis. At that time, he had been only in his twenties. A member of the law firm which represented the school board in Little Rock, John Haley had defied Governor Faubus, who "wasn't going to let those niggers in":

"You can't do this," Haley had said.

"I know I can't do it," said Governor Faubus. "I know it's illegal, but what the people want is what we are going to do."

Haley was still standing his ground. He shook his head: "Governor, I am going to do everything in my power to get you out of office."

It was a courageous thing to do and say at that time and place, and Haley meant it. He campaigned actively to unseat Faubus and was a major figure in helping Governor Rockefeller get elected. It may be that the statue of Don Quixote he keeps on his desk is a significant clue to his character.

During my meeting with the governor and Eisele, I outlined my strategy and goals. My long-range goal was to eliminate the exploitation of inmates by other inmates or by non-prisoners for personal gain. I wanted to change the purpose and effect of the institution and change the inmates' life in the institution.

I believed that the Arkansas prison system could rise from the worst in the nation to become one of the best, in a fairly short time, because it would not be necessary to go through the evolutionary steps other states had experienced. Arkansas prisons had no investment in concrete and steel that could hold us back. The prison farms could be converted to a camp system—that is, a system of small, minimum-custody institutions with emphasis on productive labor. The camp system is the best and most workable plan used anywhere for a large portion of the prison population.

No one seemed shocked. In fact, Governor Rockefeller and Tom Eisele thought I should take over both Cummins and Tucker. They wanted to fire O.E. Bishop, who was then in charge of Cummins and the prison system.

I felt that that would be creating a problem instead of solving one, though. I wanted to take over Tucker first, where there was a vacancy, and learn more about the system. At the same time, I could develop a cadre and staff which would give me a commando crew to attack Cummins later on.

It was agreed that although Bishop would still have titular charge of the system, Tucker would be autonomous, and I would have full authority to hire and fire there. There were only thirty-four civilians for the two institutions of nearly two thousand inmates. I would have to phase out the trusties gradually, substituting a civilian staff of my own selection. I made it clear that my initial plan was to bring in key people from outside the state, which would inevitably cause criticism from Arkansans with vested interests in the existing system.

The second part of my relationship with the Arkansas penitentiary system was to serve as consultant to the governor's office on prison affairs as well as to the prison study commission, which was then being formed.

We also got into a general discussion about the philosophy of penal reform. I pointed out that reform of a prison system rests with the people. I had talked with people in Arkansas, briefly, and I was aware of their tolerance of the abuses in the system. It was plain that we had to demonstrate publicly how bad the system was, so that after re-

Accomplices to the Crime

form it could never revert to the horror of the past. I warned the governor of one thing: "I cannot operate without a free and open press," I said.

"I wouldn't have it any other way," the governor said.

"There will be some sharp edges here and there, and you'll have to see me through some rough spots. You'll have to be really committed to the project."

The governor assured me that penal reform was the number one item on his election platform of thirteen state reforms; that this was the first of the items he had attacked; and it was of primary concern.

"My commitment is sincere," he said.

Governor Rockefeller accepted my plan completely. "You will have the full support of my office and all my resources," he said. "We will not expect you to go through the hard work of reform and then dump you for someone else. When a department of corrections is formed, you will be commissioner."

At the end of the meeting, the governor told me that his staff would check on my background. "If you check out, you'll be hearing from us within the week."

That night as I drove back to Illinois, to my wife and children, I considered the economics of the job. The salary of the superintendent was fixed by law at $8,000 plus full subsistence and housing. At that time I was making $12,000 a year at the university. But I knew that Margaret, my wife, would feel that I should take the job, because it had to be done.

I thought I could do it, and I didn't know of anyone else who could or would, because it meant laying one's professional reputation, and possibly one's life, on the line. No one else had applied for the job.

I also knew that in the end I would be fired. That was the theme of my conversations with Margaret during the next few days. We knew that as soon as I branched out into real prison reform, I would start treading on toes. A quiet institution suits a lot of the "important" people, but a quiet institution is not necessarily a good one. If you are going to make changes, things have to be a little upset all the time.

I would not have much time. The governor had only a two-year term, which meant I had to complete the basic reform before his first term ended. Whether he won or lost the next election, I wanted the structure, physical facilities, and ideology to be established along the correct lines.

On February 11 Eisele telephoned me and said, "Your references check out. You're the man for us."

"O.K.," I said. "How soon do you want me in Arkansas?"

"Tomorrow will be soon enough," he said.

I made immediate plans to return to Little Rock. The day I arrived, the governor met with O.E. Bishop and told him I had been hired to run Tucker, which was to be autonomous. He would be responsible only for Cummins, and he was not to interfere with me in any way. If he didn't like it, he would be fired and I would be given his job.

Later I met with the governor and Bishop. To be certain there was no misunderstanding, Rockefeller repeated the terms of his commitment to me:

1. Tucker was to be autonomous, under my supervision.
2. I would have full authority to hire and fire.
3. I would be consultant to the governor on correctional matters.
4. I would be consultant to the prison study commission.
5. If and when a department of correction—which would include probation and parole and juvenile matters—were established, I would be the commissioner, so that I could guide the development and evolution of the correctional system.

Bishop accepted the news quietly. "I didn't want to mess with Tucker anyway," he said. "Maybe we can all learn something about penology."

My appointment was announced, however, not by the governor but by Bishop, superintendent of Cummins Prison Farm, who was also in charge of the state prison system. The fact that Bishop instead of the governor made the announcement made it seem that I was appointed by and working for Bishop—a troubling note.

I took over Tucker Prison Farm less than a week later.

Arkie-ology

The Arkansas prison system consists of two massive farms. The principal farm, Cummins, has 16,600 acres; a small section of it is set off for the Women's Reformatory. Tucker is a little over fifty miles to the north, and has 4,500 acres. Both farms are in poor rural communities, ironically named: Jefferson and Lincoln counties.

As in most of the rural south, the areas the prisons are in are benighted and backward, and local governments are frequently in the hands of underpaid and ill-educated white officials. A local chief of police, for example, admits he can neither read nor write.

The town of Tucker has a population of sixty-seven souls, of whom all but half a dozen are Negroes. On the one main street there are a gas station; two liquor stores; and a general store, founded in the nineteenth century, which still stocks a variety reminiscent of that era: ready-made fabrics, coal oil lamps, brown jugs, crocks, harness, feed, and seed. The stores are run by the only whites in town.

Many of the Negro families in Tucker live in squatter shacks without doors or windows. The unpainted shacks sit about three feet off the ground, set up on pilings to keep hogs, dogs, and snakes out.

There is no law enforcement officer in Tucker. The community depends on the prison guards to come into town and pick up any escapees or prisoners who, for one reason or another, have an excuse to be off the farm, and get tanked up in one of the local bars.

From the air the Tucker area appears to be a crazy

patchwork of flat, desolate, treeless areas, water-logged fields and dilapidated shacks, with the prison farm sprawling like a gigantic telephone pole across its middle. The prison has a long, central hallway, or "yard"; the auditorium, dining hall, and offices are attached to the hallway. Three barracks, or wings, extend from the hallway; a fourth wing incorporates the death house and Tucker's only cell block. Half its fourteen cells are for men under sentence of death, the remainder for prisoners in isolation, the "hole."

Arkansas' is one of the few remaining prison systems in the United States that does not routinely house its inmates in cells. One of the nineteenth century's major achievements in penology was to replace barracks with separate cells for all prisoners, but Arkansas passed it up. Barracks one, two, and three are about fifty feet wide by a hundred feet long. There are one hundred beds apiece in them. Barracks one holds the rank men—the lowest classification of prisoners, which includes the new arrivals, called short hairs. Barracks two holds the do-pops, an intermediate group of inmates, so named because traditionally they are supposed to pop doors open for superiors. Barracks three holds the trusties, presumably so called because they can be trusted.

Each barracks opens onto the central corridor, or yard, and has heavy steel bars extending from side to side and from floor to ceiling. The rank men and do-pops are locked in at night, but there is no lock on the trusty barracks.

There was a regular system of protection in the barracks when I came to Tucker. Everything, valuable or not, had to be left out in the open, so during the day an inmate called the building tender was left in the empty barracks to see that nothing was stolen. He was paid a small sum by each inmate for protection of his property.

When the inmates returned from work at night a floorwalker took over as guard. His function was to see that there was no stealing, no fighting, and no homosexual assaults. He too was paid by the inmates.

Of course, if the floorwalker or building tender wanted to make a homosexual assault himself or do "some creeping" (sneaking up on a man), there was little the inmate could do—either submit or get his head bashed in.

The men had a remarkably active social life at night.

Accomplices to the Crime

Each barracks had its own casino, with poker tables, green eye shades, dice, and almost every card game you would find in Las Vegas. Everything but slot machines. I heard of one poker game in the trusty barracks where there had been $3,800 lying on the table at one point.

Sometimes gambling debts were paid off with personal favors. The gambling was one of the things I intended to stop—not for the sake of morality, but because I wanted to put the loan sharks out of business. If I did, I would cut down on personal exploitation and some of the bitterness that frequently erupted into fights.

From what I knew of the daily routine at Tucker, it started at sunup when the Longline went out to the fields. The workday usually ended twelve to fourteen hours later, when it was dark.

The Longline was guarded by trusties armed with a variety of weapons ranging from high-powered rifles and shotguns to heavy-caliber side arms. When the Longline left the building for work, the inmate guards moved out to provide perimeter security with a "rider," or foreman, followed by two "high powers"—guards on horseback, carrying carbines. They in turn were followed by two "shotguns," on foot, who kept a distance of fifty to seventy-five yards from the working party. Two more shotguns and a sub-rider (assistant foreman) brought up the rear. Two more high powers stayed farther away from the main body, to back up the shotguns in case they were rushed by the inmates, and to see to it that the shotguns themselves didn't escape or fire on the high powers.

Two unarmed state troopers in a sedan drove behind the lines, guarding the inmate guards who were guarding the inmates.

The head of the trusty guard force was called the yard man. He was responsible for getting the work done and had a goon squad to enforce his orders. He could and did sell jobs and assignments, usually sharing the proceeds with The Man. In fact, in Arkansas, the yard man ran the prison.

The practice of using armed prisoners to guard other prisoners has been forcefully condemned by correctional organizations and experienced prison administrations everywhere. It is dangerous for the public. It is also dangerous for the prisoners, who are entitled to be protected from injury while they are serving their sentences. In Arkansas, when a trusty shot another inmate, assumed to be escaping, he would be granted an immediate parole as a reward—as long as the "escaping" prisoner was dead and unable to protest his innocence.

One may wonder how anyone could justify putting rifles, shotguns, and pistols in the hands of men serving time for crimes of violence. According to Arkansas logic, men convicted of violent acts were just the ones to be given weapons under such a brutal system, because they had already demonstrated their willingness to assault others.

The best description of the trusty-guard system was given to me some months after my arrival at Tucker by inmate Gurvis "Buddy" Nichols, who was extremely perceptive.

"When the press compares Tucker with German concentration camps, they aren't exaggerating," he said. "They had their kapos and we have our trusties. I'm a trusty now and I understand how those kapos operated.

"The oppressed become the oppressors is what happens. You would be in the rank barracks for a while getting beat and kicked and walked on with cowboy boots and then sweep a floor all night long and go out the next morning at daylight and work in the field and the rider would beat you all day out there.

"So, they offer you a job to beat the other inmates and you take it because there are two types of living conditions: you exist, or you survive.

"If you existed, you walked around in the barracks with an army blanket around you—no underwear, no T-shirt, no socks. You wore a pair of rubber boots for house shoes. If it was summer, you wore a pair of brogans and because the blanket was too hot you wrapped a sheet around you.

"A trusty had underwear because he took it away from a rank man. A trusty occasionally had milk on the table and salt-meat—a rank man had weevils and beans.

"A trusty was surviving; a rank man was existing. So, you became a trusty and were glad to do it."

Incredible as it may seem, the inmates were in complete control of Tucker. The gates, towers, cell blocks, kitchen, hospital, dog kennel, chicken house, barns, and everything else, were all supervised by the inmates who, in turn, were watched over by other inmate guards and the troopers. Inmates carried weapons, and they would not allow the state troopers to have weapons. A first step in gaining control of the institution and weakening the power of the trusties, therefore, was to get the state police armed.

So, early on my first morning at Tucker, I had a strategy meeting with Captain Brown and his assistant, Lieutenant Jimmy Lowman. We decided on a plan that called for us to go around to the four towers and gate houses and ask the guards for permission to arm the police.

On our first visit to Tower Number One, I asked the guard what his job was.

"To guard the prisoners," he said.

"And why are the state troopers here?" I asked.

"To see that nobody escapes, too," he said.

"O.K.," I said. "The troopers have a badge and are authorized to enforce the law so why not let them help you out in this particular case?"

"No reason why not that I can see," said the guard.

By such logic I finally got all the tower guards to allow the troopers to be armed, even though it had been the tradition for them to be unarmed. But I was the first to question the trusties about the practice and suggest that the troopers and the trusties had a common goal.

The visits to the towers at each corner of the prison yard were profitable on another count: I saw for myself the interiors of the towers that were supposed to provide security against escape.

Towers One and Three, which were made of concrete blocks, had never been finished, because the 155 sacks of cement needed to complete construction had been packed off the farm by former employees. The guards in the unfinished towers could not see anything outside the towers but the fence—which had never been completed either.

All the towers were filthy. They had no toilet facilities; to relieve themselves the guards leaned over the edge or out of the window.

The tower guards were locked in. When it was time for a change of shift, the new inmate-guard drew a key from the armory, went out and unlocked the tower. The outgoing guard locked the new man in and returned the key to the armory. This was ridiculous: the guards in Two and Four could climb down the outside of the tower, and Towers One and Three were reached by ladder. The men left their posts whenever they wanted to.

Each of the tower guards had a different weapon: one had a .357 magnum pistol, another a 30.06 rifle, a third had a Remington automatic rifle. The guard in Tower One had a rifle, a shotgun, and a pistol. When we first met I thought his name was Latch-Eye. It was sometime later before I learned that Latch-Eye was really an Arkansas slurring of Glass-Eye—he had one glass eye. I found out that Latch-Eye was serving twenty-one years for murdering someone with a rifle. There he was at Tower One, the crucial point for all traffic on the farm.

Later, I made a survey of the other guards. Half of them were in for murder. I suppose they were appropriate choices, by a perverted logic, for guards, but it is frightening to consider a situation in which a man commits a criminal act of violence and is punished by being sent to prison where he is given not only a rifle, shotgun, and pistol but life and death control over both inmates and the civilian staff.

On this brief visit to the towers and the gate house I noticed there were no fire extinguishers. In fact, further inspection showed that there were no fire extinguishers on the entire 4,500-acre farm.

After we toured the towers and the gate, I gave the order to arm the state troopers. My first battle for control was won when I saw Captain Brown strap his holstered pistol around his waist.

My first official act, which was duly recorded in the institution log I established the Monday morning I assumed command, was to abolish all forms of corporal punishment. I also designated Captain Brown as the assistant superintendent of Tucker.

I fired the inmate in charge of the radio, telephone, and inmate records, and replaced him with a state trooper. For the first time in the history of the prison, control of communications at the farm was taken away from the inmates.

Late in the afternoon I learned I had a visitor in the

office. "Captain" O.E. Bishop of Cummins wanted to speak to me about "certain matters."

On my way to meet him, I was stopped by the guard at the hospital, who introduced himself as Chainsaw Jack. He explained that while sleeping on the ground with a companion, the latter made a homosexual advance. In the struggle, Jack grabbed the man's hair by one hand and sawed off his head with the other.

Chainsaw made a pleasant speech of welcome and rambled on about several matters before getting to the point. "You may know quite a bit about penology but you have a lot to learn about Arkie-ology," he said.

I asked him what he meant. Chainsaw told me that Arkansas prisoners and culture were different from other places. "There's no logic to us'ns," he said. "Arkies are tough, and we think different from other folk.

"The old heads inside don't want you breakin' up their cliques and the free people aren't goin' to let you stop their stealin' from the prison."

Chainsaw's point about the illogicality of the Arkansan was brought home to me a few minutes later during my conversation with Bishop.

My only other meeting with Bishop had been the day of the press conference when he had appointed me superintendent of Tucker, and I had not been particularly impressed. He seemed the prototype of a Southern sheriff—which he had been for some years before taking over at Cummins. I also knew he enjoyed a reputation as an excellent politician.

We talked in my office for some time before he took off his horn-rimmed glasses and got to the point.

"Look, Tom," he said. "I realize you're running this place over here separate from me and I'm running my own show. That's the way it's supposed to be—but you know the word has gotten back to Cummins that you have abolished the strap here, and that makes it kind of rough on me, because some of my boys want the hide removed over there.

"Every time you make a change here they know about it over there, so it makes it more difficult for me. So how about you just saying that you might use the strap, and that'll help me out a little bit over at Cummins."

Since such a move was completely contrary to everything I believed in, I said no firmly.

Bishop argued the point, repeating that it didn't matter if I really used the strap or not, just as long as I said I might.

He was genuinely distressed when I again refused to cooperate and was not in a good frame of mind when he left my office.

Almost as soon as Bishop left, Sergeant Turner, the desk officer, sent word that the trusties were uptight. The inmates had told the yard man, who, in turn, told Turner, that they had heard on TV that I didn't believe in inmates carrying guns and I was going to replace the trusties with men from outside the prison. If I was going to do that, the trusties intended to turn in their guns and go on strike.

If the trusties went on strike I would have to shut down the institution. I knew it, and so did they. The trusties controlled the prison, and without them and the guns there would be no control and no farm work would be done.

I decided the time had come to inform the inmates about my plans, starting with the trusties, who were obviously the key men. I had wanted to speak with them first, and alone, because they were, in effect, my staff.

I talked to the trusties in the main prison auditorium adjoining the mess hall between 7 and 8 P.M. I stood at the edge of the boxing ring and they sat on the floor all around me. They were very quiet. It has always been my experience that when inmates are unusually quiet, trouble is brewing.

It was easy to spot the wheels. They were the men with knife-edge creases in their trousers, tailored shirts, and boots. And they were the best fed. Any man who stood out like that was important in the power structure. I noted them, planning either to use them or remove them from positions of power.

I was well aware of the figure I cut in my blue jeans, lumberman shirt, and work shoes. I didn't look like a prison superintendent, and I didn't intend to talk like one. I was going to have to throw away the book, since nothing in it applied to the situation I faced. The best I could do was make a compromise with reality and tell the inmates, "We'll run the prison together," hoping they would allow me to have at least part of the action.

I started off by saying, "My name's Murton and I'm the superintendent. Normally when I take over an institution I come in and say, 'This is how it's going to be and this is the way we're going to run things.' But this is ridiculous in a situation like this because you guys have the guns and the keys and you're running things so there's no way I can take over."

The men laughed and we were off to a good start.

"We are going to have an open press policy," I said. "The administration must be honest and the people outside must know it's honest.

"The newspapers have accurately reported me as being opposed to the trusty system but we will have to continue with it for at least two years because there isn't enough money to phase out the inmate guards and hire freeworld people. I give you my word that I will never put a trusty in the ranks,[1] so you need not fear for your lives . . .

"Among the first things I'm going to do is to set up a school program to teach those of you who want it how to read and write. And as soon as possible I'm going to set up some kind of vocational training program so you can have a skill when you get out. . . .

"And I'm going to help keep you from eating like animals with a soup spoon. Next week we're going to issue knives and forks. It's ridiculous to consider kitchen knives a weapon when you already have knives and guns so I'm going to buy cutlery and ask you to leave them in the kitchen. . . .

"And I want you fellows to know that I'm not stupid. I am aware that there's a lot of gambling going on and boozing—but because I don't think that's one of the most important things to take care of at this time I'm going to move on to other priorities. So for the time being you can keep your booze and keep on gambling. When I'm ready to stop all that I'll give you plenty of advance warning."

I heard a sigh of relief from the wheels because booze, gambling, and money lending were a major part of their power. By saying that I didn't intend to interfere with any of

---

[1] That is, I would not "rank" one—demote him to the common labor force and move him to the rank barracks—an action that would result, very likely, in the trusty's death, as the rank men revenged themselves.

these, I had reassured them that their positions in the power structure went not immediately threatened.

At the same time, I had put them on notice that I was aware of what was going on. In another institution it would have been possible to establish a rule banning gambling and drinking and enforce it with civilian manpower, but here I had to be more subtle. I knew that at some time in the future I would take away the brozene (prison currency), which would automatically cut out the gambling without making an issue of it.

One of the trusties stood up and said, "They can donate blood at Cummins so then they can get money. How about us doing that over here?"

"I'll look into that," I said. "Maybe we can get the same program set up over here because it's a legitimate way to get some money."

Then I summarized for the trusties my plans for the future, including redrafting legislation to get a liberalized parole law, and investigation into the records to check on their "good time"—reductions in sentences, earned through work and good behavior. I knew that in the past the superintendent had taken away good time illegally and I was going to attempt to restore it. This gave the men an incentive to play along with me a while.

After about forty minutes I finished my talk and asked if there were any questions.

"What happens if a prisoner starts to escape?" one of the trusties asked. "Do you want us to shoot him?"

"You're a guard and you're on my staff so I expect you to shoot him. I'm going to try and give you all target practice so you can be more expert and perhaps wound a man, but I expect you to stop him. No longer are you going to get paroled for killing an escaping inmate but you will not be disciplined for killing an escaping inmate. So, if some of you know that you are not going to stop a man from escaping, now is the time to turn in your guns."

This was possibly the most ridiculous suggestion I could make to a group of inmates: to ask them to turn in their guns if they wouldn't shoot another inmate—but that was Arkie-ology. At the end of the meeting two inmates did turn in their guns. One of them, Allen Cash, a shotgun guard, said he didn't think he could shoot another inmate and he felt everyone knew it. He said it would be best for all of us if he turned in his shotgun.

At least one trusty considered "us" as part of the community. I agreed he was right and promised to find a replacement job for him.

On my second night in charge of Tucker, at about the same time, I had the remainder of the inmate population brought to the auditorium. They had already heard through the grapevine what I had said to the trusties and I could sense the eagerness, edged with disbelief, that greeted my opening statement.

"The trusties are no longer going to abuse you or use corporal punishment," I said, "but they are under orders to shoot if a man is trying to escape so don't mistake humanity for weakness.

"You are going to be fed and clothed and you will know that you are going to come back at night and won't be buried out in the field. What I am trying to do is eliminate tension and fear in your lives but until I do, and you are convinced that the trusties won't be beating up on you any more, you can keep your weapons. Some time later I'll set a box outside the barracks and ask you to turn your weapons in. . . .

"Meanwhile you are going to be promoted on merit and not by purchasing your jobs. There will come a time when you will no longer be exploited by other inmates and you will not have to pay for a meal. But in order to get to that time you're going to have to work with me."

I talked about the "open press policy," and introduced newsman Tucker Steinmetz of the *Pine Bluff Commercial*. He was, I believe, the first reporter to be allowed the freedom of Tucker prison premises in almost half a century.

As part of my plan to educate the inmates as well as the public, I discussed comparative criminology in other states and frankly said that "Arkansas has probably the worst prison system of any state in America," a statement that drew cheers from some of the men. I touched briefly on the fact that I was going to look into their good time and parole eligibility (more cheers), and then got into a discussion of the educational and vocational training programs I wanted to set up, and halfway houses that would help the inmate adjust to civilian life.

I covered much the same territory that I had covered with the trusties the night before, and mentioned some of the changes they could expect soon in the visiting schedule and the processing of mail. I authorized the mailing of privileged communications to the attorney general, the governor, the courts, and the penitentiary board. These letters could be sealed and mailed without inspection.

I reiterated that there would be no rapid change to free-world guards. My acceptance of the inmate staff was a reality and I would continue to work with them. I reminded them that corporal punishment had been abolished, and that disciplinary action would take the form of deprivation of privileges.

I closed the meeting, after an hour and a half, with some comments about freedom from tyranny's requiring collective responsibility to one's own society.

In my log I noted, "The meeting went quite well. It was well received. The atmosphere was excellent and there was much laughter and good concentration."

The following day the rank men put me to a test. Six of them refused to report for work under an inmate rider named Henderson, who, they claimed, had a reputation for brutality. They said they were afraid for their safety.

This was a serious charge against Henderson. Therefore, with the aid of Captain Brown and Lieutenant Lowman, I conducted an investigation that lasted about five hours. I wanted to show the inmates that it would no longer be possible for anyone to lie about anyone, or as they say, "put a story down." The investigation exonerated Henderson, and we put him back in charge.

The message conveyed to the inmates was that we were going to investigate all charges. If a man was right he would be backed up; if he was wrong, he would be disciplined.

Since there were no privileges yet to take away from the six rank men, I ordered some sidings taken from an old building and placed the men on extra duty chopping wood. In earlier days, they would have been flogged.

Weevils and Beans

One of the first things any prison administrator should do when he comes into a new institution, even if it is a good one, is see what's going on in the kitchen.

When a man is doing time in prison he is pragmatic; his concern is not how to do fifteen years, it's how to do tomorrow. The inmate's interest is in whether or not he will have weevils—worms that grow in flour or beans and, in a soup, float to the top of the pot—for dinner. This was the only meat most inmates were ordinarily served.

Many disturbances in penal institutions stem from dissatisfaction with the food.

When the CID investigators went into the Tucker kitchen, they found the entire area filthy. Flies were everywhere, and the food and meat were piled on the work tables, completely exposed. Tin cans with the tops cut out were being used as cups. All the cooking utensils were in a state of disrepair or damaged beyond repair.

For inmates with no power or money, the food was a very thin, watered-down serving of rice—one large spoonful per inmate. The bread was a tasteless cornbread, one medium slice per inmate. The kitchen personnel told the investigator that meat was served to the inmates only once a month, on visiting Sunday, and then only in small portions. Milk and eggs were drawn from Cummins, but they were used only for cooking for the trusties. Kitchen personnel said that the ordinary inmates got one egg per year, on Christmas morning, and were never given milk. One kitchen helper suggested that the food supply records

Weevils and Beans

should be examined, as most of the meat was either being sold by the kitchen rider or carried out the "back door" by the wardens—civilian employees.

The kitchen at Tucker is in the center of the mess hall. The ranges, steam kettles, and other kitchen equipment are in the middle of the room with tables on both sides. On Sundays, this area was full of inmates and their visitors. (An inmate could have visitors once a month; one-fourth of the population had visitors each Sunday.) Little food was prepared on Sunday, and the kitchen looked like a camp ground. Visitors arrived at Tucker carrying tablecloths, jugs, picnic baskets, and enough food for an army. Inmates who were not fortunate enough to have visiting relatives either bought food from the commissary or scrounged from someone else.

During the other six days of the week, the kitchen was open twenty-four hours a day. Different meals were fed to each of the groups of prisoners at different times. The groups ate separately because of the hostility between the guards and the guarded.

The trusties ate best of all, of course. Many of them had steak for breakfast, and pork chops and hamburger. The last trusty was out of the mess hall before the first do-pop came in.

The do-pops ate almost as well as the trusties, because most of them were able to buy food in the commissary or had the money to bribe the cooks for better portions of food. Since the do-pops were halfway to being trusties, and used in privileged positions, they too were hated by the rank men. The do-pops had to be out of the mess hall before the rank men entered.

The rank men—the lowest classification of prisoners—had the worst food. Prior to the arrival of the state police, meat had been served only once a year. Then they had hog's head stew and pig's knuckle soup. Only the few rank men with money were able to improve their menu.

The rank men had never eaten their noon meal in the mess hall. They ate out in the fields on the turn rows (elevated rows for turning equipment around) with a spoon as their only utensil. At 10:30 every morning a mule-drawn wagon called a doby wagon came back from hauling garbage to the dump, and was driven around to the kitchen.

Accomplices to the Crime

Several uncovered fifty-gallon barrels would be carried onto the wagon with a few dozen loaves of bread. While the wagon was pulled out to the field by a team of decrepit mules, wheels kicking up dust and dirt, the flies from the earlier trip gorged themselves on the rapidly cooling contents.

When the wagon pulled onto the turn row in a final burst of speed and dust, the Longline rider would shout, "Make it up!" The inmates would come from the field, keeping their lines but shortening the distance between each man.

The buckets always contained weevils, beans, and collards, in a kind of soup mixture. The rank men carried their own spoons in their hip pockets along with their cigarette "makings." They formed a single line in front of the wagon, where they picked up canteen cups or tin cans and the water cart boy spooned the stuff out.

Old pecks—inmates who had served a lot of time—made it a practice to be at the end of the food line so, when the boy dipped in with his spoon, they got less water and more beans. Inmates with money paid the boy extra for a little piece of fat back. The loaves of bread were torn into hunks and thrown to the rank men.

Trusties usually had lunches specially packed for them in the kitchen, and wheels among the rank men could buy meat or a decent sandwich from the water cart boy, who ran his own commissary. He shared the profits with the yard man, from whom he had bought his job, and the Longline rider.

The biggest hazard at meal times was not the food, however. Rank men never knew whether they were going to survive the lunch break and smoking period. Before my arrival at Tucker it had been a frequent sport among trusty guards to shoot the heels off the men's shoes while they were eating.

The rank man ate his evening meal immediately upon arriving at the main institution, before he even had time to wash any of the sweaty dirt and fertilizer from his face and hands. The supper after a day of grueling work in the fields was rice, soybeans, corn bread, and ice water. Little wonder that most of them were forty to sixty pounds under their normal weight.

I needed help with the kitchen and I needed it fast. And I knew that the farm itself was going to turn out to be a mess, so I called two old friends of mine who were living on their own farm in Willow Springs, Missouri. Frank and Bea Crawford responded immediately to my cry for help, as I knew they would.

The Crawfords offer quite a contrast to each other. Bea is big, full, and expansive. I had known her in Alaska, where she had been a cook for seven years in the institution at Wasilla. She was ideal to be the first woman ever to work inside Tucker. A plain, simple countrywoman, whose size alone commands respect, she is an excellent cook and dietician; at Tucker, she soon became known as Big Mama.

Frank is her physical opposite. As Bea herself once put it, "Why, that dried-up little old man wouldn't weigh 130 pounds dripping wet."

They arrived together within the week, and while Frank was out checking over the farm, Bea and I went on a tour of the kitchen. Bea was appalled at the filth; it was worse than anything she had imagined or anticipated.

There were other problems besides filth, too. For instance, we found more than four gallons of poisonous disinfectant and ten gallons of bug spray on the pantry shelf stored in bottles labelled "syrup." The consistency of the poison was the same as that of syrup.

I called together the thirty-two inmates who were working in the kitchen and introduced her. I told them they must take orders from her and warned them I would back her one hundred per cent. The first thing she did was put them to work scrubbing ranges, utensils, and tables, and she scrubbed too.

Within a few days Bea and I had arranged for a bus to bring the men in from the fields to the mess hall at noon. Knives and forks were purchased and distributed to the men. Under her supervision everyone, including freeworld staff, had the same meals. The innovations were simple and basic, because the kitchen equipment and mess-hall tables at Tucker were modern, having been installed in 1966.

The kitchen operation had been more of a private enterprise than an inmate service. Many of the kitchen workers were profitably in business for themselves. They bought raw products from the commissary and used the institution's equipment to bake their wares, which they sold in the barracks. I preferred that the inmates get the food they were entitled to, in sufficient and equal amounts, without paying for it in money or any other way.

The kitchen had been open around the clock to enable these entrepreneurs to carry on their business, so we ordered the kitchen locked up at night. This was not the simple move one might think. The back door to the pantry, which was the outside door between the institution and the free-world, had never been locked. It took some doing even to find the key.

One day Bea and I went to question some of the inmates assigned to the mess hall, hoping to learn something about their function in the overall setup. As was to be expected, the majority of the inmate staff had bought their jobs or were running side enterprises.

Four men from the night shift were still hanging around. Asked what they were doing, they said they were in the cigarette business. They bought bulk tobacco and paper and spent the day in a corner of the kitchen making cigarettes to sell in the barracks.

Their story was typical. The total operation was so unbelievable that we broke up laughing, and the inmates realized the ridiculousness of the situation and laughed at themselves as well.

We reorganized the kitchen so that rank men, do-pops, and trusties ate together three times a day instead of having at least seven or eight feedings with some men eating five times a day. Many of the trusties who worked in the towers had been eating four meals in the mess hall and then taking a lunch packet when they went on duty. We cut the kitchen staff back by a third.

Within a few days we were serving some type of meat at meals three times a day, and were using farm produce on the tables. The quality and quantity of the food increased, and milk and condiments—salt and pepper—were on the tables for the first time. The men were getting eggs and green vegetables.

Although we were able to straighten out the food and the schedules, we had a problem trying to cut down on the home-made booze operation, which had traditionally been conducted in the kitchen because all the ingredients were there. The making of home brew was probably the biggest and most enterprising, if not ingenious, of all inmate ventures.

As in the freeworld, liquor offered a form of escape. Inmates had needed this antidote to the cruelty and drudgery of their lives. Former superintendents had recognized this, accommodated to it, and sometimes used it to make a profit for themselves. Drinking was generally ignored and sometimes even encouraged by the staff as a way of cutting down escapes. If the inmates could get liquor at the prison, they wouldn't leave the farm to buy it.

I cut off most of the supply sources of freeworld alcohol, but it was almost impossible to stop the inmates from brewing their own booze. You can put anything with a grain or sugar content into a jar, and when water is added and it is allowed to set for forty-eight hours, it will start to ferment. The longer it brews, the higher the alcoholic content.

At harvest time the inmates traditionally got drunk on home brew. They made wine out of strawberries, apricots, raisins, prunes, and other dried fruits from the kitchen. We had acres of rice, which they made into a good wine almost like sake. And it was easy for an inmate to gather up two handfuls of corn as the basis of "white lightning," a ninety-proof brew of the south that guarantees instant drunkenness and a heavy hangover.

Fruit ferments on its own, but it ferments faster when a little yeast is added. Since we baked our own bread at Tucker, it was impossible to keep an eye on every spoonful of yeast, and buckets of it disappeared. If the inmates were unable to get at the yeast itself, they took the bread dough and used that as a starter for their alcohol.

There were one-gallon jugs all over the farm. The labels read "syrup," "mayonnaise," "coffee," or "preserves," but the contents were booze. There were bottles buried in the ground, hidden in the barns, and stashed in silage pits, and every shakedown of the barracks turned up jugs hidden under or in the bunks. When the mixture was ready for drinking, the inmate gave a building tender or floorwalker a shot for "protection"—and they were both off on a bender.

Accomplices to the Crime

From time to time, we would discover a bottle hidden along the entry road to the prison. The drop-off place had been selected on a previous visiting day. Someone driving a prison vehicle would be tipped off and would share the contents for making the pick-up.

We locked up the yeast; we cut out the use of dried fruit in the kitchen; and we instituted frequent shakedowns. For the first time, there was no rice wine made there in the fall of 1967. We were never able to wipe out booze-making altogether, but we made it a lot tougher.

The Tucker Time Tunnel

When Frank Crawford took over as livestock manager at Tucker he gathered his men together and told them he was there to make the farm a better place to do time. His men sullenly shrugged off his short speech and made no comment. Frank asked a few questions—where things were located; how things had been done in the past. Instead of answers, Frank got cold, hard looks. He sensed resentment and fear every time he was with the men. Despite his small size, Frank is a persistent and determined man. One day he asked the men why they were afraid of him. One of the men admitted that in the past they had never been allowed to talk or to be friendly with the wardens and if they were distrustful of him, it was because they were waiting for the day when he would turn on them.

Later, as the men began to feel more at ease with him, they told Frank that in the past each time a warden came around any man who spoke out of turn would be whipped. One of the men asked Frank if he had ever seen the strap. He admitted he had and asked if any one of the men had been whipped. With only one or two exceptions, every man in the group of thirty said yes.

One of the prisoners who had recently been transferred from Cummins was not doing his share of work. Frank called him off to one side and said he would have to pitch in more.

"I can't do any more than I am," the man said.

"Why not?" asked Frank.

"Because I was beaten before I was transferred."

Frank asked the inmate to come to the office and show him the marks on his body. Inside the office, the inmate dropped his pants, pulled up his shirt, and showed Frank his backside. There wasn't a sound piece of flesh from the back of his neck to the calves of his legs.

The memory of what he had seen on the man's back was still fresh in Frank's mind the day he toured the premises and outbuildings with me. Frank asked me why the man had been tortured so badly.

I explained that the inmates were beaten primarily to make them work harder, on the theory that a man can more easily be driven than led. The Arkansas prison farms had been traditionally operated as businesses to exploit inmate labor for the profit of the state and selected individuals.

"But he was beaten by the superintendent," said Frank.

I recalled my interview for the superintendent's job, when one of the first questions Governor Rockefeller's aide had asked me was, "Do you happen to know anything about agriculture?"

I had told Tom Eisele that I had grown up on a farm in Oklahoma, had a degree in animal husbandry from Oklahoma Agricultural and Mechanical College, and had taught farming in Alaska. He was in a state of euphoria, because although a prison superintendent in Arkansas is not expected to run the prison, he must manage the agriculture to show a profit.

The superintendent must see to it that the okra is picked, the peas are in, the cucumber contract is fulfilled, the hogs are fed—and, incidentally, that the prisoners don't run away. There are fifty-six different hand-harvested crops grown at Tucker, including 17 acres of strawberries, 50 acres of cucumbers, 70 acres of cane, 100 acres of potatoes and corn, 1,118 acres of rice, 306 acres of cotton, and 110 acres of oats. The superintendent's primary function is to see to it that the penal slaves make money for the state.

In order to run the farm, former superintendents made accommodations with the yard man, who ran the institution and made all the assignments. The deal between The Man and those trusty inmates was simple. He told them, "Get the crops in and keep the men quiet, and I will give you extra privileges. I don't care how you manage. Use a lead pipe, anything. Just do it. And you can keep anything you make on the side."

Frank found it hard to accept that in this day and age men were beaten to force them to work harder. But that was the way it was and, presumably, had to be, on a prison farm being run by the inmates themselves, supervised by a sadistic staff, employed by a corrupt system sanctioned by an apathetic society. The Longline worked fourteen to sixteen hours each day with no shoes, gloves, or jackets, with weevils for food—they were cold, hungry, tired, and hopeless; a man beyond despair responds only to brutality.

Slavery was never really abolished in Arkansas. The Negro slaves were freed one hundred years ago, only to be replaced by penal slaves. The peculiar jargon and vocabulary of the prisoners had clear roots in the slavery days. Inmates talked about people outside the front gate as free people who lived in the freeworld. The table where the freemen ate in the mess hall was the freeline mess table. Non-prison clothing was called freeworld clothing. "The Big House" used to be the common term for a plantation owner's dwelling.

When I arrived at Tucker there were three freeworld people, including myself, in charge of three hundred inmates and a wide range of work on 4,500 acres of land. On the day I arrived, the business manager resigned, which meant there were only two freeworld people employed in the institution. The state troopers were there only on a temporary basis.

Everything had been left in the hands of the inmates and it took over half the prison population to do the housekeeping and maintenance jobs. Of the other inmates, around fifty were guards, fifty were staff, and only between fifty-five and sixty men were working in the fields.

As could be expected, the men who were in the fields made the work accommodate to them rather than accommodating themselves to the work. We discovered on our tour that all the buildings were in a poor state of repair. It was obvious that no maintenance had been done for years. The farm work that should have been done six months earlier had been neglected. The land needed to be disced, seed beds needed to be prepared and levees to be broken

Accomplices to the Crime

to prepare for the coming crop year and to assure continued prison revenue. It was obvious we needed a crash program and on March 9th the penitentiary board entered into a contract with the Hartz Seed Company, one of the major seed processing companies in Arkansas. They authorized the acquisition of $50,000 worth of machinery and the seed company sent an expert supervisor to help manage the rice and soy bean crops, which were the two major cash crops.

The livestock had been as ill-treated as the inmates. The silage pits were empty, the hay supply was practically exhausted, there were no harnesses for the mules or pads for the collars. Bare tug chains without proper leather protection were used on the mules so each mule had scar tissue about eighteen inches long and four to five inches wide on each side, where the chains had rubbed the hide raw.

Fences were down, gates had fallen off, and manure had built up in the barns to the hay loft. No cattle on the farm had ever been identified. The penitentiary board had, for years, refused to allow branding and ear-notching of livestock, claiming it was "not humane." The actual reason for the lack of branding, however, was that at least one of the former superintendents used to run his own cattle on the farm until they had been fattened up at state expense. Then he would return them to his own spread along with prison cattle and brand them with his mark.[1]

The calf crop was about one-third of what it should have been, considering the number of breeding cows and bulls. Frank and I counted 55 calves when there should have been 150. Most of the calves had been removed from the institution after weaning time—a plain case of cattle rustling, but an accepted form of personal profiteering by past management.[2]

Most of the hogs were ruptured and some had pneumonia.

Slaughtering of livestock was done with a large-bore rifle, which meant much of the meat was destroyed.

The slaughter house was a tin shed, open at both ends,

---
[1] According to the CID Report.
[2] According, again, to the CID Report.

with inadequate sanitary facilities. The cows were dragged through the mud from the slaughter house to be loaded onto doby wagons.

Frank and I looked through the main chicken house and found about 950 laying hens. Many had lice, however, and we were losing one or two a day from illness. In the main prison compound we found a locked tool shed. We pried open the door and there was a single chicken inside; one inmate obviously had planned a fried chicken dinner. The single chicken was arrested, taken into custody and placed in our care. Apart from the chicken, the tool shed was empty. There were no tools other than one sledge hammer and three claw hammers.

Like most southern prisons, Tucker had a dog kennel with bloodhounds especially trained to track down escapees. At Tucker, the inmates did the training. From time to time, the training procedures went amiss. A few months before I arrived at Tucker, four inmates who were supposed to be training the hounds had disappeared while laying a trail, leaving the dogs behind.

The dogs were well cared for, but the inmates responsible for them were living in squatter shacks that they'd built. I entered one of the shacks—a real crud hole—and saw three dozen brown eggs. The eggs in the main chicken house were white. Asked where the brown eggs were from, the inmates said they came from "their" chicken house, which was a former dog kennel.

The kennel had been converted into a chicken house and there were thirty-two Rhode Island Reds in there, the personal property of James Pike, an escapee then in custody in Oregon. Pike had transferred from Cummins with his chickens and had had a daily egg route, with regular customers among the inmates. The men on death row, for example, were among his best customers, since they could not "jungle" for themselves as other inmates did. Some of the condemned men had ranges in their cells on which they fried their own eggs. Some game chickens in the group belonged to another inmate, who was raising them for cock fights.

Another outbuilding had apparently been used for years as a toilet. There were thirty-five outhouses within throwing distance of the building, but custom decreed that the men defecate on the barracks floor, in the field, or in other buildings. I was never able to find out why. So I was not surprised some time later to find an outhouse that had been on the property for at least twenty years and discover that the hole had never been used. I posted a notice (see p. 47).

In addition to all the other disorganized clutter on the farm, there were about a dozen squatter shacks occupied by trusties who had seniority and tenure.

Because there were no privileges, former superintendents had allowed a few selected trusties certain fringe benefits. A trusty with money and power in the structure would scrounge some lumber and build himself a shack. He would give the electrician a couple of steaks to get power installed. He would get another inmate to pipe in gas. Next he would buy a TV and a range, and become a squatter. When he was paroled or left the prison he sold his job, house, and personal property to his successor. The squatters did not escape because they had the best of prison life. They had power over the other inmates; the former superintendent allowed them to have women; and they were permitted to go in town to get whiskey.

The men on the garden squad, who raised the vegetables for the inmates, were set up in an ancient barn with their own radios, ranges, and personal gardens. Nearby we discovered five collie pups living in a house along with several men who had cooking equipment and refrigerators.

The situation defied a shakedown. In any other institution the food would have been confiscated—because food equals power, and leads to exploitation. Here, there were so many squatter shacks that it would have disrupted the entire operation if I had done things too quickly. I tried to get the men to clean up their shacks, hoping that I could at least protect their health.

Not only did the men have shacks, but some of them even had cars. One day as I was going out the main gate, something came chugging by that resembled a motorized vehicle. I flagged the thing down, and one of the two men aboard jumped off and pulled a wire on the spark plug to bring it to a halt. The drivers were two inmates.

They explained that they were test-driving their new

TUCKER STATE FARM

To: All Inmates
From: Mr. Murton
Date: June 16, 1967
Subject: Defecating

"Defecating" is the art of removing fecal material (manure) from the bowels through the anus. To put it somewhat more crudly, you may know it as "taking a crap" or something even more blunt.

It has been said that Man is the only animal which will defecate in his own nest. I now believe that this is true. As one goes through the buildings on the farm either looking for equipment or space to store supplies he constantly finds feces squishing between his toes. I have never worked any place before where inmates consistently chose to defecate in houses and buildings rather than use the provided outhouses.

I just burned down a backhouse the other day which had been standing for at least twenty years as indicated by the rotting of the structure. While the hole was twelve feet deep, it was uncontaminated with any deposits.

I would like to remind you that as the season becomes increasingly warm and the flies and maggots tend to thrive on the accumulation of feces in these buildings, this leads to a situation which not only causes an unpleasant odor to permeate the air but constitutes a health hazard.

I am at a loss to understand why you do not use the backhouses provided and prefer to defecate in larger quarters without paper or stool. Possibly we could issue each man a small shovel each day to carry to work for the purpose of covering his feces. Even a cat has the intelligence to bury it. I have assumed that you have more intelligence than a cat but perhaps this was being over optomistic.

In any event, I am tired of discussing this situation with you and it is my responsibility to provide minimum protection for the health and welfare of the individuals on the farm.

Henceforth it will be a violation of institutional rules for anyone to defecate in any structure other than those specifically designed for this purpose. For those of you who are unfamiliary with a backhouse, they are usually built of wood (although some are made of brick), are about four feet square, have a door, there is usually a vent shaped as a crescent moon or some other design, there is a bench inside with an oblong hole (sometimes two) upon which one is to place his buttocks until such time as the spirit, and the bowels, move.

It also should be noted that rolls of soft paper are usually hung on the wall. This is to replace the corn cob or stick you have been using.

It is expected in the future you will take advantage of these new modern facilities. Anyone failing to follow these procedures will promptly be subjected to disciplinary action.

Tom Murton
Superintendent

vehicle, which had four different-sized wheels and tires. Basically it was a frame with a steering mechanism, chain-driven by a Wisconsin engine hooked to the drive axle. One of the difficulties with it was that they had not devised a braking system. I suggested they check an anvil out of the shop and attach it to a log chain, then shove it overboard when they wanted to stop, instead of jumping out and pulling a wire on a spark plug.

Little wonder that after my first three weeks at Tucker I summed up my reactions to the project in the daily log: "It seems like we can't get hold of this institution. It's just one big can of worms, and wherever you grab one piece, you shake up the whole enterprise.

"There are people cooking all over the farm, they've got their own houses, their own refrigerators, their own stoves, their own cooking equipment and food. There are still payoffs, purchases of goods and services. We've got dope inside. It's just one big funny farm. When you want to make one minor change you have to revamp the entire system. The complexity of the operation is beyond belief. I've dubbed this place the Tucker Time Tunnel. Enter this institution and you go back one hundred years in penology."

The Real Heroes

Chainsaw Jack was an old peck who had spent most of his fifty years in southern prisons. He was short and heavy set, had a ruddy complexion, wore glasses, and had a low, mellifluous voice which ran on and on whenever anybody would listen to him. He was bright, as many old pecks are bright, from listening to newscasts, constant arguing in the barracks, and hard thinking during long hours in solitary.

Jack loved roses and had rose bushes planted alongside his guard shack. Whenever I drove by his shack, he would stop my car and point out his blooms, and then we would talk a bit, his big head inside the car to shield his eyes from the sun.

He was a storehouse of tales, and after a while I began to catch glimpses of his past. He never told me the whole story, just bits and pieces. He was a country boy from Louisiana who had gone barefoot and worn faded, torn Levis to school. After school he had chopped cotton until dark.

For years he was in and out of fights, jails, love affairs, barrooms, and courtrooms. He paid fines to the city and county authorities as regularly as most men pay mortgages.

After serving a sentence in Louisiana, he went on to Wyoming; eventually he made it into Arkansas, where he committed the crime that earned him his nickname.

Jack was a poet, and I never tired of hearing his poems, written and committed to memory when he was in the hole.

In them he spoke of the not so distant days in Arkansas when a prisoner prayed to live out the day because death

Accomplices to the Crime

and torture were as much a part of his sentence as time. In one of the poems, which he called "The Arkansas Pen," he told of his joy at meeting a trusty who was from his old home town and of how:

> . . . *I struggled and strived and made it 'til noon.*
> *Then the captain drove up a little too soon.*
> *He parked his truck on the old head land*
> *And when he left the cab he had the hide in his hand.*
> *Then here rider was on the head land jumping up and down saying,*
> *"Come here, Cap'n, and meet old home town.*
> *He thinks 'cause I know him I should let him slide*
> *So give the dirty rascal a taste of that old hide . . ."*

The poem that was one of my favorites ends:

> . . . *This place is no church house, it's plain to see*
> *But doggone if it hasn't made a Christian out of me.*

Jack had seen superintendents come and go during his twenty years in the Arkansas prison, and he played it cool. Until I came to Tucker, Jack's only interest in who the superintendent was or how the prison was run, was so he could figure out how to survive; reform was a word on a campaign platform.

Jack believed now that the changes we were making were good for the inmates. He gave me the best compliment I ever received when he told me:

"You make an inmate feel like a human—which he never felt like before."

So Chainsaw Jack Bell was on my side. There were others, too. Many others.

When I first went to Tucker, the hole was full of hard cases from Cummins because the latter had no cells. These men had a reputation for raising hell with the administration by ribbing and agitating, and slow-playing. I couldn't break their power by firing them, as I could with freeworld staff members, so my strategy was to use their proven leadership for prison reform.

I met Arnold Rhodes on my fourth day at Tucker, when I visited death row and the segregation cells with Austin MacCormick, a visiting penologist. MacCormick stopped to talk with Rhodes and asked him what he thought about the new administration.

The Real Heroes

Rhodes, who was in solitary confinement but still in touch with prison life through the grapevine, said that the new superintendent seemed to be on the right track. He said that as an inmate he was looking forward to change.

During the conversation I was standing next to MacCormick, who asked Rhodes, "Do you know this man?"

Rhodes didn't know me. MacCormick, a big smile on his face, introduced us.

At this first meeting with Rhodes I was impressed by his forthrightness. He didn't look impressive: he was around five feet nine with a copper complexion, dark hair, and jet black eyes; but he was taut as a wire. Later I learned he was part Cherokee Indian and had the stoicism of his tribe; he could be killed but not broken.

I checked him out and found he had been sentenced to life imprisonment in Arkansas when he was just twenty-one years old. The police considered him the most dangerous criminal in Arkansas because of his constant escapes. He was then in the hole after an escape attempt during which he kidnapped a woman.

I also found out that he had been a cook. When problems arose in the kitchen and I decided to replace the rider in charge, Rhodes came to mind. I was cautioned by the state police to leave him alone because he was a dangerous criminal with an escape record, but I believed he could be trusted. When I appointed him, I told him, "Well, if you leave, send me a postcard."

Rhodes wasn't a poet like Chainsaw Jack, but he had a good eye for truth and he understood what we were trying to do. "Those kids that come here today off the street don't know nothing about what it was like before," he would say. "They are enjoying everything here that somebody had to pay for. Any time anything good happens, somebody has got to pay for it."

As Rhodes proved his trustworthiness I gave him more authority, which meant more opportunities for him to escape. Instead of tightening security on Rhodes, I relaxed it—in my opinion the key to good prison management is that the administration must make the first move. None of the men I put in trust ever escaped during my administration.

Some time later I asked Rhodes why he hadn't taken off.

"I've had a bad life all my life," he said. "I've no family, no one ever cared for me, but I'm psychic and somebody can walk up to me and tell me something and I can look at him and know he's lying. I talked to you a thousand times and you never told me a lie, not one time. Never. If it was yes, it was yes and if it was no, it was no. That's something I like. I would rather not have a long story about nothing.

"I've always been pretty bull-headed, and if I took a notion I didn't want to work I sat in the barracks and if they wanted me I let them come get me. I've been whipped by the captain, but there ain't no Longline rider or goon squad can whip me. I'd just get tired of working, and the way they treat you and the way they feed you. You wasn't even allowed to go to church. If you wrote a letter to your people and said something out of the way, they tore it up. If they had an AA [Alcoholics Anonymous] meeting and you was caught talking to a freeworld person, you was whipped.

"I done twelve years and busted out three times. Each time I set myself up to leave. I'd been drove to a spot and I'd no hope. My patience was gone. I couldn't reason with myself no more. I just didn't see no way out at all, and a year ago I didn't look at things like I do today. Now, I could run away today, which wouldn't help me a bit in the world, but it would hurt a lot of other people."

Rhodes is one of a handful of heroes in my story. While I had laid my reputation on the line when I agreed to reform the Arkansas prisons, the inmates who worked with me like Jack Bell, Jim Nabors, Otis Standridge, Charlie Mann, Reuben Johnson, and others, put their lives in jeopardy.

All the inmates who worked with me suffered for it, and frequently there was nothing I could do. Rhodes was called "Tom Murton's man" and because of it, in the summer of 1967, they threw the book at him on an old escape and kidnapping charge. He got twenty-four years for the same offenses that brought three and one-half year sentences to other men in the dock with him.

Another man in the hole when I came to Tucker was William King Jackson. He was a writ writer, and there is

The Real Heroes

nothing a corrupt prison system can tolerate less than a man who complains to the courts.

Jackson had protested against the use of the strap while at Cummins, and his writs, sent to the Attorney General, had produced results: a series of rules governing the use of the strap were issued, though generally ignored. When he testified in court, Jackson told how "Big Mose" Harmon, a six-foot-two, three-hundred-pound freeworld warden, had laid sixty-eight lashes on him. When he returned to prison from court that night, Big Mose came up to Jackson and said, "Well, I heard you did a little talking in court today."

"That's right, Cap'n," said Jackson.

"Lay down," said Big Mose. Jackson was spreadeagled on the floor and Big Mose laid sixty-two more cuts with the strap across his back. When he completed the last lash he asked Jackson, "How many is that?"

"Eight, Cap'n," said Jackson.

Big Mose laid on the strap again until Jackson was unconscious.

As further punishment for his writ writing, Jackson was sent from Cummins to Tucker with orders that he was to be "buried"—in other words, put in solitary confinement in the hole.

He was in the hole—a group of cells that back up on death row—when I first saw him. He had been in solitary for several months and looked frightening, although he claimed he liked being in the hole because people left him alone to do his own time.

I talked with him from time to time, and one day early in March he sent me a message: "I want out of the hole and am ready to work for you."

I required every inmate to work at least thirty days in the Longline before giving him a break, because I wanted him to demonstrate that he could pull duty. Jackson was medically unfit and couldn't work in the line, so I placed him in the garden squad. When he had been there a few weeks, Jim Nabors, the yard man, came up to me and said, "Man, you're really moving."

"Why?" I asked.

"Jackson has been in the prison for ten years and never worked for anybody. He was setting back there in the hole

Accomplices to the Crime

and volunteered to work for you because he believes in what you are trying to do."

Gurvis Nichols had been sixteen years old and still in high school in 1960, when he was sentenced to twenty-one years for murder.

Like Chainsaw Jack, he wrote poems in isolation, and I still remember some stanzas from one of them:

> *You will think the worst is over*
> *But you'll quickly change your mind*
> *When you settle to the routine*
> *Of the Tucker prison grind.*
>
> *Poets talk of the sunny south,*
> *Singing promises to the stars,*
> *But they never tell the story*
> *Of the man behind the bars.*
>
> *Of how he eats corn, rice and syrup*
> *And meatless potato stew,*
> *And works like hell from morning to night*
> *For some half-breed prison screw.*
>
> *So you live the life of Riley*
> *That you dreamed of in your cell*
> *But you are just another victim*
> *Of the road that leads to Hell.*

Nichols had worked in the kitchen at Cummins for two years when the freeworld warden, "Captain" Ray Deam, accused him of not picking up a tray of scrap bread.

Nichols explained that it was his job to clean the floor and the baker's job to pick up the bread. "You're sassin' me back, you little bastard!" Deam said, and took Nichols to the gun cage where he kept his bullhide. He ordered Nichols to "make a spread" in front of the cage. Then he laid nine licks across Nichols' back, chewing him up so badly he was hospitalized for two weeks.

Deam was called "The Cheater" by the inmates, because when he whipped he turned the strap sideways, gashing the man's buttocks or back an inch and a half deep, chipping out chunks of flesh with every cut of the whip. It was then that Nichols got the nervous tic that earned him his nickname of "Nervous Gurvis."

Nichols had chances to escape during my administration

while he was out on furloughs. I asked him why he didn't cut out.

"Two and a half years ago I would have cut out," he said. "But now I would lose everything I have."

I pointed out that he still had several years to serve on his original sentence before he would be eligible for parole.

"Yeah," he said, "but I can do it. I won't be but twenty-nine when I get out and I'm learnin' a lot. You have me in the library and other places where maybe it don't apply directly to my getting a job on the street, but they are jobs where I can learn to accept responsibility.

"Why go out and run off where I couldn't even get a job? I never held a job down in my life. I was a student in school when I was arrested, but with you here I know I can make it back."

Jim Nabors was one of my best men. Nabors, who was serving fifteen years, was an easy-going Arkie in his late forties who could charm the birds out of trees if he wished. Most people liked him instantly, and because he was a good listener he picked up information every place he went.

He disliked doing heavy work and avoided it whenever possible, which may explain why he had been in and out of prison most of his life. He was a mass of contradictions. Although an excessive drinker, he never drank while he was on duty, and he was responsible for knocking over several of the stills on the farm. Placid by nature, he was capable of standing up and fighting for what he believed was right.

It was Nabors who urged me to reinstate the rank of inmate sheriff. When I asked him to explain what that was, he said, "Well, Mr. Murton, the sheriff is a convict who drives a prison truck, operates the police radio, carries a gun, and makes sure the trusties do their job."

"You've got to be kidding," I said.

"No sir. It takes a convict to understand the convict mind. I know who's goin' to run, I'll keep the trusties awake, and I know all the escape routes from the farm. Make me sheriff and you won't have any more trouble."

At the time, I shook my head in disbelief, but later I bought him a badge, gave him a gun, and appointed him sheriff with authority over all the other inmate guards. It proved to be a wise decision.

Accomplices to the Crime

Ronnie Crabtree, who was a trusty, began to emerge as an important agent for change in the fall of 1967, when he took positive action to help me even though it put him in personal danger. A weatherbeaten six-footer who looked like a typical hillbilly, Crabtree was completely fearless and tough. In his late forties or early fifties, he too had spent much of his life in prison.

Otis Standridge was another. I first met Otis on the day that Frank Crawford and I toured the farm and outbuildings. A powerful man, well over six feet tall, Otis thought of the prison as almost a second home and he had two or three brothers in at the same time. Because he was a trusty and wise in the ways of survival, he had made a good life for himself.

I found that he had been on an all-fried-meat diet before we stopped all that. He was not eating in the kitchen; he took his meals in his shack, where he had a range and refrigerator and an inmate to do his cooking.

In the course of a conversation with Standridge I asked him where he got his meat.

"Well, I'll be honest with you," he said, looking me straight in the eye: "I steal it."

Since Standridge was being candid with me I was equally candid with him. "O.K.," I said, "you're an inmate and I'm the superintendent, and as long as you can get away with stealing, lots of luck. But don't let me catch you stealing or I'll have to rank you."

"I understand that," he said.

"Don't ever let me catch you getting meat out of cold storage," I said. "I don't care where else you get it because I'll worry about chopping off that source later."

"O.K.," said Standridge.

I demanded only one thing of the inmates who worked for or with me: honesty. Standridge and the others were always honest. They were not "yes" men or boot lickers; in fact, many times we disagreed on matters of policy. Though I made my own decisions, which many times varied from their opinions, I listened carefully to what they had to say.

And these men saw reform for what it really was: a program that would enable them to survive with some

The Real Heroes

dignity as human beings while they served their sentences.

They came to my side of their own free will. There was no way they could be coerced into working for a superintendent or a system.

They were the ones who really changed the prison, not I or the governor, not the public nor the various investigating committees or prison boards. I used selected inmates as change agents on the assumption that an inmate is not a moral pauper. He may have one or two defects in his overall character, but there are still areas in which he can function normally and positively. Therefore, I had to find inmates who had the same dedication and zeal that motivated the freeworld staff.

I was not so concerned about why the men were in prison as I was about their relationship to me and the other inmates. The crimes they'd committed on the street were only important when I was going to give a man a gun or put him in the freeline housing area, where he might become involved in an incident.

I believe one of the mistakes most correctional departments make is giving a man an assignment on the basis of his record rather than on a character evaluation. If you stick to the old labeling procedure, a man is pegged for the rest of his prison life, and he will never get a chance to function normally and positively in a new role.

My basic assumption was that most of the inmates could accommodate to me and my methods, just as they had accommodated to the superintendent before me. A prisoner is not a different kind of man from a man in a freeworld corporation who finds himself with a new boss. He learns to adjust and to do things the way the new boss wants them, or he gets out.

I tried to make deals with the men I felt could be most helpful to me. If they would do things the way I wanted, I would keep them as trusties.

Sometimes I would call an inmate in and say, "This is what you've been doing but you can't do that under me." I had such a conversation with the laundry rider, who wanted to become a trusty. I laid out the details of our agreement quite clearly. "I don't want anybody paying for laundry any more, and I'm going to make you a trusty if you guarantee me that nobody will pay for laundry. But if I hear of anybody paying you a dime, down the tube you go."

He said O.K., and it worked out fine for a couple of weeks. But a few weeks later he began to charge for laundry again, and I had to replace him with someone who would not exploit the inmates.

Under the old system, the trusties worked for the warden directly over them. They were not concerned with the prison administration or with the superintendent; from their point of view the warden really was The Man.

I wanted to get the trusties to work for the administration, that is, for me. I wanted them to do what I wanted, and I didn't care what someone else told them to do. They were not to go against my wishes.

One day two trusties came to me questioning an order of warden Thomas Gann, who had told them to burn down a barn. They didn't think I wanted it done. That was the beginning of a big change, the first indication that the inmates were really responding to my wishes and could discreetly challenge the orders of the old wardens. It meant I was getting through to them. For the first time they were identifying with the new administration.

One of the major problems at Tucker, as in all other institutions, was communication. I wanted the inmate population to be able to tell me quickly about news of sensitive areas and priorities for change. Then I could respond quickly. At the same time I wanted to be able to get information out fast to the inmates by some means other than memo or announcements.

In Alaska, earlier in my career, I had developed a "camp council," made up of members of the inmate body who truly represented them. The system worked there; it might work in Arkansas.

Early in March I spent a great deal of time talking with the men about such a council—planting the idea in their minds. I had to start from scratch explaining secret balloting and the technique of a primary election.

We held the primary election one night in mid-March in the main auditorium. The men from each barracks were brought in one group at a time. There was a portable blackboard set up at the end of the room. Gurvis Nichols was in charge of the mechanics of voting. I issued the ballots, which had blank spaces where the men could nominate two names. I emphasized the type of inmates to be selected, and said that it was in their own best interest not to select wheels as candidates.

The inmates filed up to the blackboard and dropped their folded ballots in a box. A group selected at random by the inmates were the election judges. The ballots were spread out on the floor of the boxing ring and counted. The judges signed the results, certifying that they were correct, and Nichols wrote the names of the four candidates who had received the most votes on the blackboard.

We followed the same procedure with each of the barracks and the following night held the general election. All the ballots were stamped with a date stamp, and I took great pains to make sure all the procedures were in the open so that the inmates would be convinced that it was honest and above board.

The election ended up as a short course in civics. The inmates were pleased with the results, and so was I. None of the men elected as Farm Council members—two from each barracks—was an operator. None of them had had any power before, and none of them had bought or sold jobs.

Only a few of the inmates, like Otis Standridge and Chainsaw Jack, argued with me about the council. They never understood that inmate power itself is not evil; it's the type of power that matters, and we were trying to substitute legitimate self-government for the goon squad.

The Farm Council met on Saturday afternoons in the superintendent's office. We sat down at a table and reviewed the inmate files before going through the same classification procedures that a civilian staff would use in other institutions. None of the men classified for minimum custody by the council ever attempted to escape—which showed that the inmates were functioning more effectively than the freeworld staff. They made certain the men they appointed as trusties or do-pops were not people who wanted to escape.

Half of the members of the Farm Council formed the disciplinary committee, which met in the death house because most of the men coming up for disciplinary action were in the hole. There were four members including William King Jackson and myself. Each of us had an equal vote, although I reserved the right to veto any action. This committee heard all complaints against inmates; decided guilt or innocence; and rendered judgment.

We reviewed each man's files, read the disciplinary report on the inmate when he came in and then, in rotation, discussed the situation with the man, one of the members of the committee taking the lead in questioning him and getting the full story. We also questioned any witnesses. The man was sent back to his quarters, and we made a decision later in the evening.

All the inmates had an alternative: they could have a hearing either before the committee or before me alone. It was interesting to note that with only two exceptions they chose the committee, which was inevitably harsher than I would have been. Yet I never felt it necessary to use my power of veto over committee decisions.

Committee members determined punishments. For example, it was agreed that men who were returned from an escape would lose all visiting privileges and would be allowed to send only one letter a week out, although they could receive all incoming letters. They would also be denied all commissary privileges. Their confinement was to last a minimum of thirty days, but could go to sixty days, depending upon their attitude.

Although the punishments were not so harsh as in former times, when the strap would have been used indiscriminately, they turned out to be just as effective in maintaining order and control.

I believed that with the proper classification and disciplinary methods we could eventually get complete control of the prison. The fact that we were using prisoners themselves for this would send chills down the backs of most penologists, but I had every confidence that the system could work effectively. It did.

At Tucker we had among the inmates a father and son, Frank and Jerry Harrison, and for some time I tried to get Jerry into the garage where his father worked, hoping he would have a positive influence on the boy, who always seemed to be in trouble. I was not willing to accept the argu-

The Real Heroes

ment that the father was to blame for the son's wrongdoing. Jerry had served a sentence as a juvenile at the Arkansas Boys' Industrial School at Pine Bluff[1] and I believed he was more a product of the system than of his parents' influence.

Jerry was forever getting into skirmishes at the prison and was never on the Longline long enough for me to promote him to the garage.

One day, he was brought before the disciplinary committee for an infraction of the rules. I was all for putting him in the hole but Jackson took me aside and said, "I can straighten that kid out. He's exactly the way I was ten years ago. Let me be personally responsible for him."

"You want to play parole officer?" I asked.

"Yeah," said Jackson, "let me be his parole officer. Move him into the barracks I'm in where I can keep an eye on him."

I told Jackson, who had been promoted from the garden squad to floorwalker, that if the boy messed up he would be ranked too and sent out to pick cotton.

"Give me a chance with the kid," said Jackson.

I asked Jerry if he would work if he were paroled to Jackson. He said he would.

Jackson told the boy, "I'm going to take you into the barracks with me and keep you out of trouble. In return, I expect you to keep your business straight, or else you'll have trouble with me."

The boy went to the Longline, where he worked for thirty days and kept his business straight in the barracks. I was able to put him in the garden squad next and finally move him into the garage where his father was working. There were no further difficulties with Jerry, and he was eventually paroled.

The freeworld staff members could not have brought about this change in the boy, but inmate Jackson, who had been buried in the hole by the former superintendent, in this instance turned out to be the most effective change agent in the prison.

---

[1] This institution was one of four training schools—separate facilities for Negro and white, boys and girls—for confinement of delinquent children. As in the regular prison, the boys work on farms. There is no minimum age for commitment; at the time, an eight-year-old boy was serving an indefinite sentence at the Pine Bluff institution.

The Freeworld Missionaries

The only men in Arkansas with experience as prison guards were ex-inmates. Because of this—and my curiosity—I decided to hire former inmates as officers. At least they had had on-the-job training.

There was not time to train freeworld people who had no experience. I believed, anyway, that the correctional authorities should demonstrate that we believed what we were preaching—that inmates are human and can be trusted to function properly, with adequate supervision.

Herman Helton was the first ex-inmate I employed. He was paroled to me on September 21st and hired at his former job as gate guard. Helton became an excellent officer; later I hired four other former inmates, who did equally well.

This criminological innovation at Tucker was made easier by the general acceptance of the notion of giving inmates authority and because of the total lack of understanding in the freeworld of what was going on.

It takes a special kind of man to work in a prison without being corrupted by it himself. Put any freeman on a job and it's likely an old peck can break him in the way he wants to, because the freeman relies on the convict to show him the ropes. Before the freeman is broken in, the inmates will have something on him—perhaps just a minor infraction of regulations—but the convict will have the freeman in his power.

I needed the inmates on my side, but, equally important, I needed to have outside help. The ratio of freeworld staff

The Freeworld Missionaries

to inmates in Arkansas was one to sixty-five; the national average is one to seven. One of my first plans was to employ freeworld people to take over the essential areas of the institution, so that I could begin to phase out the armed trusties.

Since no one would go to Arkansas for the pay, which was dismal, or the prestige, which was nil, I had to find people with missionary zeal, integrity, and the ability to straighten out some of the simple administrative problems. The processing of the inmate mail, for instance, was a major headache. In the past, an inmate had been sent into town unescorted to pick up the mail. On his return to the farm he was supposed to open the mail and take out all the money; theoretically it was given to the clerk, who entered the amounts in the inmates' personal accounts.

As I suspected, not all of the money sent to inmates reached them. In the case of money orders, the inmate who received the draft had to sign it and acknowledge receipt of the total amount, even though he got only part of it. If he refused to sign the receipt, he didn't get even part of the money, which was given in the form of brozene—bronze coins.

I wanted the mail system changed. There was a money swindle; there was too great a time lag between the mail's arrival at the prison and its delivery to the inmates; furthermore, one inmate had access to the contents of all letters, which gave him control over the others. That inmate knew who was having problems at home, and he could use the knowledge to his advantage. He knew who had received money, too, and this meant he could tip off the loan sharks for a fee if the inmate withheld money he owed.

Fortunately for me my former roommate at Oklahoma A & M, Don Bassett, was then living at Fort Smith, Arkansas. Bassett had a degree in business management and twelve years' experience as a troubleshooter for Western Auto Stores. He agreed to come to the penitentiary to help out and straighten up the books, put honesty into the business management, and start proper purchasing procedures to get us the materials we needed.

It was several weeks, though, before the inmates actually believed that if they got $5 in the mail, Bassett would give them $5.

Accomplices to the Crime

As a first step in doing away with the inmate guard force, we needed a chief security officer. I wrote to Harold Porter, who was then with the prison system in Australia. He had been the first officer I'd hired at the Ketchikan jail when the new jail system for the State of Alaska was instituted.

He agreed to leave his job immediately and travel twelve thousand miles to Arkansas. As might have been expected, the Arkansas penitentiary board hesitated to pay for bringing a man from Australia. What finally clinched it was the fact that he had been born in El Dorado, Arkansas. O.E. Bishop said, "We ought to bring the Arkansas boys home." Luckily the board didn't know Porter had been born in El Dorado because his parents were traveling from New York to Texas; his mother went into labor in Arkansas and he had spent only the first three days of his life there. Because of his recent ties to Australia, Harold soon became known among the inmates as Captain Kangaroo.

Victor Urban, another from the original Alaska cadre, was a case worker for the federal bureau of prisons at Terminal Island in California. He had valuable experience in probation and parole and had long ago told me of his ambition to become a superintendent or warden. I believed he could develop parole procedures at Tucker and could eventually become a superintendent, or director of pardons and paroles.

I arranged for him to fly to Little Rock to meet with Governor Rockefeller. I told the governor what I thought Urban could do in the Arkansas system, and said he would be a potential prison administrator who would be able to supervise Tucker when, later, I went to Cummins.

The governor personally provided funds for Urban's move to Arkansas, and Urban's first assignment was to examine inmate records to see if time had been taken away from them illegally. We found some men still at Tucker who were eligible for parole, and some who had actually finished serving their sentences. One man was five months overdue for release because his "good time" had been taken away illegally. Within a few weeks we were able to release more than two dozen inmates who had served their sentences but were still in prison because of the inefficiencies or corruption of the system.

This small group of people whom I brought to Tucker in

The Freeworld Missionaries

the first few weeks of my takeover were dedicated to the job. They knew that prison reform takes time and patience. They were not rigid, and this is important; it takes a very special kind of person to survive on the staff in the Arkansas prisons.

I made one mistake in staff that was nearly tragic. We had an application from a student I had met who was working on his master's degree. He was a student of penology and had intermittent experience in some other institutions.

He visited the farm along with a couple of other people we were considering, and I agreed to hire him. He arrived at the farm the first week in April with his wife and child, and as an introductory assignment I made him postal officer.

He went beyond his area of responsibility and got hung up on the total decadence of the system, wanting to move too fast and accomplish everything at once. He was experiencing the traditional conflict between theory and practice. In reforming a prison, timing is most important in making changes, and decisions about timing are primarily based on experience.

He had difficulties right away. He started to interfere with the other crews and complained that the inmates were not working with him. He was intrigued with the cops and robbers atmosphere of the prison, and wanted to play Dick Tracy.

He went to England, a farming community nine miles from Tucker, and saw the chief of police and told him he was available in case he, the chief, needed any help. Then he got a gun and went out supervising the guard force, even though that was not his job.

He became nervous and anxious, and eventually stopped eating. He seemed completely unable to get the mail processed on time, and this created hard feelings and interfered with the operation of the institution. I had some heart-to-heart talks with him, telling him that he would probably work out but he had to consider himself a nonparticipating observer for a while.

It was against my policy for an officer to perform personal services for an inmate but he was carrying cookies out to the front gate guard to "establish rapport," as he termed it.

Later the gate guard came to me to ask, "What's with this new mailman we've got?"

"Well, what do you think he's up to?" I asked.

"He's trying to get information from me."

A couple of days later I asked the officer what he was doing. "I've been out blowing smoke," he said, meaning he was covering his trail.

He was unable to relax. He saw too much to do and everything shocked him. I kept telling him to take it easy. You can't do everything overnight. But he wanted instant reform.

One day, a week after he arrived, he went in town and bought a fifty-foot dog chain so the tower guard could lower his key from the top and be let out. He bought some red and green bulbs to put in the tower for signaling and a mirror so the guard could flash the yard officer and let him know if anybody was getting oversexed in the yard on visiting day. He also bought a fluorescent compass so he could find his way to the towers at night.

The next day he ordered the hogs butchered, shot in the heart with his own gun, thus destroying much of the meat. That afternoon I received an urgent phone call from the yard and learned that his wife had fled her home with her baby, and taken sanctuary with my wife. She was afraid he was going to kill her.

I went to my house for a talk with his wife, who said she was afraid her husband was a borderline psychotic and had reached the point where he was a threat to himself and everyone at the institution.

While I was talking with her, Margaret, my wife, received a call from him in Tower Number Two. He had left his keys locked in his car. He said he had barricaded himself in the tower and planned to stay there until she brought over a duplicate set of car keys.

I told his wife to get her keys from the house. While she was gone, I strapped on my shoulder holster and a .38. When she returned, I took the keys and went to the building, telling Lieutenant Lowman to stand by and back me up in case of necessity.

The man came down voluntarily when he saw me, and I realized he was very disturbed. I suggested we go to my office for a talk.

The Freeworld Missionaries

We talked for almost four hours, during which time he became hostile, began quivering, and practically lost control of himself. I told him he was not doing his job properly. He demanded he be confronted by other members of the institution, to see what they thought of his contributions. So I arranged to have Don Bassett come in but Bassett came close to hitting him, and almost brought the interview to a close. Harold Porter confronted him and said he wasn't suited for this kind of work. The Crawfords were equally candid, as was Lieutenant Lowman.

I called the boy's father, an army officer in Texas. He wanted no part of caring for his son, and suggested we have him committed to an institution in Arkansas. I then terminated him and restricted him to his quarters, so he could sleep for a day before he left the premises.

This failure to adjust to life at Tucker was largely a result of his having studied theory at college without any actual practice in the field. His experience in other institutions had been as an observer rather than a participant. Also, the limited experience he had, as well as his studies, dealt with the usual institutions found outside of Arkansas. Even officers with experience in other prisons found it difficult to function in Arkansas' unique system.

I have often seen that a formal education can be a hindrance rather than a help to survival in the prison community. More than 25 per cent of the Tucker inmates were illiterate, and the one or two college-educated men were of little value to me because they believed themselves to be above the system rather than part of it.

One inmate, who was serving three years for burglary, was a case in point. After four years of college and three of law school, he was convinced he was the smartest man at Tucker. He worked his way quickly into the front office as a clerk because he could type and make computations. But he wasn't satisfied.

He never admitted to himself that he was an inmate. He set himself apart from the other inmates, who were naturally resentful. I tried him at a number of jobs, but he didn't know how to survive and maintain his presumed status. He wanted to wheel and deal at the expense of other inmates and give them nothing in return. Few things can wipe out an inmate or officer faster among the prison population than his belief that he is better than they are. This inmate caused so many problems that I finally had to send him out with the Longline, picking cotton, and eventually gave him a punitive transfer to Cummins.

Meanwhile something else had come up, which indicated to me that I needed good professional help quickly if I was to do away with the excesses of violence and cruelty that had been the order of the day before I took over.

An old peck named Dick Williams said he knew of five inmates who had been shot and then buried in a hole in the Warren Field, about two miles southeast of the main Tucker buildings.

"And there's others buried there, Mr. Murton," he told me.

Williams had already served twenty-five years in the penitentiary of a life sentence for murder. He claimed he could still see the sink holes out on the grassy knoll where the ground had collapsed, long before tractors were used on the farm.

Other old pecks had told me more or less the same story —that bodies of murdered inmates were buried on the farm—and it seemed to me that if I could find the bodies I could begin on my plan of educating the people of Arkansas about the past evils and we could do away with the myth that Arkansas had a great prison system. Shock was needed, to gain public demand for change. Some Arkansas citizens might approve of homosexuality, brutality, excessive punishment, working fourteen and fifteen hours a day, lack of clothing, and the even more harsh treatment of the Negro inmates, but I doubted that there were many people even in the State of Arkansas who would condone the murder of inmates.

One afternoon I suggested that Williams join me in a little archeological exploration on top of the knoll. We worked for about an hour, digging a hole about five feet deep in an area that appeared to be depressed, but we found nothing.

I borrowed a bulldozer from Cummins on the pretext of digging a trench silo. We used the dozer for about a week, excavating the alleged grave site, but found nothing. I gave up on the project for a while.

The Convict Posse

During my first month at Tucker there were three escapes. The second month there were eight more, and on one day alone in the third month there were six. Although most inmates were captured after a few hours, there was a Keystone Cops quality to some of our manhunts. Sometimes I wondered how we ever did manage to get the prisoners back inside.

One day word came that two rank men had overpowered their shotgun guard and escaped in a doby wagon full of goat manure, which had been destined for the strawberry patch. The shotgun man had hobbled into camp minus his gun, two hours after the escape, to report that the men had taken off. There were five major escape routes from the farm, and we knew roughly which route they must have taken.

I notified Frank Crawford, who was in charge of training the dogs by then; the "dog boy," who handled them on hunts; and the state police. Then I took off in a truck with the shotgun guard to the site of the escape. We found the doby wagon at the edge of the bayou, which had risen as a result of heavy rains.

While waiting for the dogs, I studied the bank of the bayou, looking for tracks. There were none. I unhitched the mule team, tied them to a tree, and left the shotgun man standing by to show Crawford over the area.

At the farm, the escape procedure was already in motion. The police set up roadblocks throughout the area, and an inmate posse was formed. Six trusties were issued guns, and three of them went out on horseback, with instructions to phone in from time to time from some place along their routes; the other three went off in trucks with the same instructions. They had to use public phones too, because we had only one car radio.

Crawford loaded his truck with men and dogs and drove to the escape site, where he found the spot where the men had crossed the bayou and made it to the other side. He was hot on the trail when his pickup truck got stuck on a country road.

Claude Overton, the farm manager, who was following him, was unable to get by in his pickup because the road was too narrow. Overton's truck had just come back from Cummins loaded with flour and butter when it had been commandeered for the chase.

When I arrived at the scene, the dogs were baying, the butter was melting into the flour, and the carburetor from Crawford's truck was laid out neatly alongside the road in pieces.

We could not continue the chase until we got Crawford's truck out of the way. I suggested that they pick up the carburetor and that Overton push Crawford's truck. The trucks were about to make contact when I shouted, "I don't think that will . . ." There was a crash: all the headlights on the second truck were broken.

I called in on the radio for a wrecker to come and tow Crawford's truck. We loaded the dogs into their cages, put the butter, flour, inmates, and guards into Overton's pickup and mine, and backed down the road.

While all this was going on, the three mounted inmates were off searching the bayous. Mindful of their orders to check in, one of the inmates, a rather seedy looking character wearing a six gun, stopped at a house in the woods, knocked on the door, and tipped his crumpled hat in Tex Ritter style to the housewife. "I'm from Tucker Prison Farm, ma'am," he said, "and I would like to use your phone to report in where I'm at." Understandably the lady slammed the door in his face.

He finally located a pay phone, but couldn't get through to the prison. The line was busy. The next time he called our Mickey Mouse switchboard, he got J.D. Niven's General

Store. On the third try he made contact and was told that the prisoners had been apprehended by the state police at a road block. Like most of the inmates who attempted to escape, the men were unsuccessful because they were loners and took off without any plan in mind, and without any money or contacts. Their only aim was to see their families, or to get into another state, where they might find asylum.

Some states, such as Oregon, tended to resist extradition attempts. One Oregon judge, for example, refused to return four Arkansas escapees on the grounds that he did not believe "the courts of Oregon should encourage Arkansas by aiding and abetting her in the management of her institutes of terror, horror, and despicable evil. No court in an asylum state has a right to ignore practices involving substantial and systematic deprivation of constitutional rights."

Circuit Judge Lyle Wolff, speaking from the bench in Oregon on June 2, 1967, said that "undisputed evidence . . . establishes that Arkansas conducts at her two penal institutions, Cummins and Tucker, a system of barbarity, cruelty, torture, bestiality, corruption, terror and animal viciousness that reeks of Dachau and Auschwitz.

"The people of Arkansas are chargeable with the neglect, wrongdoing and failures of her governing officials.

"Her legislators cannot plead ignorance of these revolting conditions. The legislature establishes and generally provides institutions for the execution of sentences. The legislature in its appropriation and general policy-making functions is guilty either of indifference and failure to visit and to inspect, by committee or otherwise, institutions, or of cynical and deliberate refusal to take positive, decent and civilized action to remedy the conditions in her institutions.

"Her governors in the past could not possibly have been unaware of these ruthless and deliberate violations of the constitutional rights of prisoners to be free of cruel and unusual punishment, if the chief executives of our sister state were attending to their responsibilities in the area of prison management."[1]

He also noted that "the subjection of the prisoners to

---

[1] *Pine Bluff Commercial*, Pine Bluff, Arkansas, June 4, 1967, p. 12.

Accomplices to the Crime

physical violence if they are returned and probably to death itself is not mere speculation."

The surprising thing is not how many prisoners escaped but how few. Almost any time a trusty felt like leaving he could simply take off. Many of the trusties had guns and cars at their disposal, and were permitted to be on the roads or in the towns during the day. They were, after all, staff members.

Frequently there was confusion about a prisoner's intentions. One day a Cummins inmate was sent into Dumas to get a truck repaired. He was given a gate pass. After leaving the truck at the garage he went to lunch, had a few drinks in a neighborhood bar, and then went to shack up with his girl. Late in the day he picked up the truck.

By then, someone at the prison had noticed he was missing and sent out an all-points bulletin. He was picked up at a road block but as he was headed in the general direction of the prison it was assumed he was in fact on his way back. Only in Arkansas was it sometimes impossible to determine whether an inmate had actually escaped or not.

The rank men were usually under the gun in the fields, but it was still fairly simple for them to escape by bellying along a turn row and wading the bayou or a drainage ditch till they reached the woods. There were at least five well-traveled escape routes from the farm, and it was impossible to guard them all.

Before I went to Tucker it was the rank men who most often escaped and the trusties who stayed. The reason was obvious: the rank men were mistreated and the trusties had it good. When I began to attack the power structure, the rank men stayed, because their lives and living conditions were improved, but the trusties began to bust out. Many of the trusties who escaped were simply unable to live in a prison society without the means of exploitation.

It was impossible to break the power structure I found at Tucker without removing the medium of exchange. Having begun to pull the institution together, I had started to take away the brozene, and replace this prison money with a ledger system. The men could not gamble with money in ledgers, because transfer of funds from one inmate to

The Convict Posse

another was prohibited. They could still play dominoes, checkers, and poker, for pop and candy bars, but nobody was going to get stabbed over a Juicy Fruit.

One afternoon in mid-April, I went into town to buy some cattle with Jerry Cullum, rider of the beef herd. Jerry, an ex-cowboy, had been raised on a ranch in Arkansas. He was one of the trusties with a squatter shack—a minor wheel in the power structure. As we were driving into town he told me, "Boy, I sure hate to give up that brozene tomorrow. It was bad enough giving up the freeworld money."

"Why can't you give up the brozene?" I asked.

"The only thing I got going for me is gambling," he said. "How else am I going to get the money to buy extra things?"

"But you know why the brozene has to go," I said.

"Yeah," he said, "but I can't live without it."

"There are only two things to do," I said. "You can go back to Cummins or you can cut out."

Cullum and the other trusties had not protested my taking the freeworld money from them because it was contraband anyway. Brozene, however, had been legal tender in the prison for the past fifty years, and they thought they had a right to it.

The order to turn the brozene in the following day had been posted for almost a month. The next morning I had a bus backed up into the compound in front of the institution. "Any man who doesn't turn in his brozene can get on the bus and go to Cummins," I said. Cummins had not abolished whippings and the food was not good.

All but one of the men turned in their brozene and received credit on the new ledger system. Only one inmate chose to go to Cummins rather than turn it in. But that night Jerry Cullum cut out with two other men. Cullum left for some very specific reasons. I had threatened to burn down his squatter shack; I had told him that in a few days I was going to pull in his cooking stove; and he knew he was going to have to quit slicing steaks off the carcasses to sell before he turned them over to the meat house. His little empire was crumbling, and now I was putting an end to his gambling.

During the next ten days we lost about twenty-five prisoners, including the convict doctor, the barn rider, and

Accomplices to the Crime

several other trusty guards in key positions who suddenly woke up to the fact that they had lost their cars, shacks, chickens, women, booze, and currency.

The rash of escapes pleased me. It meant my attack on the power structure was becoming successful—and it also speeded up our reform program by as much as sixty, and maybe ninety, days. It gave me justification, in the eyes of the inmates, for burning down squatter shacks, conducting shakedowns of the barracks, and reclassifying inmates. Before I had had to move more slowly, getting the inmates' acceptance for each innovation. However, my annoyance over the escapes and having my own position jeopardized justified my taking harsher action.

The state police and the governor's office did not share my view, however, and as luck would have it, on the day I held a press conference in the prison's chapel-auditorium to explain the number of escapes, one of the cooks took off in an unmarked police car. The press conference was interrupted when Harold Porter, the prison security officer, came in to announce, "Gentlemen, there's been another escape."

It happened that while I was with the press the only state trooper still assigned to the farm was taking a shower. Luther Priest, a cook at the Big House, who was serving a five-year term for burglary, took the car keys and the trooper's billfold from his trousers. He made the nine miles to England, Arkansas, before a patrol car passed him and, recognizing the car, radioed in news of the escape.

Before the conference ended, however, I was able to report that Priest had been apprehended at a road block near an ice-cream stand.

All of the men who escaped during April were captured without incident except one. He was Paul Moore, a harmless, happy-go-lucky Canadian who had been sentenced to five years in prison for forgery. A trusty, he was assigned as a picket guard at the hospital. One night late in April, while the night sheriff, Johnny Gates, was making a routine tour, he stopped by the hospital to check it out. The inmate doctor, Jackie Wood, took Paul Moore's gun from him, held it on the sheriff and locked him up. Then, with Moore and Clarence Haynes, one of the prisoners in the hospital, he took off.

The trio took the sheriff's pickup truck and headed out

through the new south gate, which I had tried to have installed properly that same day but could not, because we were lacking four "I" bolts.

The men were found the following day north of Pine Bluff, holed up in a barn. The police called to them to surrender but they refused. In the shoot-out Jackie Wood was shot twice in the upper left arm and Paul Moore was shot through the head. Later, I talked with troopers who'd been at the scene; it was obvious they had not intended to take the men alive. Wood and Haynes had thrown down their guns and come out with their hands up.

Wood had been living a good life as a trusty. As the inmate doctor, he'd lived in the old hospital where he had his own refrigerator, kitchen, separate bedroom, and TV. He was able to push pills and make profitable deals with inmates who wanted to be on sick call or buy medication. He knew we planned to open a new infirmary; it was only a matter of time until he would lose his former privileges. There was nothing he could do about it but leave.

Moore died without regaining consciousness. I noted in the log: "It is a sad thing that this death occurred. When I think about the minor things which could have prevented it—if I had not assigned Moore as picket, thinking I was doing him a service; if the black pickup had not been stolen earlier in the day the night sheriff would have been driving the blue pickup, which was easier to spot; if we had had the four "I" bolts for the south gate, Wood and his crew would never have made it out.

"I was talking with Wood and Moore only the evening before they escaped, and maybe there was a clue then that I should have noticed. In any event, somehow we have failed; a combination of events has resulted in the death of an inmate."

Immediately after the series of escapes, I shut the prison down tight. I told the desk officer that all inmates other than tower guards and the night sheriff were to be permanently restricted to their quarters in the main building day and night. Only really vital work, like feeding livestock, would be allowed. No inmate could leave the building for any purpose without my written authority and without an officer's accompanying him.

I got the inmates together and told them that if they

wanted to go back to the old system, they were setting about it in the right way, because my opponents were going to use the rash of escapes to organize my downfall.

I told them their only hope lay with me, and that furthermore I did not intend to have them help my opponents. Therefore, if anyone stepped outside the door without permission, he would be shot.

I wanted them to get thoroughly sick of the barracks and to feel the frustration of being locked in all the time. That might make them hesitate before messing up on the outside.

I talked to some of the trusties because I needed their help to run the farm meanwhile.

"Right now it means getting your feet muddy, and I can't promise you any reward other than a furlough[1] when it's due you."

The inmate tractor drivers parked their equipment and worked the rice levees, killing snakes and flooding fields. They were hip deep in mud while the rank men sat in the barracks watching television and getting bored.

After a while, I let more trusties out, and then a few do-pops. About three weeks later, I let out some of the men on the rice squad, and gradually all the men went back to work, this time on an organized daily roster system. My strategy worked.

It was now ninety days since I had arrived at Tucker. But in those three months we had broken the inmate power structure. Now we really had psychological, if not physical, control of the prison and its inmates.

---

[1] Selected trusties could be granted up to one week's leave from the institution each year. A number of American prison systems use furloughs to reward inmates for particularly cooperative behavior.

The Condemned Prisoners

During my first week at Tucker I visited death row, which housed the only Negroes at the prison—a convenient arrangement, since state law required racial segregation. There was one white man on death row, who had a cell of his own; some of the eight Negroes were doubled up.

To my horror, I found that some of the men had been there for as long as eight years and during all that time had never been allowed out of their cell block. The former superintendent had had a policy of allowing them out of their cells only for three or four minutes every New Year's Eve. Then they had been permitted to walk from one end of the corridor that fronted on their cells to the other. One man— who died before I came—had spent fourteen years in his cell, leaving only twice, with his lawyer, for hearings.

They had not been allowed to communicate in any way with the other inmates. They had no newspapers, magazines, books, or radios. One inmate had a TV set in the hall. They were completely isolated from the rest of the population and were even unaware of the usual prison activities; not even the grapevine reached them.

The condition of their six-by-nine cells was beyond belief. Each of the two men in a cell had one shelf at the back of the cell for all his personal effects. The cells had bunk beds with thin mattresses, a vitreous-china commode, and a wash basin. The only pieces of furniture were a steel table and bench affixed to the wall and the floor.

The cells had years of encrusted dirt caked on the concrete floors and walls, which had never been painted. The

Accomplices to the Crime

only light was a huge floodlight outside each cage, which focused on the inmates day and night. The bulbs must have been torture for their eyes, but hopefully they gave off some heat during the winter, as something was wrong with the heating in the block and temperatures would drop to as low as forty-five degrees.

Some of the cells had wire leads running from the lamps to ranges, which were necessary because the condemned men had to do their own cooking to supplement their prison diets.

The whole area stank. The air was heavy with the smell of dirty clothes, sweat, and stale air, and the entire atmosphere reminded me of a zoo. In fact, Jerry Johnson, one of the Negro inmates on death row, told me later that the guards had been in the habit of walking down the corridor and poking the men in the cells with sticks, and throwing food and water on them as though they were animals.

After my first visit to death row, I sent the men newspapers, magazines, and library books. I knew that almost all of them were illiterate, but one or two would be able to read aloud to the others; and all of them could enjoy looking at pictures. I also bought them a TV set from the Inmates' Welfare Fund.

After later visits, I allowed the men to walk two at a time in the corridor in front of their cells for thirty minutes a day. Soon four men were allowed out at once and could play checkers, dominoes, or cards.

The men were allowed to paint their cells, and given their choices of colors. Paint and brushes were distributed, and the first painting project at Tucker began on death row. The one white man on death row, Frank Harris, painted his cell a psychedelic mixture of dark green, yellow, and pink. Walter Brown and Jerry Johnson painted theirs blue, and the rest used pastel shades. Some painted their bars grey. I tried to talk them out of this, but they wanted the bars grey and some even wanted them black.

Meanwhile I began to check around the state to see if legal aid could be arranged for the condemned men because, from the records, I felt sure that at least half of them were victims of the white power structure in Arkansas, and not guilty as charged.

Governor Rockefeller was opposed to the death penalty.

Although he had been challenged by the state's legal system to set dates for executions, he had skirted the issue. If we were able to get some of the cases reopened, we might be able to produce evidence that would justify his commuting their death sentences.

For the next few months, I explored all available avenues of possible legal aid for the condemned men. I presented the problem to the Arkansas Bar Association, the Legal Aid Society of Little Rock, and the University of Arkansas Law School. Ultimately I was successful in obtaining a $25,000 Ford Foundation grant, which was awarded to the University of Arkansas for the purpose of providing legal aid to condemned prisoners under the guise of conducting a general Executive Clemency Study. The purpose of the study was not so much to obtain a new trial for the defendants as to document the procedural errors in a brief which would be provided to Governor Rockefeller, thus giving him a rationale for commuting the death sentences.

One of the first cases I hoped to investigate was that of James Williams, who had been sentenced to death for allegedly raping a white woman. All the available trial evidence indicated to me that he had been railroaded into prison. Since my arrival at Tucker, I had received many reports that Williams was steadily losing contact with reality and showing signs of becoming dangerously psychotic. The other condemned men were free in their cell block now during the day, but Williams had to be confined in a cell by himself, now, for the safety of the other condemned men.

One day after his exercise period, Williams refused to go back into his cell until he got a fair trial. I knew that his rebellion against the Arkansas system of criminal justice was understandable. I also knew that he had to get back into his cell.

I heard from Harold Porter that he was roaming around the cellblock. Porter could have handled the situation with force, but he was well aware what a tricky business it was. I decided to go into death row myself, although I rarely became involved personally with these problems, because if the superintendent can't handle the situation he loses face.

The death row inmates were in a panic. The inmate guard had locked himself in a cell with one of the condemned prisoners. The other men on death row had gone

Accomplices to the Crime

into their cells and shut their doors, leaving Williams alone in the corridor. He was pleasant and cheerful, but rock firm when he said to me, "I'm not going into that cell."

"What's the beef?" I asked him.

"I ain't going to talk to you, man," he said. "You're nothing but the head trusty and I want to talk to the man up front."

I considered the wisdom of using force. Williams was a powerful twenty-eight-year old. He was about six feet two and weighed 250 pounds. He was also a weight lifter. If we used force, someone was surely going to be seriously injured. I had six or eight men standing by, but I wanted to try strategy before force. Still, I hadn't a clue to what my next move ought to be. The best I could do was stall for time.

"Why don't you just watch TV a while and we'll talk about it later?" I said, and withdrew my men.

While we were debating strategy outside the cell block, Gurvis Nichols came up to me. "Let me see what I can do," he said.

Nichols was the librarian. He was half Williams' size, but he asked for permission to go into the cell block. "I can quiet him down," he said. I don't know exactly what happened between Nichols and Williams, but in a few minutes the little man led the big ox into his cell, and locked his cell door. Then he let the guard out to unlock the other men.

When Williams saw the others leaving their cells he went berserk. He got on his bunk and jumped down on his commode, smashing it. Then he tore apart everything else in his cell. We would have to get him to the hospital. It took three hours and five men to drag him out of the cell to the car, and we finally got him to the state hospital in Little Rock in irons.

By the time he returned in the fall I had given the men on death row even more freedom. As they responded to trust, we left the cells open all day, only locking them in at night.

One Saturday in July, I asked the group how they would like to go outside to help make a baseball diamond. I will never forget the scene. Some of the men had been there eight or nine years and had never been out of the cell block. They walked out into the yard, they kissed the ground and lifted their faces to look at the sky in wonderment. They ran wildly, kicking up dirt like a bunch of skittish colts that had been locked up in a barn.

I wasn't aware of it then, but during all the years that the men had been caged in death row, some of their hostility toward the outside world had turned them against each other. One of the men had even threatened to beat up all the others if they ever got outside the cell block.

After they had worked off some excess energy, they began to accept and return old challenges. I sent a man into the institution to bring out a set of boxing gloves.

It was a ridiculous, and a pathetic, sight. The men had the opportunity to go at each other but they had been cooped up so long that most of them were exhausted and puffing after the first two or three minutes.

They wheezed and feinted, looking for an opening. When one came they were too out of breath to take advantage of it despite loud encouragement from the others. They went back to their cells exhausted and happy.

The baseball diamond was completed in record time, and it was only a matter of weeks before some of the trusties went out to play with the death row team. Although the trusties were southern whites, they had real compassion for the condemned men who had been so brutalized in the past. Mutual deprivation had resulted in mutual empathy.

After one of the ball games, Arnold Rhodes, who was the kitchen supervisor, came to me and asked, "Why don't we let the death row men eat in the mess hall?"

I feigned reluctance; but I finally agreed, on the basis that it was too much trouble to have the men carry the trays of food to the cells. At first the death row Negroes ate by themselves on one side of the mess hall. After about three weeks, however, Rhodes asked why we didn't put them on the other side at a spare table.

Suddenly the mess hall was integrated, and there was only one incident. One morning Jerry Johnson found his table full. He sat down next to a white inmate at another table, the white got up and said, "I'm not going to eat with no damn nigger."

Johnson said nothing, but Rhodes heard the comment. He went over to the white inmate and said: "I'm runnin' this kitchen, and if you're gonna eat here, you're gonna eat

Accomplices to the Crime

the way I want you to. If you open your face one more time like that I'm gonna knock your head off."

The white inmates initiated further integration. Soon the condemned men were attending church services and movies with everyone else. This might not seem like an important step forward in race relations, but generally black people do not sit with whites even in the Arkansas freeworld.

At the same time another type of integration, this one of criminological significance, was taking place. By August, the condemned men were moving around within the prison and working at regular job assignments. To my knowledge this was the first time in the recent history of prisons anywhere that men condemned to death were not confined to cells but allowed to be part of the over-all prison community. I regard this as a major achievement in the handling of condemned men.

Two death row inmates were working in the kitchen, one who had been a tailor for twenty-four years on the outside was in the laundry, another was in the commissary, another was a porter in the minimum custody section of the main building, two were on the paint crew, and one was on the permanent carpenter crew. They worked without incident, and there was never any thought in my mind that any of them might try to escape—which was saying a good deal for them and the system. They were already condemned to death; what did they have to lose, other than their privileges and self-respect? That was all the deterrent needed. It was demonstrated once again that if a man is treated like a human being he will respond like one.

The Swinging Preacher

Traditionally the pastor of the First Baptist Church at Sherrill, Arkansas, was chaplain at Tucker. His duties were minimal. He went to the prison farm once a month to deliver a sermon and was on call to prepare a condemned man for his death the week before his execution. It was also the chaplain's duty to walk with the man to the electric chair and be with him when he died; but he was kept completely away from the other inmates, and allowed no personal contact with them.

Attendance at the monthly services was compulsory. The inmates were marched to and from the old mess hall across the bayou, where services were held. Our chaplain, Jon Kimbrell, told me he'd spent many Sunday afternoons looking through the mess hall window wondering what the men thought about being forced to come to a church service to listen to a preacher they did not wish to hear, talking about matters that held no relevance to them.

Kimbrell often wondered what would be appropriate for a sermon. How do you reach a man under these circumstances? What could he possibly say that would be of any value to men forced to listen to him by armed guards, men who were not allowed to shake his hand or speak his name. He saw justifiable resentment on their faces and admitted to me that had he been in their position he would have rebelled and probably got his head whipped going to and from the barracks to church, because he didn't like to be pushed; and he was certain they felt the same way.

The only real contact he established was on a Sunday

Accomplices to the Crime

when services were being held at the same time the National Football League was holding its championship playoffs. He knew there was TV in the barracks and the men were more interested in football than religion. As soon as they marched in and were seated, he told them if they would be quiet for thirty seconds while he read a passage of scripture, he would then pronounce the benediction and they could go back to the barracks and watch the game. This suited the inmates just fine. For a while he was known as The Football Preacher.

When I arrived at Tucker I didn't know we had a prison chaplain. I wasn't enthusiastic about the chaplains I had met in the past. I didn't want a crusader out to save all the inmates from hell when most of them couldn't write. And I didn't want a preacher jumping pews and stirring the men up emotionally—the situation was already tense enough. I asked Kimbrell what he wanted.

"Do you want an office so you can sit up here with your feet on the desk, so you can be a wheel inside the institution and people can put in little request slips to see you for counseling?" I asked.

Kimbrell admitted that might have been the role I had seen played in other institutions but it was not what he wanted. What he had in mind was to have my permission to move about within the institution with complete freedom. He wanted to be able to go into the barracks and spend his time there with the men. He wanted to get acquainted with them and be their friend, and then advance to the point where he was, in their eyes, a chaplain.

He said the words I wanted to hear. In my mind, I began to assess him differently. He was granted permission to come and go as he wished.

Kimbrell's movement into the barracks was not very spectacular. In the rank barracks, an inmate walked up to him bristling with resentment and hostility, and snarled, "Hey, you son of a bitch. I want to tell you something I've been waiting to say for a long time. I hate your damn guts. They used to march me over to hear you preach and I hated you then and I hate you now."

Kimbrell made no attempt at that time to establish any sort of religious program. He was more interested in just trying to establish himself on the grounds that there had to

The Swinging Preacher

be communication between the inmates and himself. He wanted the men to feel that he could be trusted and was a friend who understood at least some of their problems.

It was hard sledding for the first few months. Church services consisted of just one inmate named Chuck and himself. Chuck sat in the front row and the chaplain preached a sermon to him. Then he sat down beside him.

Once the men became aware that they were not going to be marched to church and given a dose of religion whether they wanted it or not, they started seeking the chaplain out with their questions and problems. In time his involvement became deeper and deeper and his commitment to the institution became greater; the prison came to require more and more of his time. He was there almost every night, sometimes at ridiculous hours.

One night while circulating in the barracks the chaplain heard Rainwater, the prison barber, picking out chords on an old guitar. He sat beside Rainwater and listened as he played fragments of songs, spirituals, and mountain hymns, in the Ozark style. When Rainwater finished playing the chaplain congratulated him.

"You know, preacher," Rainwater said, "we got a boy on death row named Jerry Johnson that can sing the blues. He has a lot of ability. I wish you could hear him some time and maybe we could have a band."

His words made Kimbrell come back to a discussion he had been having with me for some time. Kimbrell felt we ought to develop a band. It would give the inmates a social activity, and it would be something he could be involved with, which might speed up his acceptance.

One or two of the inmates had their own guitars. They made a flat-top guitar from parts of one that had been junked. By then I could see that they were really serious about starting a band. They even had a name, The Tucker Themesters. Kimbrell was nicknamed The Swinging Preacher—soon, The Swinger.

The bandleader was James Russell Smith, a convicted forger with a reputation as a real troublemaker, who had spent considerable time in the hole. Kimbrell took several of his songs, which were quite good, into Nashville to try to have them published.

Although there were instruments at Cummins they were

Accomplices to the Crime

not available to us. So one day in August I took Smitty—the trouble-making forger—into Little Rock, where we bought $2,000 worth of instruments including an electric guitar, microphone, amplifier, drums, and an electric bass, with money from the Inmates' Welfare Fund.

The band members built a platform in one corner of the auditorium for the day when they could have their first show.

In my log for September 2 I noted: "This evening the farm band put on their first recital, so to speak. This is a group of inmates who have been playing instruments together for the past two or three weeks. It is one of the programs I have been extremely interested in but one where I have waited for them to take the initiative. Reverend Kimbrell has brought in some strings for one guitar and purchased another. We have also bought some strings for one of the fellows in death row.

"This past week or so I have been allowing the death row men to work out with the band in the library.

"The leader of the band is James Russell Smith and the main vocalist is Leon Goins. Rainwater, Harold Munger and Charles Schultz play guitar. The two men from death row are Jerry Johnson and Walter Brown. Johnson sings and plays guitar and Brown sings and is the drummer.

"They started about 7 P.M. with Gurvis Nichols as MC. I haven't got an accurate count yet, but it looks like 150 to 175 men participated. One of the interesting things about the evening was that there was integration in the band with no problems whatsoever. One of the fellows from death row came to watch and some of the white fellows sat down beside him. Even more interesting is the fact that the trusties and rank men sat indiscriminately beside one another throughout the auditorium.

"This is an amazing feat and never would have taken place six months ago. When I first came the trusties had to sit separately and were totally segregated from the rest of the inmate community for fear of reprisals from other inmates.

"Now we have noticed that tensions have dissipated, the institution has settled down to a very relaxed atmosphere. . . . At last, we have a community formation. In the past,

The Swinging Preacher

the men never smiled, never laughed, never talked to anyone. The place was one of mutual distrust and hate.

"Tonight, for the first time, we have seen a feeling of community developing. I am going to encourage this band as much as possible. And this is the way I want the AA group to develop. Initiative must be taken by the men, from inside, if anything is to succeed."

After the band stopped playing, Kimbrell got up on the stand and gave a short sermon. I wish I had recorded it because it was great.

He told the men that he did not share the traditional and puritanical view of Jesus Christ and of religion. He said it was his theory that if Christ was alive and in the world today he would be in Tucker prison sitting in the auditorium. And if there was a marriage feast, he would be making wine and, in all probability, drinking some of it himself.

Kimbrell said that Christ never intended man to construe and twist His thoughts and teachings and the spirit of His life so that it seemed He was against a man enjoying the life that God had given to him.

At the end of his sermon the inmates applauded. For the first time, I felt the chaplain was in solid with the prison community. The men felt that to some extent he was one of them.

During the month of September the band played at a barbecue at Reverend Kimbrell's church in Sherrill. On September 30, they entertained the freeworld staff and wives at Tucker. On that night there were two of the colored death row inmates playing in the band, and the others were in the audience.

"I was sitting beside one of them," I wrote in the log. "Other officers were sitting with the inmates. The do-pops, trusties, and rank men were all mixed together. A phenomenal experience when compared to the situation when I first came here. Once in a while when you are involved in a situation like this it all seems worthwhile."

The band, including its black death row inmates, also played at the state mental hospital in Benton. There was a wonderful interaction between the patients and the prisoners. Each believed the other group was worse off than they were; the inmates danced with both patients and staff, all without incident. There was, of course, an officer—unarmed—there at all times.

After one of those sessions I noted: "It was almost pathetic watching the mental patients trying to involve themselves in this social activity. Anybody who would want to discourage our participation there would have to be a sadist."

Quietly we began to allow the condemned men to leave the prison farm on various assignments. Some of them went with me into town to pick out band instruments. Lonny Mitchell was allowed to attend the funeral of his grandmother in El Dorado, Arkansas, escorted by Harold Porter.

George Douthit of the *Arkansas Democrat* heard that the condemned men were in the band and traveling around the state and asked if he could do a story and take some pictures. The men went to the state hospital at Benton to play for the second time, and Douthit wrote a story that was good and accurate. Happily, nobody in Arkansas knew what a prison was supposed to be like. So when another of my newspaper friends did some ad-libbing and said it was done in all prisons, nearly everybody assumed it was part of modern penology and grudgingly went along with it.

This two-way integration process of black and white and condemned men into the general prison community was subtly and effectively taking place without incident when I received a call from Elijah Coleman, Executive Director of the Human Rights Council for the State of Arkansas.

Mr. Coleman, a Negro, went before the penitentiary board and made a formal request, later released to the press, demanding that Tucker be integrated. I had done what he wanted surreptitiously, but he wanted to make a public display of integration by having Negroes transferred to Tucker from Cummins.

Bishop was delighted. "This is what I've been telling Tom," he said. "We ought to send over a busload of them black fellers."

What he had in mind was not the noble goal of integrating Tucker. He hoped to start a publicity rodeo that would end up with my being bucked out of the saddle.

The Swinging Preacher

Elijah Coleman and I talked for some time. I told him that we were integrating quietly, and that if he focused integration publicity on us, we could lose all the other reforms that had been made—including the elimination of the strap. But Coleman was adamant. He thought public integration in Tucker was more important than all our reforms.

I was finally able to get Coleman off my back by telling the Southern Regional Council that he was setting integration back rather than moving it forward. As for the importance of our reforms, I suggested Mr. Coleman talk with the Negroes in the Cummins barracks. They would tell him there was nothing more important to them than ending corporal punishment and brutality. Their prime concern was to be fed and treated decently and to know they would not be tortured and beaten. They were not concerned with "equal rights"; they wanted human rights.

Sex and Isolation

Hazel was six-two and wore bib overalls—which he would drop at the sight of any man standing still. He was a good worker—but he was very open about his sexual appetite, so I had to keep him moving from place to place.

One day Jimmy Carlin, the tractor squad rider, came to me and said, "I've had it. You've got to get Hazel off my crew."

I asked him what was the matter.

"Well," he said, "he or she or whatever it is, is always out in the ditch laying one of my tractor boys. Every time I see a tractor with nobody on it I find Hazel down in the ditch blowing someone. Hazel is getting all the action and I'm not getting any plowing done."

I moved Hazel to the carpenter squad. One day I went to check why a new duplex wasn't finished on time. Hazel was to blame. So I moved him to the vegetable shack. Again he disrupted work.

Finally, I put him in the chicken house alone. That worked out fine for a while and Hazel became the best chicken house rider we ever had. But he was lonely. He bribed other inmates to come down and keep him company by letting them take some eggs.

The incidence of homosexuality and sodomy at Tucker must have been the highest in the nation. Almost 80 per cent of the inmates either were homosexual or had had homosexual experiences. The reason was not surprising. The inmate power structure was based on exploitation, and one method of exploitation was sex.

Sex and Isolation

Every privilege at Tucker, including the right to continue living, had a price on it. If an inmate did not have money he was forced to bargain with his body. To me, it was the ultimate degradation of the system that a man had to pervert his body for physical survival.

Since there was no minimum age for commitment to the state penitentiary, we had many fourteen year olds, who were ripe for becoming punks. The average age of the prisoners at Tucker was twenty-three, and most of the inmates were under twenty.

There was just no way to segregate the youngsters from the predatory older males because we had group living in the barracks. There was no place in the prison where an inmate was safe from homosexuals, who didn't seem to care where or when they made their advances.

One afternoon I heard rifle fire and discovered that one of the guards had put a .30-.30 bullet through an outhouse. When I went to investigate, I found that two men had been in the outhouse together. Presumably they were performing some homosexual act, as it was a one-holer; the guard thought they were in there too long and put a bullet through the side near the top. Since the outhouse is only five feet high, one of the men could easily have been killed.

The men fled from the outhouse and returned to duty. I took the guard's gun away and put him on another assignment with a set of hedge clippers. Lieutenant Lowman summed up that event nicely: "The moral of the story is, don't stand up to wipe."

One way to hold down perversion was to replace the yard men, of whom three out of four were homosexual. Their punks were the hall boys—youngsters who were supposed to sweep the floors. The hall boys were usually fifteen-year-olds, who kept their soft jobs in return for favors granted.

As might be expected, the yard men tended to bestow the best jobs in the prison on other homosexuals. That meant that most of the floorwalkers and building tenders, who were directly under them, were also active sexual deviates. The yard man had absolute authority in the inmate power structure. There were few inmates who dared to cross him or his assistants.

All the building tenders had their own wall lockers,

Accomplices to the Crime

ranges, and refrigerators, plus the fringe benefit of punking anyone they desired. Most of them had their own special punks, who were given privileges—like double innerspring mattresses—and protection from other inmates. There was even a line painted across the floor at the end of the rank men's barracks. No rank man except the building tender's punk could cross the line.

As soon as possible, I arranged to have government-surplus footlockers sent to Tucker. They were painted and issued to all the inmates to replace the "Arkansas suitcases" —cardboard boxes. Then we got padlocks; the day they were issued I did away with the building tenders and replaced them with "barracks orderlies," who were responsible for keeping the place clean and making themselves generally useful. A lock could be picked, of course, but it would take time, and it would be obvious that it had been tampered with.

I also moved the barbers out of each barracks, keeping only one man to cut all the prisoners' hair, who was not to be paid for it. This way I eliminated two services which the inmates had had to pay for with either money or their bodies.

The homosexual problem remained in two of the barracks, and finally I had to send Chainsaw Jack in to solve it; Chainsaw was in prison because he had murdered a man who made a homosexual approach to him. I told Chainsaw I didn't want anyone hurt but I wanted the situation straightened out. He went into the barracks of about sixty men and called all the inmates together.

"Mr. Murton put me in charge here and you all know why," he said. "If I catch two of you in the same bed, I'm going to get that chainsaw up front and come back here and straighten you out."

Chainsaw Jack had a convincing way of communicating. I don't know whether the inmates believed him or not, but the effect was the same. While he was there, homosexuality in the barracks virtually stopped.

As another step, I tried to isolate the more active homosexuals. Whenever possible I made them trusties, gave them guns, and assigned them as tower guards—where they were alone all day.

It was impossible for me to protect the youngsters,

Sex and Isolation 93

though. We had boys there age fourteen and up, and a boy wasn't safe even in solitary. One day I went into solitary and noticed that a sixteen-year-old's eye was badly swollen. During the course of the first night in isolation the three other inmates with him forcibly raped him after a terrible assault. His eyes had been almost kicked out of their sockets.

He told me that he had been beaten nearly to death before submitting. But he refused to testify against his assailants in court. I had hoped to get a felony conviction for an incident like this, but without his cooperation there wasn't a chance. Nevertheless, I transferred one of the men to Cummins.

The irony of the situation was that the men in the cell with the boy were supposed to be in isolation from the rest of the community; we were so overcrowded at Tucker that isolation was impossible. There were twenty-eight men in seven cells, and we had unbelievable complications in selecting cell mates. Rank men could not be mixed with trusties; we had to make certain none of the men had grudges against each other; and we had to try our best to separate the active homosexuals.

Isolation in one form or another replaced corporal punishment one hundred years ago in most prisons. Isolation cells usually have solid doors and no windows, so the man inside cannot see or hear other inmates, hence, the name "the hole." At Tucker, the hole was a number of cells which would normally be lived in at other prisons.

Before I came to Arkansas, men in the hole were on a restricted diet of bread and water for two days, then given a full ration for one day. A layman might think this was good for the man's health, but it was really another form of torture. Two days of bread and water shrinks a man's stomach. On the third day the full ration extends his stomach; then the hunger pangs really hit him.

Old pecks disciplined themselves in the hole. They ate only small portions on the full-meal day and squirreled away a little food for the bread and water days. After a time, their stomachs shrank so they were less hungry on a small amount of food.

I felt it more humane to give the men in isolation the same food as the other inmates, with the exception of

Accomplices to the Crime

condiments and the beverage. Sometimes I would reduce the rations for a week or so, but the amount of food did not vary with the day.

Most men in the hole had sentences of three to five days, but men brought back from escape attempts automatically got thirty. Thirty days was generally the maximum. Sometimes a man was in the hole longer than thirty days because he committed another offense while he was there, such as tearing up a cell or throwing the contents of his toilet bucket at a guard. I would parole a man from the hole if his behavior indicated that the solitude was affecting him mentally. "Messing with their minds" is what Arnold Rhodes called it.

Lengthy isolation is much more damaging than the strap —bad as a whipping is, it is finished in short order. By the end of a day or two, a man is probably able to drag himself back to work in the field. Confinement in the hole for days on end, with fungus growing up the grey walls, puts a man uptight. So I shortened time in the hole, put a prisoner back in the barracks sooner, and took away some of the privileges I had instituted. He automatically lost visiting privileges, most privileges of writing and receiving mail, he could not watch TV or listen to a radio, he could not attend the movies, he could not buy food at the commissary, and could not have any reading material.

The loss of privileges affected most men much more than the strap. They could lie on the floor while being whipped and call out, "Oh Captain," and laugh as blood streamed down their butts, but none of them wanted to miss the next episode of *Bonanza*.

Although the cell block construction was fairly modern, the locking devices in the segregation section were ancient and useless. The locks were so antiquated the men could open them with a spoon or a homemade key, and it was not unusual for inmates to be walking around in the cell block. They weren't planning to escape. They were just juveniling and getting away with something.

I put log chains around the cell doors and secured them with the best padlocks I could get. The inmates met this challenge to their ingenuity by picking the "pick-proof" locks.

It was obvious that we were playing a game and I was

Sex and Isolation 95

losing. The men were in isolation for disciplinary reasons, and they were challenging my authority, which put my whole administration in jeopardy. I had to do something to correct the situation.

One day in mid-summer I found half a dozen inmates roaming the corridor, unshaven and dirty; there was junk all over the floor. Nabors was with me; I ordered him to turn them all out.

Nabors looked at me with astonishment. Under normal circumstances it was a foolish thing to do since there were just the two of us alone in the cell block with ten or twelve inmates, including three serving life sentences. However, I had to do something surprising, drastic and effective.

The men still in their cells were let out. The entire group lined up facing me and waiting. Their faces were straight but I knew they were amused by the episode and curious to see what was going to happen. They were already in isolation, which was the worst punishment available—they had no more privileges to lose and they knew that I had abolished the strap. So, what would I do?

"O.K., fellows," I said. "I'm tired of this juveniling. If you wanted to be dangerous criminals you'd figure out a way to tear out the walls, get by the guards and cut out. But I know you don't really want to escape. You're not that stupid. Yet you are playing the silly games you used to play at the Pine Bluff Boys' School.

"I'm not going to play with you any more. If you want to act like adults, I'll treat you like adults. But if you want to act like kids, I'm going to treat you like kids.

"For a variety of reasons, whether you agree with them or not, you've been ordered to live in that cell and that's where you are going to stay. It's a simple thing. You are convicts in cells and I am the superintendent and you're not going to run the prison.

"My object is to get you in your cell and keep you in there and that's just what I'm going to do. And, I'm going to do it by putting you on your honor. I'm not going to worry about the locks any more and I'm not going to buy new ones. I'm going to take the log chains off and put the locks in the front office and I am going to lock you in the cells with the old keys. You know you can get out and I know you can get out. You've proven your point.

"But if I ever come back here and you are outside your cells or have something in your cells that indicates to me that you had to get out of your cell to get it, I'm going to bring the welder over and I'm going to weld you in. Are there any questions?"

The men looked at each other. No one asked a question.

"All right," I said. "This is how it's going to be. If I catch one of you clowns out here tomorrow I'll call the masonry man over here and we will put concrete blocks in the window. And you can live in the dark like a mole. And if it's not dark enough I'll put boiler plate in front of your cells with a slot to slip your cabbage through at night."

I knew that they were thinking I wouldn't dare do what I threatened because of public reaction. I was only too well aware that they mistook humanity for weakness. So, I said:

"If you think I am not going to weld you in here because it might be embarrassing to the governor's office when you get the word out, you are out of your minds. I'm going to do whatever I think needs to be done to run this prison and I could care less what people out there think. So don't think you can intimidate me that way."

I made it plain that I was not going to call the welder over to cut the bead every time the man in the cell needed something too large to be handed through the bars. That would mean they could not get their mattresses at night.

"You have your shower, your bunk, your commode, and your drinking water in the cell, and we'll slip your food through. And that's it. You can't win because you know I'm not going to give up and you can't escape so let's quit juveniling."

The men went back into their cells quietly. Nobody came out for almost a week. Then I heard that some of the men were roaming around the corridor again. I called the garage foreman, and told him to bring his portable welder over, along with some steel collars to secure the cell doors. He welded them shut.

After about ten days I felt I had proven my point and I went back for another visit.

"I'll try you once more to see if you're going to act like adults," I said. "If you don't, you will be welded in your cells until Christmas."

No one broke out again. I had made my point.

Profit-Making—Modern Slavery; Modern Medicine

At first I didn't understand why people in the towns around Tucker were so cool to us. Margaret and I took our children to the Methodist Church in the town of England, which was the hub of local social life, and although the parishioners seemed friendly they would never get involved in a meaningful conversation with us, much to Margaret's frustration.

She wanted to tell everybody that what was going on at Tucker was the most marvelous transformation she had ever seen, but nobody would listen. They never asked questions, and they avoided the subject if they could.

Then, when the inmate power structure began to crumble, resulting in many escapes, there was a lot of joking. Suddenly people did want to talk about Tucker. "Well, I wonder who-all is escaping from Tucker now?" they would ask me, or: "How many escapes have you had today, Mr. Murton?"

We were angry and hurt. We were also perplexed, until we found out from the minister of the church that Jim Bruton, the former superintendent, had been a solid member of the church community for many years. The minister had been his spiritual leader and very close to him during the time when Mrs. Bruton had been dying of cancer.

Like most Arkansans, the people of the congregation refused to believe that this good, staunch Christian, Jim Bruton, could have done all the things the newspapers said he did. They blamed us for his exposure, and resented us because of him.

Whenever I drove through a small town the police

would fall in behind and clock me through, presumably hoping I would commit some violation that would give them a reason to stop me.

Once I was returning from a trip out of state when a trooper stopped me to relay a message. As we talked he told me, "You know, while I was down there at Tucker as a guard I thought you were just another of those smart asses from out of state. I was suspicious of you at first. You were a big joke among us police. I didn't approve of anything you were doing there, but I can see now, after talking to other people, that you're on the right track."

When I went for a driver's license in Little Rock, the examiner spent half an hour telling me how to run Tucker. "Bring back the strap, boy," he said. "Don't be a damn fool. That's the only way to handle convicts. It's the only thing they understand."

A few days later, Henry W. Smith, a circuit judge, criticized us from the bench in Pine Bluff for doing away with the whippings. The judge made his comments after the father of a seventeen-year-old boy accused of burglary told the court he had given the boy "a good whipping." Judge Smith said, "You use better sense than some of the people down at the penitentiary. You know they don't allow the strap any more at the penitentiary."

Some of the citizens of the towns around Tucker warmed up to us a bit, eventually, but they never discussed the prison except to tell me how they used to get their horses shod while visiting the Tucker freeline or how they had ridden the prison horses or had their cotton picked by the prisoners. As they told me these things, I understood that for them the prison had been a place where you could get favors done if you knew the right people. Now all that had stopped, and they didn't like it much.

No one seemed to be aware of the bestiality, cruelty, and inhumanity that had gone on at Tucker. They were like the townspeople of Dachau who didn't want to find out what caused the constant greasy smoke from the concentration-camp chimneys. The people in the towns near Tucker would not believe that men they knew could take part in murder and torture. They still don't, to this day—and that's the whole problem in Arkansas. With a few rare exceptions, people refuse to acknowledge that their prisons are evil places, worse even than concentration camps because they exist in a civilized country.

There was another basic reason for much of the hostility toward our attempts to reform the Arkansas prison system. The success of reform meant the death knell of profitable exploitation.

The state prison farms had long been self-supporting. Traditionally, they were run for the profit of the state and of a few selected individuals. In 1966 the penitentiary system made a profit—for the state—of $300,000. The profit in 1967 was $220,000. The profits that went to individuals have not been tabulated.

The state, fond of its profits from what amounted to slave labor, was not willing to relinquish more than a little of those prison profits for operating funds for the maintenance of the prisoners. The prison, therefore, functioned with a minimum of money. There was little mechanization. The bulk of farm work was done with mules and convicts who labored in the fields ten to fourteen hours a day, six or seven days a week. Within the prison, the needs to maintain discipline and meet work quotas were the immediate causes of the brutality which sometimes resulted in murder. Nothing was to get in the way of production for profit—men were beaten for minor infractions. (See p. 100.)

Neither Tucker nor Cummins had adequate medical services. The penitentiary dentist visited Tucker the third Sunday of each month and was paid by the extraction. No teeth had ever been filled by any dentist in the history of the institution or the recollection of the inmates. Although dentures were supposedly provided at prison expense, the inmate dental assistant charged patients $15.

Most prisons in the United States have vocational training projects. Arkansas didn't. The work programs used in the institution were designed for two ends: profit, for the state and individual freemen; and for the inmates, degradation. There was absolutely nothing an inmate could learn in the Arkansas prisons that he could ever put to use in the freeworld, unless he planned to be a sadist or a criminal.

Accomplices to the Crime

```
     A R K A N S A S   S T A T E   P E N I T E N T I A R Y
                       PUNISHMENT REPORT
             P. O. Varner,  ARK., DATE 5/6 195-7

Asa Bohnert, Secretary
Board of Pardons, Paroles & Probation

Captain Lee Henslee, Superintendent
Arkansas State Penitentiary

Gentlemen:

I have today corrected  Robert Cumitry

Register Number_____ Crime_____

Term_____ Color_____ County_____

For what offence corrected  not covering - up
_____

_____


How corrected  10 lashes

                                Yours truly,

                                _____
                                Warden         Camp #

Witness:

  F D Leim
```

The best he could do was continue as a slave. Penitentiary commitment in Arkansas was penal slavery, and the parole system was indentured slavery.

To get a job, a parolee had to have a sponsor, and sponsorship of penal slaves was a privilege generally accorded people who had contacts with the parole board. As late as 1966, Arkansas inmates had been furloughed or paroled to state senators for two or three years at a time, to work on their farms.

In all this morass of inmate exploitation, I kept hoping

that somewhere there would be a "good guy." There had to be somebody connected with the prison situation who was honest, decent, and not interested solely in making a buck off the convicts. I was wrong. Everyone involved with the prison seemed committed to exploiting the inmates, and the inmates had become so accustomed to this treatment over the years that they rarely dared complain. If a complaint was uttered in the barracks, it would be stilled by the goon squad, and on the rare occasions when the press ran a critical story, it was soon hushed with the usual clichés about convicts being subhumans and liars by definition.

This whole system of exploitation began in the days after the Civil War, when the farmers and plantation owners who were forced to free their slaves looked for a new source of cheap labor and found it in the prisons. The same thing happened intermittently in other states, but it became a way of life in Arkansas.

State records show that on May 5, 1875, "the entire penitentiary, its buildings, equipment and the labor of all convicts confined then or after," were leased to a Mr. Jno. Peck for ten years.[1] State supervision of such an arrangement was minimal, and anyone who submitted critical reports would be dismissed by the Penitentiary Commission. During this period, up to 10 per cent of the prison population might die during one year.

As early as 1890, the prison board did attempt to abolish corporal punishment, but pressure from the lessees of the penitentiary was too strong. The board was, however, able to establish rules limiting the use of the strap and requiring that only wardens that the board had specifically authorized could administer punishment.

In 1892 the penitentiary lease earned the state a profit of $32,128.42. The next year, the highest bid for a ten-year lease was $31,500 a year. As a result, the state decided to

---

[1] Some of the sources relevant to the history of penology in Arkansas are: *Legislative Audit Report*, State Legislature, Little Rock, Ark., June 30, 1963; *Survey of Prison Labor Problem of Arkansas*, Prison Industries Reorganization Board, Washington, D.C., Nov. 25, 1936; *Arkansas Gazette*, Little Rock, Ark., Jan. 22, Oct. 6, & Dec. 12, 1936, Jan. 30, Feb. 14, 1937, Sept. 4, 1940, March 13, 1941, Jan. 4, 1943, March 6, April 6, April 7, July 6, July 23, Aug. 11, Sept. 5, Sept. 9, 1949, May 17, 1951, May 9, July 22, 1952, Aug. 9, Dec. 14, 1953, April 10, 1955, Feb. 13, Dec. 18, 1956, April 15, May 26, Aug. 27, Nov. 1, 1965, Jan. 19, 1966.

eliminate the middle man and lease individual prisoners and groups of prisoners. In the one-year period from 1898 to 1889, over two hundred inmates died in mines, quarries, and turpentine camps.

A public scandal ensued, and the prison board had to restrict the type of labor for which a prisoner could be leased. The leasing of prisoners was formally abolished in 1912, when the governor, George W. Donaghey, pardoned more than four hundred prisoners and broke the back of the system.

Correspondence and investigative reports on file in the office of the State Board of Pardons and Paroles show that until the late 1940's, influential citizens would let the board or the superintendent know that they were looking for "likely Negroes" to work on their farms. Paroles or indefinite furloughs for "boys" who met the plantation owners' requirements would then be arranged. The exposure of this practice led, in 1953, to the establishment of a rule that anyone who wanted to provide employment for an inmate on parole had first to submit a request for a specific prisoner by name. However, the practice of furloughing inmates to individuals continued until 1967.

Although the parole system was tantamount to indentured servitude and an extension of penal slavery, there was little we could do quickly to reform it other than release about twenty-five men who were over their release date and then start to determine parole eligibility of the other inmates.

According to Arkansas law, a convict who had more than one sentence had to complete the first before he was eligible for parole on the second. As most men were serving more than one sentence, there was no way for them to get out on parole in a hurry.

Traditionally, parole in any state is an extension of prison outside the walls. The parolee is a prisoner with time yet to serve, and although he is allowed to serve his time outside the prison, he can be controlled almost as rigorously. If an inmate has a three-year sentence and is paroled at the end of one, he has two more years to serve. If he serves one year on parole and then commits a violation, he is returned to the institution to finish out his last year.

A prisoner's eligibility for parole is determined by a

parole board, which in Arkansas was composed of the five-man penitentiary board—the governing body of the prison system—and a director. The members are political appointees named by the governor. They cannot, however, be removed by the governor. Nevertheless, during Faubus' terms, the board members had been puppets of the governor's office. They were told who was to be given parole and whose sentences were to be cut.

The average age of four of the board members was around seventy-five years. The fifth member was thirty-two-year-old John Haley, who was Governor Rockefeller's first appointee.

One member, R.E. Jeter, was partially deaf and in his eighties. He slept through most of the board meetings, snoring loudly, until someone punched him and said it was time to vote. Between July, 1967, and January, 1968, he was so physically incapacitated he never attended a board meeting.

I found it difficult to tell him apart from Grady Wooley. Wooley was in his mid-seventies, had white hair, wore glasses, smoked cigars, and spoke with an Ozark drawl. Jeter was a Wabaseka farmer, and Wooley a former sheriff from El Dorado and a long-time friend of O.E. Bishop, superintendent of Cummins.

Jeff Wood was an active man in his sixties, with thinning white hair. He constantly fingered a pencil or his coat buttons; and he seemed to consider his task of moderating board meetings an agonizing ordeal.

L.A. Green, the secretary, was in his late sixties. He was a dapper man with a mustache, and perhaps the most alert member of the group.

The Director of Pardons, Paroles and Probation was W.P. Ball. An elder of the Methodist Church, he was almost seventy. In addition to being chairman of the meetings, he was executive secretary.

The board met the last Tuesday and Wednesday of the month at Tucker and Cummins respectively. No proper parole evaluation was prepared, as is standard practice elsewhere. Instead, board members had simple forms with the prisoner's name on it, and spaces for comments on his "attitude" and "work ability," the only two things they cared about.

The chosen inmate would appear before the board.

"You keeping your business straight?" he would be asked.

The answer was Yes, of course, and the board would then pass some comment such as, "He looks like a nice boy," or, "I know his pappy," or, "He goes to a good church."

If the inmate had a written offer of a job, at $10 a day plus room and board and a forty-hour week, a board member might ask—and frequently, he literally did—"You never got arrested in church, did you?"

The proper answer, of course, was No, and parole would then be granted with the comment, "Old Ned's a good man. He'll take you to church every Sunday. He'll take care of you."

Charles Noyes is a case in point. He was paroled in May of 1967 to the owner of a Little Rock bowling alley who promised him a forty-hour week at a fair salary. Within a month, Noyes telephoned. "I'm uptight about the job," he said. "Can I come down and talk to you?"

I said, "Sure, come on down."

When he walked in I scarcely recognized him. He had lost at least twenty pounds and his face was haggard, his eyes bloodshot. He had been working sixteen hours a day, seven days a week, and getting considerably less money than had been promised, even though he had got married on the strength of his having a job. The long hours were also wreaking havoc with his domestic life.

Noyes was also forced to do heavy work, although a condition of his employment specified that he be given only light work because of an earlier back injury.

When he told his employer he couldn't keep on working under such conditions, he was told that if he complained or tried to get another job, the employer would call his parole officer and Noyes would be sent back to prison.

Noyes asked me if he could come to work at the prison. I cleared his employment with the parole director and became Noyes's parole sponsor as well as supervisor. He worked out extremely well, and a few months later we hired his wife, too, to work as a secretary.

Noyes's story was typical. This was the psychological situation of the convicted prisoner, from which there was no escape but the grave, because he could not legally leave Arkansas while on parole. And if a parolee managed to make it through his parole period, he still lived on the razor's edge between the freeworld and the prison, because the system, once set in motion, continued to work against him.

Local authorities were well aware that he was a former prisoner. If he was ever picked up again on any charge it was most likely he would be sent back to prison. In Arkansas, as in most other states, a convict's word is worthless in court. Any kind of sentence in Arkansas for any offense, resulting in imprisonment in the Boys' School or the prison farms, is tantamount to a lifelong sentence of apprehension, anxiety, and harassment.

One of the principal problems a parolee or ex-convict faced in the freeworld was repugnance, and reluctance on the part of most people, including farmers, to hire him. There was little we could do to educate the entire population of Arkansas, other than discuss the human qualities of the inmates in public speeches. But there was something we could do to equip the prisoners to return to the freeworld. We discovered that the Arkansas-Louisiana Gas Company, Arkla, had been trying to set up a vocational training program at the prison—since 1949. They needed about four hundred small-appliance repair men each year, and the prisoners would have been ideal trainees. Previous superintendents had refused to allow the men to take training courses, even though Arkla was willing to provide the instructors and equipment. Such a program would not cost the state anything, and it would not interfere with the operation of the prison, but the prison authorities were determined not to do anything for the convicts; only to work them.

I explained the idea of the program to the inmate population, and asked the men to sign up if they were interested. Fifty students registered for the first class, twice the number that could be accommodated. The group included one of the men from death row. Although he was under sentence of death and might never be able to use the training, I believed that if his mind was occupied fruitfully by classwork it would relieve some of his tension, so he participated in the program.

The instructor from Arkansas-Louisiana Gas was so inspired by the inmates' enthusiasm for the project that he agreed to conduct two sections of the same class. We released the men from work in the field to attend classes—the first time that training had taken precedence over punitive—and profit-making—labor.

During the eight weeks of the first vocational training course in the history of the penitentiary system, the prison auditorium looked like a gigantic kitchen. There were ranges and small appliances all over the room in various stages of assembly. We made plans to conduct additional classes after that course was completed. When the inmates attained sufficient proficiency they could qualify for an apprenticeship with the gas company, and a position upon release from prison.

One of the several purposes behind vocational training in prisons is to prevent the men from being exploited when they get out. Some basic general education is helpful in the freeworld too. One of the reasons these inmates were so easily exploited was that few of them knew anything about the law or could even read newspapers. We arranged with the state department of education to give literacy tests, and to my horror—but not surprise—I found that in the group of three hundred we had four who knew only their ABCs, about fifty-five functional illiterates, and forty more who were just beyond the "see Dick run" stage. With the exception of the two college men, and a few with some high-school background, most of the men had only a grammar-school education.

Armed with this information, we were able to get the department of education to set up a fund to hire six teachers, including four women, from the Plum Bayou School District. We set up school for grades one through nine, with classes held two nights a week for three hours at a stretch in the prison auditorium.

Canvas curtains were draped from the ceiling to make school rooms. Each class had around twelve men learning such basic essentials as how to read and write their names.

My wife, who is a certified school teacher, insisted on being an instructor. At home, after her first class, Margaret told me she had been nervous because the prisoners at Tucker were tough convicts. As time went on she felt more and more comfortable with them. After a few weeks, she told me that although for the most part they were emotionally immature, they were very attentive in class and tried their best to learn.

Margaret was especially impressed that at no time was she treated with anything but the utmost courtesy and respect. The inmates were, in fact, better behaved than her regular school students had been.

As a by-product of the educational experience, I began to bring more women into the institution. To my mind this was an important factor in helping inmates adjust to their future life in the freeworld. Again, we were taking a giant step forward, as women are not generally on staff inside men's prisons in the United States.

But the freeworld society is heterosexual and heterogeneous, and one of the basic problems of penal institutions is that men don't have any contact with women. If, upon release, the inmates are going to be able to communicate with women and relate to them in the world outside the prison gates, it is important that they do it in a positive fashion.

One of the two female secretaries—whom we hired at Tucker to replace inmate clerks—had previously worked in a construction office; the other had worked in a retail store. They both told me they were treated with more courtesy and respect by the inmates than by the freeworld personnel they had worked with before.

The men reacted to the presence of women in the institution in a most predictable way, and Margaret noticed it almost at once.

"When I first came to Tucker," she told me, "I didn't have to turn around to know an inmate was standing behind me. I could smell him. But after a while, the only odor they had was of freshly washed clothing."

We also attempted to do away with medical exploitation of the inmates and provide them with an adequate health service. The former prison physician, Dr. Gwyn Atnip, had spent half a day, five days a week, at Cummins, and visited Tucker about once a month, until April of 1967, when he was discharged. His dismissal followed the death of Luther Bailey, an inmate on death row, who had never been out of his cell in fourteen years. Bailey had died of peritonitis as a result of a lack of medical attention. Dr. Atnip had refused to attend him for three weeks, and had never come to the main building to see anybody.[1]

Most Tucker medical services were provided by the "convict doctor," who had no medical training but had established his own empire at the prison. He pushed pills, and he sold medical passes so inmates with money could goof off in the hospital—one of the most corrupt places in Tucker.

The prison hospital at Tucker was the oldest structure on the farm. Originally built as the death house, in 1922, it was across the bayou from the main building and had a levee around it to keep the water out when the bayou was up. The levee didn't always work. After heavy rain storms the water inside the building was sometimes a foot and a half deep, with fecal matter floating around. When that happened, all the patients stayed in bed until the bayou went down.

There was algae growing on the floor and the wiring had been condemned. Gas was piped through the building in water pipes. Cooking was done under the least sanitary of conditions. The shower was a pipe hanging down from the ceiling in the corner of a cell. Fire-fighting equipment consisted of a box on which was written, "In case of Fire, RUN!"

Although the hospital would not meet any acceptable standards, the state department of health had issued it licenses yearly since it was "converted" to a hospital in 1948. In April, I wrote a letter saying that in my opinion, it ought to be condemned. When the state health inspector came, he agreed.

Rather than attempt to get funds to build a new hospital, however, we decided to convert the "new" death house—built in 1948, when the older one had become a hospital—into an infirmary. It had already been used as a temporary

---

[1] Sources for this information were statements by convicts and Captain R. E. Brown's investigation (Brown was in charge of Tucker shortly after this death). See further the Little Rock *Arkansas Gazette*, Feb. 4, 1967, for an account of this death. The superintendent of the state hospital refused to perfom an autopsy as requested by the governor, although it was required by statute. An autopsy was eventually performed, at the request of the victim's attorney, but a copy was never provided to the governor.

operating room. There had not been an execution in the state since 1963 and it seemed a shame to let the space go unused. The structure was poured concrete with security steel, and there were barred windows, drains, an operating table, and leg-operated water faucets with hot water. The facility was attached to the main building.

The morgue, where the bodies of legally executed prisoners were examined and prepared for burial, could serve as an excellent examination room. A third room, where the jumbled electrical switches were installed, had enough space to hold dental and optical offices and serve as a records office for the medical technician.

Old Satan, the 22,000-volt electric chair, had to stay, so it was boxed in, and the rest of its room was used as a ward for ten beds.

By May, the new infirmary was in operation. James Hargraves, a licensed medical technician, was in charge. Hargraves picked up an eye examination unit through surplus channels. With the assistance of Dr. Morrow in the town of England, he set up a program for examining the inmates' eyes and providing them with prescription lenses. For the first time in the history of the penitentiary system, we had a regular optometry program.

We could not do much more than this to improve medical services for the inmates, except cut out the corruption. We were effective in stopping the "blood-sucking program," run by Dr. Austin R. Stough, who had the contract for blood collection at the prison. Dr. Stough paid each inmate $5 for blood plasma, which he sold to Cutter Laboratories for $15. John Haley studied the books, and estimated that Stough made between $130,000 and $150,000 a year from this contract. One dollar of the inmate's money went to the Officers' Welfare Fund and another dollar to the Inmates' Welfare Fund. At Cummins more than $73,000 in "blood money" was in the inmates' fund, but the inmates derived little benefit from it. All they got was the immediate $3 for each donation.

John Haley filed a report about the program with the penitentiary board, and in May got approval for a nonprofit foundation (Medcor) to take blood from prisoners, at Cummins. Under the new arrangement, which went into effect in November, the inmate donors received $7, and profits went into a prison fund to provide better medical care for the inmates.

The only problem with this arrangement was that we had to transport our men by bus to Cummins, and many inmates were reluctant to go through the plasma program because outbreaks of hepatitis were blamed on it, and they believed there were certain inherent dangers in this blood plasma program.[1] For those inmates who did not want to take the risk we set up an alternate plan. A firm in Little Rock sent nurses to Tucker weekly and drew whole blood, for which they paid each inmate $7.

We also instituted a program in collaboration with the University of Arkansas Medical Center, under which trusties went to the medical center for a couple of weeks and engaged in a research project of a noncritical nature. While they were there they ate well, got to watch color TV, and were paid. They considered it a paid vacation from the prison.

Our men were not anxious to go to Cummins hospital, because many of the inmates working there were homosexual and the drug situation was almost completely controlled by the inmates. They even had a price for aspirin. For six months Tucker could not get medical supplies from the Cummins hospital, because the inmate doctor refused to fill our requisitions.

We also had problems with the Arkansas State Hospital at Little Rock, which consistently created confusion whenever one of our inmates had to be transferred there for special medical treatment. We spent weeks in profitless correspondence with the superintendent of the hospital, who was forever changing his policy.

Early in June, Dr. Elizabeth Fletcher, who was in charge of one of the departments at the state hospital, refused to admit five of our men on the grounds that there were only so many beds available for prisoners. In the past, we had used bed space and the business manager at Cummins had not paid our bills. She said she didn't see any reason why the inmates should be admitted anyway. Two of the men

---

[1] It seems they were right. The *New York Times* (July 28, 1969, pp. 1, 20, & 21) carried a fourteen-column article by Walter Rugaber titled "Prison Drug and Plasma Projects Leave Fatal Trail" exposing this abuse of inmates.

Profit-Making—Modern Slavery; Modern Medicine 111

had shot lighter fluid intravenously with a hypodermic needle, and one of them was in very serious condition.

To help upgrade the medical services, we contracted with Dr. Willie Harris of England, Arkansas, in April, 1967. He was young and capable, had no previous relationship with the prison—and he cared about the inmates' welfare.

Dr. Edwin Barron, Jr., a director of the Medcor Foundation and a lifelong friend of John Haley, was hired in September at a salary of $20,000, to be the prison physician, eventually freeing Harris for his private practice, and to upgrade the Cummins hospital, which was reasonably modern and well-equipped. He never came to Tucker to see a patient, although this was among his duties. We sometimes used medical students who came to Tucker to hold sick call. If an inmate needed treatment, we had to arrange to have him driven 110 miles round trip to Cummins and back, without any guarantee a doctor would be there to see him.

Dr. Barron, who was nicknamed "the Red Baron" by the inmates, was an aviation enthusiast and flew around Arkansas making calls in his "Sopwith Camel." During a week of good flying weather, he might spend a total of eight hours at the Cummins prison hospital. The inmate doctor screened sick-call patients for him, signed his signature better than he did, and admitted and discharged patients at will.

When one of our inmates came back to Tucker from the Cummins hospital, he would be accompanied by reams of forms—many of which were still blank—supposedly a medical report of his stay in the hospital.

Each man who transferred to Tucker also arrived with an impressive medical file prepared by the staff at Cummins. My attention was directed to at least two inmates whose official medical reports didn't match with what laymen observed: their vision was rated as "normal" in each eye by the prison physician, but they both complained of poor vision, and the Longline rider told me that they couldn't see well enough to clean the rows. I referred them to Hargraves, our medical technician, for examination. He reported that not only did each man have very poor vision in one eye but, in each case, the other eye was glass.

Committees, Consultants, and Commodes

At least once a month our normal routine at Tucker was interrupted by visiting "pilgrims"—people with official connections. A typical visit was that of the twenty-five members of the state legislative council, who inspected Tucker Prison Farm in July. They arrived in an air-conditioned chartered bus, with a loudspeaker inside for tour comments.

I knew they were coming because they had already lunched at Cummins, but I made no special arrangements. I did not want to pull men in from the fields to spruce up the barracks, and I wanted the council to see Tucker and me on a typical day. I wore my work clothes.

The legislators spent most of their time in the hospital. The medical technician in charge was elsewhere on an emergency case, and consequently the room had not been cleaned properly.

While in the converted death house, a legislator sat down in the electric chair and let his fellow tourists strap him in. Others of the jolly group pretended they were trying to find the switch to turn on the chair while the seated legislator insisted hilariously that he could feel some current. The other members then took turns photographing each other in the chair as souvenirs of their visit.

After a hasty tour of the barracks area, a legislator said he had counted about forty men on their bunks who were not working. I explained that twenty-four of the men were off-duty guards, some of the others were laid-in by the

Committees, Consultants, and Commodes

doctor, and the remainder were off duty from the kitchen staff.

Another complained about the flies—some flies and one cobweb were all they could fault in the kitchen—and said he hadn't seen them at Cummins. "They were waving them off you at Cummins," joked one of his companions.

"Why didn't you get a detail of men to clean Tucker?" a legislator asked.

"I could let the okra go to hell, plow under the beets and onions, and instead, clean up the barracks," I said. "But somewhere you've got to decide a priority. The place may not be spick and span, but the question is, what do you shut down to clean it? Right now I have a total available work force of thirty-five men and seven hundred acres of cotton to be chopped. I believe in cleanliness, but you've got to put everything in some kind of order."

Another legislator asked what was my biggest problem at Tucker. I answered that we needed facilities to segregate the fourteen, fifteen, sixteen, and seventeen years olds from the other prisoners. This was not the kind of answer they wanted.

They saw only the superficial. O.E. Bishop had followed our lead and abolished the strap—he claimed. But even if Bishop really had stopped the whippings, something far worse, in my estimation, was going on at Cummins. The visiting legislators had had difficulty maintaining their footing on the wet floors of the isolation building, where they saw wet mattresses, clothing, shoes, and socks. They seemed untroubled by the fact that thirty-six Negro inmates, in solitary confinement for staging a sit-down for better food and working conditions, were hosed down several times a day with a short fire hose that exerted enough pressure to pin a man to the wall.

When the legislators went through the Cummins isolation unit,[1] they saw at least two of the prisoners lying doubled up with chills on the wet floor. Another of the prisoners told the legislators he had not had more than two hours sleep in the seventy-two hours since they had been placed in solitary.

---

[1] My knowledge of the Cummins tour comes from newsmen who accompanied it.

Accomplices to the Crime

The council members did not discuss the hosing, and apparently not one of them was aware that the day before their visit to Cummins, the governor's assistant on prison affairs, Bob Scott, had witnessed a whipping. Three Negroes had been taken from the chow line and whipped in the hallway in front of the other prisoners. Scott called it a "sickening sight," and regretted that he had seen it.

Blood from the beaten prisoners' buttocks had just been washed off the floor when the council members came; the legislators were satisfied with clean barracks, a good meal, and obeisance from the superintendent. They had had lunch at Cummins on white tablecloths, at banquet tables set up in the auditorium. There was a convict behind each legislator, waving flies away with a fan.

Mr. Bishop had dressed himself in a suit, and draped a white napkin over his arm, maitre d' style, to take their orders. The legislators had a choice of three cuts of meat, with potatoes and butter beans. While they ate, the ten-piece prison band played rock 'n' roll, popular songs, and Strauss waltzes.

The group was then guided through the barracks area at Cummins, which had been spruced up for the occasion: even the pillows were at attention.

My work clothes, the fact that I had not brought men in from work details to polish the institution up, and my candid answers to questions, militated against me. The legislators reported to the press that Tucker was "filthy" and that I was "disrespectful."

They may have had a point about my personality. Still, I was aware that they were only interested in the superficial; they cared nothing about making a real investigation, probably because they didn't know how, or what to look for.

It took abrasion to rub through their shell of ignorance. It sometimes took fireworks, or what the board called "rudeness," to spark off action and get things moving. Other ways had proved hopeless. There is no way to tiptoe through the quicksand of social and bureaucratic inertia.

Instead of verifying or discounting the charges of brutality and exploitation made in the CID report, or taking them as true and investigating the progress, or lack of progress, the legislators ignored the CID charges and submitted their own criticism of Tucker. Their report said

Committees, Consultants, and Commodes 115

that the Tucker "grounds were not well kept, the barracks were dirty and the beds unmade . . . the prisoners were unkempt . . . many prisoners were idle . . . there appeared to be an attitude of lax discipline . . . Murton did not appear to have a proper attitude toward the prisoners and thereby did not command control over the institution."

The legislators' report distorted the image of reform again. An unaware and uninformed public was left to believe that a military atmosphere and military discipline were the signs of a well-run prison.

The fact is that most politicians in Arkansas seemed determined to fight prison reform, or to hamper it. State senator Knox Nelson, for example, considered the Arkansas penitentiary system one of the finest in the nation. He claimed people from all over the United States came to study it so they could model their own system after it. They may have come to study it, but not for the reasons he imagined. Another state senator claimed that the Rockefeller administration was stirring up a prison scandal for political reasons.

Committee after committee was formed to investigate the prison system. Their reports invariably ignored the real and obvious faults.

I had been brought to Arkansas as, in their words, an "expert" in criminology, and had been promised the job of commissioner of corrections. I was therefore distressed to learn I had been eliminated from any official capacity with the prison study commission formed to investigate the prison system.

Bob Scott, the governor's aide, claimed that when I accepted an appointment as Tucker superintendent I became a part of the system, and thus forfeited any possible consultant relationship to the study commission.

I told Scott bluntly that I hadn't come to Arkansas only to be superintendent: Governor Rockefeller had also assured me that I would be the consultant to the prison study group, and I would help them channel their efforts productively.

Scott assured me there was nothing to worry about concerning the commissionership. (Inconsistency was a hallmark.) A few days later, Governor Rockefeller came to the prison for a personal tour, to give me some kind of endorsement in front of the inmates. He, too, assured me that I would play an active role with the study commission, and he repeated his promise that I would be commissioner of corrections.

Meanwhile the study commission went ahead without me. The official chief consultant was seventy-five-year-old Austin MacCormick, who believed that Arkansas prisons, because of their agrarian base, should be patterned after the system in Texas. He suggested the commission look to Texas for immediate help and recommended discussing the situation with George Beto, head of the Texas prisons. (Beto has a doctorate in educational administration, and he was formerly an instructor at a Lutheran seminary in Illinois.)

I told the members of the commission that in my opinion experts from other states were not qualified to evaluate the Arkansas system. I recommended that before doing anything else, it would be best to develop a philosophy of what the prison should be,

However, George Beto and his director of agriculture, Byron Frierson, came to Arkansas. They spent two days touring Tucker and Cummins and reported that the prisons were "not clean."[1] Beto also said that he had never seen finer pieces of farm land, and that Arkansas had the potential of having "the best feeding [eating] program of any prison in the nation." He said the agriculture operation offered "a priceless opportunity in providing a work program" which would have "tremendous rehabilitative value."

He ignored the primary fault with the prison system—the exploitation of inmates for profit—and occupied himself with how the exploitation could be made even more efficient.

"The Arkansas penitentiary system has the potential of becoming one of the best in the country," he said, without giving any indications of the steps that would be necessary to make it so. Like most experts, he confirmed his position with the members of the establishment by saying only what they wanted to hear.

His primary recommendation was that we should not

---

[1] Beto's remarks were reported in the *Pine Bluff Commercial*, Pine Bluff, Ark., April 30, 1967, p. 8.

Committees, Consultants, and Commodes   117

dispose of any farmland. This suggestion hindered reform, because it was impossible to run a penitentiary system consisting of 21,000 acres devoted to hand-labor crops with a declining prison population. By April 1, Tucker had 140 fewer inmates than the previous year.[1] In that group were most of the hard-core cases sent over from Cummins: perverts, mentally retarded, escape risks, and chronic troublemakers. To complicate matters further, April was the wettest month in eighty years of weather reporting in Arkansas. We had eleven inches of rain, which meant we couldn't work on the soybeans until we got the rice in, and nearly half of our crop land was rice.

A consultant of another caliber was Joseph D. Lohman,[2] Dean of the School of Criminology at the University of California at Berkeley. The Southern Regional Council of Atlanta had offered to sponsor a criminologist to evaluate the Arkansas prison programs for the new administration. At the invitation of the new penitentiary board, Dean Lohman visited each unit of the prison and for several days studied the activities and emerging programs.

Lohman expressed amazement at the peaceful revolution taking place within the prison and reported to the prison board, Governor Rockefeller, and the state legislature, that a "renaissance in corrections" was taking place in Arkansas. A few listened; some heard; none understood.

The hostility of the investigative groups was trivial, however, compared with the antagonism of various state agencies which were supposed to work with us.

Our principal harassment came from the state purchasing agency, directed by Sidney Kegeles, who was a personal appointee of Governor Rockefeller. The man in state purchasing assigned to work with the prisons was Bob Hudgins, a brother-in-law of R.E. Jeter, who was on the penitentiary board that seemed determined I should fail.

Hudgins enlisted the aid of Eugene Nunn, the Arkansas State Penitentiary Business Manager. Mr. Nunn, who was called "Skinny Nunn" because of his pear shape, was quite a character. Don Bassett, Tucker's business manager,

---
[1] The average inmate population at Tucker was, approximately, 300; at this time we had 232 inmates.
[2] Lohman's distinguished career was cut short some sixty days after his visit by his untimely death.

made frequent trips to see Nunn to try and get him to cooperate with us. Bassett arrived at Cummins one June day in time for lunch. His description of the luncheon is in my log:

"After catfish and hush puppies served by the houseboy, they had three bowls of ice cream set around for Nunn, his wife, and Bassett. Bassett suddenly noticed the houseboy coming silently up behind Nunn with something in his hands. He slipped a cloth over Nunn's head and, for a moment, Bassett feared the boy was going to strangle Nunn.

"The thing in his hands, however, turned out to be a large bib which was tucked over Nunn's fat belly and neck. Nunn shakes so much from his daily fifth that he is unable to handle the spoon trip from bowl to mouth.

"After lunch Nunn takes a two-hour nap, then staggers back to work."

This was the man who arbitrarily rejected and cut our requisitions and sent us items that bore no relationship to what had been ordered.

My problems with state purchasing were endless. When one of our tractors was destroyed it took almost three months to get a replacement. It took three months to get searchlights for two of our towers, and when they finally arrived they were the wrong voltage. Our smoke house was destroyed by arson and our slaughter house and the old infirmary had been condemned. Yet it was impossible to get state purchasing to order materials for new buildings.

The day after I took over at Tucker, I discovered the steam boiler in the laundry had been condemned by the state inspector a month earlier. It was one of six experimental models built in 1913; the other five had already exploded. This one had been condemned—and restored to duty—six times.

The boiler was condemned again in February, 1967, when a state inspector examined it. He was amazed that it worked at all. Even if it had worked to capacity, it could not have met our demands, and we expected it to explode momentarily and blow the building off the farm. It took the new boiler four months to be delivered.

The situation became so bad that I finally wrote a long letter to Kegeles in April, with copies to Bassett and Eisele,

Committees, Consultants, and Commodes   119

trying to solve the purchasing problems once and for all.[1] There was some temporary relief, but conditions soon returned to the usual slow-playing.

All the produce for canning was trucked over to Cummins, where the canner was. If the produce wasn't fer-

---

[1] This was the letter:

April 26, 1967

Mr. Sidney A. Kegeles, Director
State Purchasing Department
Little Rock, Arkansas

Dear Mr. Kegeles:

I am sure you have found your new position quite exacting and possibly frustrating. There is no doubt that you have quite a formidable responsibility facing you. I am well aware that there are many state agencies requesting your services and there is a limit on the time you can devote to assisting us at Tucker.

However, it is my belief that we are becoming unnecessarily bogged down in bureaucracy. I will recite a few instances to demonstrate this. I believe there is a breakdown somewhere in your agency but, will not presume to suggest where the difficulty lies. My comments should not be interpreted personally by any of your staff.

Tucker is a beachhead and we are trying to man the battlestations under somewhat adverse conditions. I was employed to administer Tucker to the best of my ability. I have been given full authority to hire and fire, and proceed as I see fit. There is no one in the Penitentiary System, on the Board or in the state government who has sought to pass judgment on my actions; nor, in the area of criminology, are any of these persons qualified.

I know what the needs of Tucker are and have sought diligently to follow all established procedures to obtain equipment and supplies. We have consistently experienced difficulties with purchasing through Mr. Nunn at Cummins. Our requisitions have arbitrarily been rejected, the orders have been cut or partially eliminated and sometimes what arrives is not what was ordered. You have taken steps to expedite this operation by assigning certain individuals in your office to process our requisitions. We have also been advised on numerous occasions that Tucker has top priority on purchasing. Unfortunately, the results do not indicate this.

It is my understanding that within the last 24 hours the bid was let for replacement of our tractor. It has been nearly three months since the other one was destroyed and probably be some time before we can expect delivery. It has been on order since February 15th. Cummins "repaired" our other tractor at a cost of some $700 and a delay of seven weeks. When it was finally delivered, the engine had been ruined because the oil drain plug had "mysteriously" been left out. As you know, all we have for transportation here are a few pickups. The Board gave approval for a 2 ton truck which we have recently ordered.

About ten days ago I advised you of the dire need for some kind of service vehicle for the garage and rice pumps. You stated there are three '64 pickups we could have on transfer from another agency within 24 hours. We don't have them yet and Mr. Munch advises there is some legal objection to this. He also advises he is looking for a service vehicle.

We have had an order in since January 6th for steel water pitchers for the dining hall.

Two of the towers have no searchlights. We made formal requests for these on February 26th and March 21st. We listed the complete description and possible source of supply. Last Friday I was advised

mented or ruined in travel, there was a chance that it might be canned and sent back to Tucker. But Cummins, claiming they had no cans, consistently refused to can our produce. I sent inmate Jim Nabors to Cummins to investigate. He reported that Cummins had three railroad boxcars full of Number 10 cans and that they had been canning potatoes, squash, beets and carrots for weeks for use at Cummins. In short, it was a bald lie that they were out of cans. The rider of the Cummins canning operation told Nabors that he had been ordered not to can anything for Tucker. As a result, we lost $10,099.50 worth of produce in one week; there was no point in picking it, so it rotted in the fields.

---

that your office was dilligently searching a junk yard at Cummins for some lights allegedly shipped there several years ago. This was finally abandoned and I believe the order has been let.

We placed an order for paint for the barracks on March 31st and are still waiting for this. On rainy days I could use the men to paint the barracks. It is interesting to note that Cummins has been able to paint the entire building and all I have been able to paint is five cells; and that by buying paint directly.

Five weeks ago the Penitentiary Board approved a $27,000 expenditure immediately for construction of 3 staff houses, an infirmary, a slaughter-smoke house and machine shed. Mr. Bishop and Mr. Nunn said these funds were available. On April 5th, the Board reaffirmed this authorization. I have submitted want lists for materials for everything but the staff houses. We plan to construct these of wood after a fashion that can be moved should Tucker be sold. Now, I have been advised that there are no funds available for capital expenditures for the balance of this fiscal year. Also, some caution seems to have been expressed from your office about my purchases in view of the fact that Tucker might be sold.

Whether Tucker is sold next week or retained for twenty years is not material to the issue in my opinion. My infirmary has been condemned and we can only use it pending erection of an adequate structure. The smoke house burned down several weeks ago and the slaughter house has been condemned. If I am to continue preserving meat or feeding it at this institution, we need to have facilities which meet minimum state health standards.

The staff houses have been authorized and officers have been employed with the understanding they would have housing. We need to start construction *now*. We should have started a month ago. I was advised last Friday that one of your officers was sent down here to photograph the slaughterhouse to "justify" the expenditure for replacement.

The one difficulty which lies beyond my comprehension is the boiler fiasco. I reported for duty February 20th, on February 21st, I requested a new boiler for the laundry. It had been condemned by the state boiler inspector in January. I called for estimates for replacement. The Board gave approval on February 28th to buy a new one.

We later submitted all estimates to your office. The boiler, according to my information is the sole survivor of six such experimental models built in 1913. Since that time, it reportedly has been condemned and subsequently restored to duty six times. It was condemned again in February when another inspector was sent down here. All inspectors

Committees, Consultants, and Commodes 121

Meanwhile, we ordered a small canning machine to preserve the overripe strawberries for our own use. The order was delayed while our need was "investigated." The canner finally arrived the week after the strawberry season ended.

We also needed typewriters—desperately—if only to keep up with the voluminous correspondence required by state agencies. When we put through a requisition slip, state purchasing ignored a company that had the machines on the shelf and for a difference of eighty cents per machine, awarded the bid to a variety of firms unable to provide the machines for months.

It took more than months for some things. We had only

---

have expressed amazement that it runs at all. Even if it could work to capacity, it would never carry the demand by the presently installed equipment. There is the constant danger it will blow the building off the farm *when* it explodes. It breaks down constantly.

About every ten days some "expert" drifts through to assess the situation. One does not need to be a cow to know what milk is. Neither does one need to be a mechanical engineer to evaluate a boiler that could kill or maim the eighteen assigned inmates.

Again last Friday, another pilgrim visited the farm to photograph the evidence to "prove" to your office we need a new boiler. I believe your office probably has been confused by actions in this matter from Cummins.

I have asked for boxes to put inmates clothing in which has been questioned. My order for security plumbing fixtures has been held up. I have been requested to explain these purchases in view of the fact that "they never ordered them before." Also I have been advised by your office that it will be necessary for me to certify that the Bureau of Prisons and other prisons use this type of security wares.

Then of course there was the venture whereby your office questioned my request for Angus bulls because you thought I might not know what I needed. I believe your subsequent investigation demonstrated we have a good livestock management program in operation. Even so, your office wanted to make the selection of the bulls although I requested authority to make the selection.

We ordered a small canner to preserve our over-ripe strawberries for institutional use a couple of weeks ago. This got the usual delay while someone tried to determine if we really needed it. I understand it finally was ordered and your office said we would have delivery one week ago today. We do not have it yet and we have some 400 crates of over-ripe berries to dump tomorrow if we cannot can them.

I am sure you are honest and capable. I have no doubt of your motives. I assume you are trying to surround yourself with competent men and bring some organization to your office. I am very frugal by nature and have a reputation of being rather economical.

However, I believe your office is becoming too personally concerned with this operation. I have been superintendent of six other institutions, I have fought battles all my life, I have degrees in animal husbandry, education and criminology, I will hopefully receive my doctorate in June.

Mr. Rockefeller hired me to do a job. Apparently he had confidence that I could do it. I know what I am doing, but there is not time to conduct courses in criminology. I have no intention of justifying my

Accomplices to the Crime

fourteen cells at Tucker and each one had a vitreous china unit which consisted of a wash basin and commode. The units could easily be smashed or damaged, as James Williams did later, and I wanted to order special unbreakable institutional commodes made of cast aluminum. State purchasing sent a man to photograph our old units and requested I get signed statements from officials of the U.S. Bureau of Prisons and two other state systems to confirm my contention that institutional commodes were commonly used in institutions.

I didn't imagine all this harassment. Some time later Russell Kumpe, the inmate record clerk at Cummins, told me that he had been ordered by superintendent Bishop not to cooperate with us in any way. Bishop denied our request for school supplies and told Kumpe not to send us anything we requested. The wardens even told Kumpe not to put us through on the telephone when we called. They gave instructions that whenever I called, he was to say no one was available to talk.

Kumpe also said that the wardens at Cummins made fun of our activities and felt threatened because they didn't

---

requisitions with documents showing what is done in other states. As long as I have the responsibility for this institution I must have the authority also.

It would seem to me that all that is necessary for your office to determine is whether there are sufficient funds in my budget to make the purchase. I am not interested in what has been done here the past 50 years or necessarily what is being done in the other 49 states.

It is my responsibility to determine what needs to be done and advise you. If no one in the Penitentiary System deems it necessary to review my requests, I see no reason why your office should. I will be happy to give a relief of responsibility to your office if you wish.

All I am asking is that my orders be processed without the mickey mouse double checking and second guessing that has been going on. The critical nature of the current situation forces me to bring this directly to your attention.

Again, I have no specific quarrel with any of your personnel. All have been most cooperative. We just are not getting results.

Therefore, I want the boiler without any further delay. I also want my requests for building supplies processed immediately so we can get moving. We need the canner now.

I ordered all supplies and equipment for all institutions in Alaska for several years and have personal contacts as well as knowledge of what is best, what is essential and where it can be purchased.

I would not presume to suggest to you how your office should be operated and ask that you extend the same courtesy to me.

Sincerely yours,

Tom Murton
Superintendent

cc: Mr. Eisele
Mr. Bassett

understand them. He confirmed what I had long suspected: that he had orders from Bishop to pick out the misfits, perverts, cripples, and agitators, and send them to Tucker —a situation we had been aware of for some time.

Late in June, I became furious about this whole scene and prepared a nineteen-page "status report"—which I mailed to the members of the penitentiary board, with copies to the local press—charging Mr. Nunn, other Cummins officials, and state purchasing, with specific instances of harassment and interference.

O.E. Bishop responded with a thirty-three-page reply avoiding all the charges I had filed against him. He also attacked me and the press. The board reluctantly called for a face-to-face confrontation between us, to be witnessed by the press.

On July 13, the board convened in the governor's conference room. Bishop and I were asked to sit down together at the long press table. The board fumbled around until one of the newsmen asked what they were going to do.

Jeff Wood, the chairman, said that I had made a release and Bishop had made one and perhaps we would like to add something to our statements. In view of the fact that he had not read either release, Wood said, he didn't intend to go any further with the charges at that time.

He asked me if I had anything further to add. I told him some details about the recent sabotage of two trailers. There was an exchange back and forth that died on the vine. Then Bishop brought up the boiler situation, contending that we had two boilers and one of them had been installed a year before. I wiped out that argument by showing pictures of our only boiler—vintage 1913.

It was obvious the board didn't want to get involved in a discussion of any kind. The only thing that kept the meeting going was the newsmen's questions. The only board member to question us was Grady Wooley, who suggested that perhaps the inmates were responsible for the sabotage and were trying to thwart the efforts of both prisons.

Later in the week, the board had a forty-minute closed session to go over our reports again. They refused to disclose the results of their "investigation" of my charges, on the ground that they were only interested in an efficient prison system and were not there to referee conflicts between the two superintendents.

My charges did have some impact, however. The board discharged Mr. Nunn, who was my principal stumbling block, and in July he was replaced by Don Bassett, whom I had brought to Tucker to be our business manager three months earlier. Mr. Nunn, who was sixty-five, was given an advisory post until his retirement that September, thus disposing of half of our problem.[1]

The board did not address themselves to the other half of my charges, which dealt with derelictions of the state purchasing department headed by Sidney A. Kegeles. I appealed to Bob Scott, Marion Burton, and Tom Eisele, legal aides to the governor. No action was forthcoming from them, so I discussed the matter personally with Governor Rockefeller in October. He seemed genuinely alarmed by my charges that Kegeles was deliberately interfering with prison reform, and directed Scott to investigate. As a result of the investigation, Kegeles "resigned" in November, although he was allowed to remain in office until after the first of the year.

I did accomplish something important in the July meetings, though. I told the board I was getting all of the cruddy prisoners from Cummins and I wasn't allowed to send any back. After my explanation, the board gave me authority to select my own prisoners from the group at Cummins, and I was authorized to return any of the men to Cummins who did not adjust at Tucker.

The board also released a state police report that B.C. Howard, who had resigned from Tucker as business manager when I was appointed superintendent, had borrowed more than $1,500 from a Little Rock bank and repaid the loan with money from the Inmates' Welfare Fund.

The investigation of Mr. Howard came about because

---

[1] Or so we thought at the time. Immediately after his appointment, Bassett advised all vendors that only he could authorize any prison purchase—which resulted in our being unable to buy even medications, for either inmates or livestock. He denied my request to exempt Tucker from this ruling; and my appeal to Haley was no more successful. It was not until I requested intervention by the board four weeks later that the issue was resolved to our satisfaction. Even after this intervention, Bassett continued to perform his duties in a manner reminiscent of Nunn's tactics.

Committees, Consultants, and Commodes

I had been insisting, since my arrival in Arkansas, that a search audit of the records of the state prison system should be made. I was convinced that such an audit would reveal how many private individuals had made enormous profits from the sale of prison produce. I was certain it would reveal a whole variety of frauds. The authority for such an audit was covered by the act that created the prison study commission, and reads, in part:

"SECTION 2. The State Penitentiary Study Commission shall make a comprehensive study of the penal system of this State, including, but not limited to, the following . . .

"(9) A study of the financial operations of the Penitentiary, including the source of income, and the purposes for which expenditures are made . . ."

The state's prosecutor, Joe Holmes, said he couldn't understand "how this search audit would come within the purview of the act which created the commission." Despite support from three other members of the commission, the recommendation for an audit was voted down—but they did agree that they would authorize an audit of *my* administration thereafter.

Holmes was at least being consistent. He had been one of the first to discount stories of brutality at the prison, and had done his best to avoid prosecuting former superintendent Jim Bruton.

After we abolished the strap and began to use disciplinary segregation to punish prisoners brought back from escape, Holmes had contended that the segregated confinement made it impossible to prosecute the inmate in court for the same offense. He claimed this action would place the inmate in double jeopardy—a ludicrously specious bit of reasoning.

In July, an inmate named Marion Odel Morrow escaped from Tucker. Apparently he had made arrangements during his wife's visit to have her pick him up in a car outside the front gate. Word of the escape was broadcast. The couple tried to run a roadblock but a trooper headed them off, and eventually they were taken into custody by Frank Crawford and the dogs.

Morrow's wife said she had paid Otis Standridge, the frontgate guard, to allow her husband to escape. Joe Holmes promptly announced that he was going to get the people who were helping prisoners escape and this was a hard and fast case which he could prove.

The implication of his statement was plain. My front-gate guard was corrupt, and by inference my entire administration was corrupt.

Uptight

By late fall of 1967, there had been only one escape from Tucker in five months, and the farm was running like a Sunday School. The scene at Cummins was very different.

One of my sources for information was the inmates. Russell Kumpe, who had been sent to Tucker early in July because it was feared he would be killed at Cummins for having testified in court against his crime partner, told me they still had two different kinds of food: the trusties ate better than the do-pops and rank men. But even the trusty food at Cummins was not as good as our mainline food at Tucker.

Much of the bitterness at Cummins was over visiting. Visitors and their automobiles were searched on arrival. The visits were monitored in a special room, which held only forty visitors at one time. Inmates, under the supervision of officers, stood on one side of a glass barrier and yelled through a small hole. All conversations were taped, which is rarely done any more in prisons.

At Tucker, we were allowing families to come to the prison without a shakedown or search of any kind. Visiting was conducted in the fenced compound surrounding the main building, with only one officer and one supervising trusty in the visiting area.

As far back as July, Kumpe told me, there had been talk of a mass breakout at Cummins, planned for the 4th. Happily, it did not come off. The reason the men were so uptight was that Bishop had started to exert more personal control in the field. The 175 trusties who were at the root of the problem felt certain he was going to replace them with freeworld men, as we had begun to do at Tucker. Bishop was also having problems with the Negroes. Whites were no longer whipped, but the Negroes were.

Grady Mask, another inmate from Cummins, said he paid $80 to get his job on the water cart where he could sell food. This confirmed my suspicion that the buying and selling of jobs was still going on there. Short hairs still had to pay $1 for a bed on their first night, and most of the inmates had to buy their laundry back. Gambling was still going on at Cummins; and I knew of a dozen inmates who had at least $2,000 in their possession.

Ironically, many of the men I sent to Cummins from Tucker for disciplinary reasons were put in positions of authority at Cummins. I had wiped out Bob Baty for being brutal while he was a floorwalker at Tucker, yet he was given the same job at Cummins.

Conversations with inmates like Kumpe and Mask gave me a picture of the tremendous problems facing me at Cummins when I took it over—if I ever did. It was urgent that I get some of my own men inside Cummins, because it was becoming more and more apparent that I was going to be on my own when I went there.

I asked Harold Porter, who was supervisor of the inmate guard force at Tucker, to go to Cummins as an advance man for me. Prisoners had been fleeing Cummins in increasing numbers; since Bishop knew Porter was a good security officer, and had earlier asked for his transfer, he accepted Porter without hesitation. Porter took the job readily, even though it meant a cut in pay. Partly, this was because the Tucker inmates' constant use of his nickname "Captain Kangaroo" and the "boing, boing" noises they made when he passed offended him.

I also arranged to transfer my inmate secretary, Lee Rogers, to Cummins, after we had a disagreement over a furlough and he asked for the transfer in protest. Rogers was a most unusual man. In eight years, he had successfully survived five different superintendents. To do this he had to walk a constant tightrope; he knew more about the prison than anyone else but he never betrayed any confidence about past superintendents, so I knew my plans were safe with him.

Rogers dressed like a trusty and lived in the trusty barracks, but when I checked his file one day, I found he was a do-pop. I told him I was going to promote him, but he insisted on staying a do-pop.

"You know what happens to Arkansas trusties in other prisons outside the state," he said. "And maybe I'll be picked up again after I get back on the street."

Rogers had a good point. Arkansas trusties are always put in isolation when they are imprisoned in other states, to protect them from the other prisoners—an extension of the system in Arkansas, where trusties could not be put in the barracks with rank men or even put in disciplinary isolation with rank men, for fear of reprisals.

Rogers was moody but efficient and, as I anticipated, Bishop immediately made him his secretary.

Bassett had also gone to Cummins in July, which meant that my men were slowly infiltrating into positions where they could supply me with information. In the meantime, I took full advantage of less formal sources of information —such as the Cummins milk-truck driver, an inmate who delivered daily prison gossip along with dairy products.

The turnover at Cummins would have done credit to a hotel. The prisoners were still checking out in groups. Ten took off in as many days. Some of the escapees showed a strong reluctance to being returned to the prison.

During the time I lost one prisoner from Tucker, in the fall of 1967, Cummins lost twenty-eight—because Bishop attempted to tighten restrictions and because the trusties, aware I would soon be taking over, were leaving rather than face the day when they would lose their power.

The multitude of escapes from Cummins received caustic attention from the newspapers. But what hurt Bishop's administration most was the escape on September 29 of two inmates named Reaves and Crotzer. Through established, though unofficial, tradition, they had been getting occasional passes to go uptown to shack up with girlfriends, an informal benefit allowed by the superintendent for certain prisoners.

The men shacked up in a motel with two ladies. Shortly,

the men took off, dropping the women in Tulsa, Oklahoma. Some weeks later the escapees were apprehended in another state for bank robbery.

Meanwhile there was a furor in Arkansas; not so much because the men had escaped, but because it was the first time anybody with a pass had escaped.

Embarrassed members of the penitentiary board held a secret executive session and ordered Bishop, who was on vacation, to take away the brozene, the freeworld money, and the civilian clothing. They wanted the trusties locked up at night, and they insisted on a shakedown of all the barracks, because it had been ten years since the last shakedown in the trusty barracks.

Following the board's decision, Scott called a meeting with Bishop and Colonel Lynn Davis, director of the state police, to discuss the mechanics of conducting the shakedown.

Colonel Davis intended to make the shakedown for Bishop by posting eight state troopers in the hall in front of the trusties' barracks with Thompson submachine guns. Then, Davis intended to go into the barracks and have the two hundred trusties line up against the wall while their property was searched. Ten more state troopers were to shake down the men and the barracks and then move over to the next barracks. If anyone tried to make any trouble, Davis planned to rely on his machine guns to keep order.

Colonel Davis also planned to put one trooper in every second tower to maintain control. He estimated it would take eighteen troopers to control the main building and make the shakedown, and another twelve troopers to provide security for the entire farm.

Bishop said that if the shakedown were conducted in this manner, the state police should be prepared to remain at Cummins for an indefinite period to control the riots that it would surely precipitate.

Davis' reply was: "It costs the state police about $2,000 for each manhunt. You've been losing prisoners at Cummins every few days for the past several months. Our budget is almost depleted. So I have a way for you to stop escapes, if you're interested."

Bishop allowed as how he was interested and asked Davis

for his solution. According to one of the governor's aides, who was present, Davis said:

"Well, you dig a hole two feet square and eight feet deep in the compound and when you catch the escapee you put him in the hole with a heavy iron grill placed over the top. You toss him bread and water for ten days while he is standing there in his own crap, exposed to the weather and when you bring him out he won't be in any condition to run off. If the prisoner who takes off is a trusty, you leave him there for twenty days because he has violated twice as much trust."

Bishop shook his head in disbelief and, ignoring the suggestion, later ordered everyone to turn in freeworld clothing. The Negro trusties responded to the order by announcing they were going to throw all their clothes out the windows. The white trusties said they would follow suit.

Bishop rescinded the order and refused to comply with any of the board's orders or Davis' suggestions. He transferred warden Clay Smith, who had given passes to the escapees, from security warden to farm manager, thus making him the scapegoat for the escapes. Smith, however, was popular among the trusties: they responded by threatening a sit-down strike and revolt if warden Perry Kinard, his assistant, were to become his replacement.

While all this was going on, John Haley went to Washington, and Bishop used his absence to poll the various board members on the telephone. Each one reversed his previous position. Bishop considered this tantamount to a reversal of the board's instructions to tighten up the prison, although it was not legal because, as Haley pointed out on his return, official board action could only transpire at board meetings.

As it happened Jim Nabors, one of my best men, had just violated a three-day furlough by going on a bender—which gave me an excuse to transfer him to Cummins. On the day he was transferred, I told Nabors that I wanted him to try and get information out of the trusty barracks. He looked pale around the gills, but he was game.

"You're coming over to Cummins soon, aren't you, Mr. Murton?" he asked me.

I told him I was but I didn't know when.

"Better make it quick," he said, "because if you don't they're going to get me."

Nabors was clearly afraid for his life. I told him if things got too tight he should pass the word to Bassett and I would bring him back.

I knew that Bassett would get word to Porter who, although he was at Cummins, had a Tucker pickup truck on the Tucker radio frequency, which could not be monitored at Cummins. In case of emergency, Porter was instructed to call me by radio.

About November 1, Harold Porter called from Cummins to tell me that Perry Kinard had been removed as head of security, and that about twenty-four guns were missing from the prison inventory and no one could find them.

Later in the week, Nabors came over from Cummins to Tucker to pick up a road grader. He used the visit to tell me that Robert Atwood, a former trustie, had been brought back as a parole violator, put in with the rank men, and beaten almost to death. I couldn't believe the Cummins administration could have bungled things so.

Later Porter phoned again to tell me that he had just witnessed twenty Negroes and one white man being beaten. It was the first beating he had ever seen, and it had made him sick. He also told me that less than a week previously Clay Smith had given ten lashes to one of the women in the Women's Reformatory at Cummins at the request of Smith's wife, who was the head matron.

Cummins seemed more like a fort under seige than a prison. The staff wives stayed on the freeline and children were kept inside the houses. There were two men instead of one in each gun cage in the mess hall, and the tower guards had been doubled. Don Bassett carried a twelve-gauge shotgun and a Thompson submachine gun in his car. Everyone was concerned about a mass escape.

Rockefeller's Contribution

Governor Winthrop Rockefeller sat with his legs crossed at the tops of his hand-tooled cowboy boots, swished ice cubes around in his glass and took in Martinis and cigarettes nonstop as I told him how my attempts to reform the prison system were constantly being thwarted by interference from state agencies as well as his own aides. He nodded occasionally and he made vague sounds, more like the clearing of his throat than affirmative responses. When I finished, he promised to look into all the matters I had discussed. But I was not encouraged. From past experience I knew I had probably failed to reach him again; only once or twice since I had been in Arkansas had he put the full authority of his office on the line for prison reform.

Our communication failure started two days after I took over Tucker and told the trusties and other inmates that I was in complete charge, that Cummins couldn't interfere with me in any way, and that I intended to run the show but needed their help.

The next day in an article in the *Arkansas Gazette*, the governor was asked: Is Murton running a separate prison at Tucker and does he have to answer to O.E. Bishop, over at Cummins?

"Captain Bishop has the right to fire Murton," the governor said.

Although the governor's reply was technically correct[1]

---

[1] Bishop could fire me, but Rockefeller had said that if Bishop did, Rockefeller would then fire Bishop, and appoint me to Bishop's job.

Accomplices to the Crime

it was misleading and cast doubts on my veracity. You can never lie to an inmate; so it was essential that the governor authenticate immediately my statement that he was supporting me and there would be no interference from Cummins.

I got in touch with Bob Scott, the governor's aide on prison affairs, and requested that the governor publicly endorse me—to offset the negative reactions created by his statement. Scott promised to give the matter his immediate attention. But it was a full month before the governor responded by making a hasty visit to Tucker with his party.

He arrived with a cavalcade of cars filled with his bodyguards and aides—a most impressive entourage. The governor himself was in a business suit with Western string tie, fawn-colored Stetson hat, and boots.

The governor greeted me with enthusiasm, wrapped his arms around me in a bear hug, and asked me how things were going. After some small talk I got to the point.

"It would help my position with the inmates who read the papers and see TV if you would clarify my position here," I said. "They are afraid that if I am under Bishop, any of the innovations I have made are subject to change at Bishop's command. So would you mind if I called the trusties together in the auditorium and, perhaps, you could set them straight?"

The governor smiled. "Well, Tom," he said, "I'll do anything I can to help you out, and you know it, but I'm not sure about the wisdom of my speaking to the trusties. I don't think my boys here"—and he pointed to his bodyguards—"would like that."

He did, however, give me token support. He strolled the halls of the prison with me, his arm around my shoulders in a paternal manner, and gave me an occasional approving hug. During our parade, he gave me his indirect blessing by smiling at me—which I am certain he felt gave sufficient affirmative endorsement in front of the inmates.

But that was the only endorsement I was to get. It soon became obvious that the governor was caught in a bind between prison reform and political expediency. He wanted just enough token reform of the prison to fulfill his campaign promises without attempting a real overhaul of the system; a thorough overhaul could be controversial, and perhaps lessen his chances of re-election. (The governor is elected for only a two-year term in Arkansas and, in effect, must continuously run for office.)

A man of many inconsistencies, Rockefeller seemed without a mind of his own and I quickly found that where prison matters were concerned, he relied on a variety of advisors, each of whom had a limited knowledge of prison affairs and management, had no training in the field, and at best had a questionable interest in true reform. Although the governor was undoubtedly the official decision maker, the actual decisions were made by his palace guard.

His most trusted advisor was Tom Eisele, who spoke for the governor so often that he came to be known in the press as "the other governor" or, simply, "OG." Eisele was always at the governor's side, staring impassively through his horn-rimmed glasses, ready to close any of the breaches made by unfortunate lapses of gubernatorial judgment or unfortuitous ad-libs.

A native of Arkansas, born in Little Rock, and a member of the GOP since 1951, Eisele had a master of law degree from Harvard. In 1953, while he was Assistant U.S. Attorney in Little Rock, he earned a reputation as a crusader for his competent and fearless defense of Gene Wirges, a former newspaper editor who attacked the corrupt Democratic political machine in Conway County.

In 1964, Eisele managed Rockefeller's unsuccessful gubernatorial campaign, and he was campaign manager again in 1966. Although he was in private practice and not on the state payroll, he claimed he spent 75 to 80 per cent of his time on matters affecting the governor.

Bob Scott was another of the lawyers whom the governor relied on for advice. Scott had worked diligently for the Republican Party over a period of years. He was installed in executive offices, and given a random assignment to coordinate activities and information concerning the entire area of pardons, paroles, and prison matters, even though he had no background for such work and at the time was only thirty-two years old.

His initial role was to investigate and report on prison conditions for the governor, a job he sometimes approached with more enthusiasm than judgment. For example, soon after I took over at Tucker, Scott, unshaven, and dressed in inmate clothing, went through the line at the dental clinic in an attempt to expose the deficiencies in medical treatment. The newspapers made much of the story; and they referred to Scott as "Convict X." His "investigation" revealed little, however, except his naiveté and inexperience.

Scott also functioned as a channel of information between the prison and the governor, but as time went on he assumed the role of an expert. He confided to my secretary that he wanted to be superintendent himself. After a while he was effectively blocking any communication between the governor and me, thus strengthening his own position.

I had admired John Haley for his role in the Faubus school-integration crisis a decade earlier. Haley was appointed as the youngest member of the penitentiary board when he was thirty-five years old. His purpose was to suggest, guide, cajole, and coerce the lethargic board of oldsters into instituting some modest changes in the prison system—or at least to keep them from impeding the efforts of reform. Haley was soon able to influence board activities out of all proportion to his actual power as a minority member. But he, too, came to consider himself an expert on prison affairs, although he possessed only a layman's knowledge of criminology and lacked the breadth of experience essential to forming policy decisions.

Haley was in constant touch with the governor and, as a trusted confidant, was in a position to influence strongly all executive decisions. As time passed, Haley tended increasingly to make recommendations that were based on his own study of the prison history and on conferences with people who represented themselves as experts.

A fourth important member of the palace guard was thirty-six-year-old Marion Burton. Conservative, polite, and proper, Burton, who was always nattily dressed, presented an image of the self-sufficient, quiet and assured mediator. A lawyer, too, he was committed to one goal: the re-election of his mentor. Burton's chief assignment was to meet visitors who had sought in vain to obtain an audience with the governor. It was Burton's function to explain, in ambiguous terms, the governor's constant absences from the state: during one six weeks' period the governor had not been seen in his office for more than ten hours. Burton was also responsible for answering the flood of executive mail.

Like Eisele, Burton had little direct concern with prison affairs. Nevertheless he soon came to play a minor but damaging role in the reform movement.

I learned early in the game that if I wanted to reform the Arkansas prison it would be in spite of the governor and his assistants rather than because of them. And if I had problems, I was better off if I tried to solve them myself than if I involved the governor's aides.

In May, when we faced a crisis over purchasing, I was called into Eisele's office and criticized for writing an "inappropriate letter." Eisele also said that I couldn't expect instant support from the governor's office because I was a newcomer to the state and it would take a year or two before they would develop any confidence in me.

Early in May, when the governor dropped in unexpectedly on a prison board meeting in Little Rock, I asked him for help. I hadn't been able to get the release of $38,000 in construction funds earmarked for Tucker on the Cummins budget. Although the board had approved construction of an infirmary, slaughter house, and three staff houses, and I had the requisitions, I couldn't get the material.

The governor asked the state comptroller, who was at the meeting, why the money was not forthcoming.

"The funds are frozen by your executive order," said the comptroller.

"Well, take care of it," said the governor.

After the meeting the comptroller filled out a special form, had the governor sign it, and the funds were released that afternoon.

It was one thing to get the governor to take a stand on a minor administrative problem but quite another thing to get him to back me when internal prison problems were concerned. In July, for example, I had become involved in a dispute with O.E. Bishop over my charges that he was harassing my administration (see pp. 120 ff.). Instead of supporting me, the governor issued a statement that he did not "want to become involved in the dispute between Murton and Bishop." According to him, our difficulties resulted from a "personality conflict."

Then, on July 8, I attended a banquet for some six hundred of the GOP faithful at the governor's Petit-Jean

Mountain Ranch, headquarters of Winrock Farms, a 34,000-acre enterprise with holdings in Arkansas and Oklahoma. First, we were all treated to a tour of the governor's mansion, a long, low, rambling stone-and-glass palazzo sitting on the top of Petit-Jean Mountain. We then filed out along a little flagstone walk that led to an inspirational point on the bluff overlooking the valley, where Biblical quotations were prominently displayed on stone.

By dinnertime, most of the people clustered in groups in the informal gardens alongside the house were lubricated enough to relax, along with the governor, who likes his liquor, too. (He once appeared before the state legislature in what seemed to witnessing legislators a state of inebriation, speaking in behalf of a mixed-drink bill.[1])

We filed into a huge circus tent where the banquet was to be held. The cuisine was excellent and the mood jovial when the governor stood up and assessed the first six months of his Republican administration. He selected about a dozen of the men he considered the more significant members of his "team" to stand up and take a bow. Together with members of the palace guard, I received an ovation for "outstanding" efforts in prison reform.

"Murton is probably the most controversial person in Arkansas, other than myself," the governor said as he introduced me. That moment was the high point of the governor's commitment to me.

I was not naive enough to believe that his attitude toward reform had really changed. It was one thing to give me credit on such an occasion, but it was another matter to give me support when members of the press were around.

Two days after the party, July 10, I rode to Benton, Arkansas, with the governor and John Haley in the executive limousine, a maroon Lincoln sedan similar to the one favored by President John F. Kennedy. Rockefeller sat in front next to his bodyguard, who was driving, and Haley and I sat in back.

Haley was making plans then to have the board fire

---

[1] *Pine Bluff Commercial*, Pine Pluff, Ark., May 22, May 26, May 27, 1968. The issue of June 2 said, on p. 21, "The legislators were paying little attention to his message. They were snickering over what they assumed to be the governor's inebriation."

Rockefeller's Contribution

Eugene Nunn as business manager and he was concerned with what would happen if Bishop refused to hire Don Bassett as his replacement.

"I'll fire Bishop if he gives us any trouble," murmured the governor.

Haley and I pointed out that our overall strategy was to take over Cummins slowly and only after I had Tucker running smoothly. It was not politically feasible to fire Bishop before the crops were in and the stage was publicly set for his dismissal. It was agreed that the proper strategy was for me to continue to expose the Cummins administration in an attempt to refute the popular belief that the prison was being run correctly.

Later, I noted in my log that the governor's comments "were difficult to discern because of his vagueness and the low tone of his voice. . . . However, after discussing the matter with Haley it appears that the governor has given us the green light to do whatever we think is necessary and he does not plan to take any personal concern over it."

After dropping the governor off at Benton, Haley and I rode back to Little Rock together, pausing en route for a cheeseburger.

"I'm still getting slow-played by state purchasing," I told him. "Isn't there some way for you to use your authority to make it possible for me to buy the supplies I need for Tucker?"

Haley told me, over Cokes, "Your difficulties stem from lack of communication. And your problems ought to be kept within the family. Word of discord gets out and it's bad for the image of Arkansas. It might reflect negatively on the governor and his chances of re-election."

I was taken aback. "How do you expect me to resolve my problems if neither you or the governor wants to get involved?" I asked.

"They're your problems and you ought to be able to solve them. After all, we're all working together toward a common goal. And keep in mind—the governor is holding you and me responsible for the overall plan to get you into Cummins without any real problems."

I repeated to Haley what I had said in my first meeting with him and the governor; "Prison reform does not take place in a vacuum independent of the establishment. There are bound to be rough times ahead when we have to stick together on our strategy plans. It's foolish and unpolitic for me to go out setting the scene for the takeover of Cummins and then have the governor or one of his aides pull the rug out from under me."

Haley agreed and told me he had advised Eisele, who was now the Arkansas Commissioner of Administration, to remove Bob Scott from the governor's staff as soon as possible because Scott seemed to thrive on sensationalism and agitation.

Not only had Scott played Convict X in the medical line, but he kept demanding the names of prisoners who had escaped from Cummins, so he could release the list to the press; every time I made an innovation at Tucker he would try to force the change at Cummins and bypass Bishop. He apparently still nurtured the desire to become acting superintendent and was anxious to establish a reputation for himself.

But Haley's principal complaint was that Scott was operating outside the agreed-on general strategy. We feared that he could force a showdown with Bishop before we were prepared.

Haley also said that I was holding up the reform movement by not delivering a long-range proposal for the overhaul of the prison system. "I know you've been busy," he said, "but the governor is counting on you to write it. Why don't you hole up in my cabin outside of Hot Springs for a few days and get it done?"

Meanwhile, the prison study commission was going about its work without me, even though the governor had promised me that I would be their consultant. When I complained to Haley and Bob Scott about my elimination from any official capacity with the commission, Haley said, "We're stuck with MacCormick. The only thing we can do is try to work through or around him."

As part of the plan to get the commission to heed my suggestions, I took Haley up on his offer to lend me his cabin. I spent three days preparing a 108-page proposal detailing the correctional needs of the State of Arkansas. The report included: a specific program for setting up and running a department of corrections; overhaul of the probation service; suggestions for the creation of institutional services; a plan for the separation of juvenile offenders from adult offenders, with emphasis on cutting down the high incidence of homosexuality; and a feasible proposal for revamping the entire prison system. I also suggested a five-year plan for implementation of the various proposals economically and within the framework of the existing system.

Haley telephoned me on August 19 to say he had read the report and met with the governor, who was most enthusiastic and wanted it reproduced and distributed throughout the state with his endorsement. Five hundred copies went to officials and news media throughout the state.

Meanwhile, in line with our agreed-upon strategy to expose the Bishop administration prior to my takeover at Cummins, I made a speech before a YWCA public affairs forum at Hot Springs.

"Although O.E. Bishop has made significant changes at Cummins, they are more superficial than real," I said. "The Arkansas prison system has been a manufacturing process by which a man is turned into a beast."

The next day the governor, who had urged me to speak out in just such a fashion, criticized me for doing it. In a press interview he said, "Murton is doing an exceptionally fine job at Tucker," but added: "Had I been in his shoes I wouldn't have gotten involved in Cummins. I do not know that a comment such as he made is going to help the problems of the prison study commission."

Two days later the governor apologized for criticizing me and told the press, "If I stepped on his toes, when I see him I'll apologize." But he added that I had exercised "questionable judgment" in downgrading Cummins, and said that I was not hired to become superintendent of both prison farms, nor as a consultant on prison affairs.

The following day he said, "Murton was perfectly within his rights in making statements criticizing Cummins." He followed up by saying that he viewed me as more than superintendent of Tucker: he looked upon me as his advisor and consultant for the entire correctional system.

Then the lid blew off the pot. Dr. Barron, the new prison medical advisor, had been on the job only six weeks, but it was long enough for him to uncover a drug and narcotics ring operating on state-financed drugs at Cummins. He also claimed that the medical facilities were so unsanitary that it was probably responsible for an outbreak of hepatitis among the prisoners.

The doctor, who had a good eye for publicity and, coincidentally, owned a large share of a local TV station, arranged for a thirty-minute TV documentary to be made two days before the press announcement on October 31.

His exposures were genuine. He said he had uncovered the drug ring after a study of the books had revealed that the prison had been spending $8,000 to $9,000 a month on drugs during the three months prior to his coming to Cummins. He claimed that prisoners who were running the medical program sold stimulants to a clique of other prisoners, who in turn retailed them in the prison. He found half a dozen prisoners with puncture wounds on their arms.

"Anything you could get a kick from was being sold," he stated at a news conference.

Dr. Barron took great pains to absolve Bishop and the former penitentiary doctor, Gwyn Atnip, of any blame. The newsmen were not so gracious. They pointed out that both the legislative council and the prison study commission had visited Cummins and the hospital without complaining about conditions, and that members of the council had even been complimentary about the cleanliness.

The governor's office was furious at the scandal and claimed it should have been informed before Dr. Barron had held his press conference. Bob Scott issued a press release the next day saying that the drug situation at Cummins was Bishop's fault. Judge Henry Smith ("The Whipping Judge"—see p. 98) impaneled a grand jury to investigate Barron.

On November 1, while the penitentiary board was in closed session in Little Rock investigating the drug situation, Bishop resigned effective December 31, saying that "many circumstances and a number of people have rendered it impossible for me to do my job in the manner in which I think it should be done."

I heard the news of Bishop's resignation from Bassett, who was present at this meeting and stepped out to call me. My first reaction was surprise, my second was that it was a strategic move on Bishop's part. My third reaction was: when will I have to go to Cummins?

I drove to the governor's mansion in Little Rock as fast as I could and met with the governor's staff, including Tom Eisele, Marion Burton, and Bob Scott, and Lynn Davis of the state police. Eisele was in charge of the meeting. He said that the governor intended to announce that he was accepting Bishop's resignation effective immediately, instead of two months later, and that he was putting me in charge of Cummins that night. The purpose of this earlier meeting was to get Davis' reaction and mine before making the announcement at a noon press conference.

I was opposed to this plan for several reasons. First, the governor didn't have the authority to appoint a superintendent. He could fire, but the authority to hire was vested in the penitentiary board.

Second, I didn't want to abandon Tucker until the reforms I had established were firmly entrenched; I didn't want the prison to retrogress to what it had been when I had taken over. Victor Urban had only recently taken charge of the probation and parole services, and Robert Van Winkle, whom I intended to break in as associate superintendent, had been on the job only ten days. He just wasn't ready to take command.

Added to all this, we still weren't through picking crops at either prison. If I went to Cummins, we would have to shut it down temporarily until we could get control. That would jeopardize the harvest there and precipitate unwarranted criticism.

I suggested we put off my transfer to Cummins until January 1, at which time Van Winkle would be ready to handle Tucker. By then I would have had the time to infiltrate more of my own men into Cummins, and make the final plans for the takeover.

Eisele took all these points to Governor Rockefeller and at his noon press conference, the governor said he had been notified of Bishop's resignation and hoped the board would choose someone qualified as soon as possible.

On November 29, the penitentiary board met secretly at Cummins. Wood, Greene, and Wooley refused to endorse my appointment.

At the open board meeting the next day, Grady Wooley turned to John Haley and said, "How about that guy over in North Carolina you've been talking to?"

Haley stuttered and stammered and denied any knowledge of a man in North Carolina, but Wooley had let the cat out of the bag. As I had suspected, the board members had been looking to replace me.

The by-play was amusing on a second count: I seemed to be the only one who knew that according to the Arkansas law, the appointment of the superintendent is made by the board with the advice and approval of the governor, and the board cannot appoint anyone the governor does not approve.

When I told Bob Scott of the statutory provisions, he was pleased as well as embarrassed. Pleased to learn the facts, and embarrassed because none of the four legal advisors on the governor's staff had researched the legislation. Furthermore, according to the statute, Bishop could not continue as superintendent after January 1 because his resignation had been accepted and a termination date set.

Despite evidence to the contrary, a newsman who polled the governor, Scott, Haley, and Eisele, reported that they all denied there was any move afoot to "dump" me.

Six days later, the three Democrats on the penitentiary board sat like stone figures while Governor Rockefeller, with obvious irritation, told them it was their "commitments to friends" that kept them from making me the state prison superintendent. Greene and Wooley puffed silently on big cigars, and Wood fidgeted.

After the three-and-a-half hour meeting with the board, Governor Rockefeller called me into his offices.

"The board is sticking to its belief that you can't handle Cummins and there will be a rash of escapes when you go there," he said.

I pointed out that if the escapes continued at the present rate there would be no problem because there would be no prisoners left.

"Agreed," Rockefeller said. "But the board also claims you have overspent on the Tucker budget, you have refused to comply with their instructions, and you're not qualified as an administrator because you have failed to fill all the personnel vacancies at Tucker. They want a man from the

Rockefeller's Contribution

U.S. Bureau of Prisons to do the administrative work, leaving you at the prison as a penologist."

"Forget it," I said. "I'm not going to accept that job. For the good of the prison system I've got to be head or nothing —as we agreed. And you know as well as I do there's no one from the Bureau of Prisons capable of familiarizing himself with the prison system here in less than six months. By then there won't be an institution left."

"Okay, what can we offer them as an alternative?" the governor asked me.

"I'll go to Cummins with Lieutenant Lowman of the state police 'to maintain security' and a handful of my own men," I said.

"It's your head, Tom," the governor said.

That was the way it had been from the start; it was my head if I got in trouble, but if I was successful he would step in and take credit for his administration.

The Eleventh Hour

The events of December, 1967, read like a chapter from a James Bond novel. There were mystery, suspense, hired assassins, "evil women," and the threat of a major prison revolt. Unlike 007, however, I was not always cool and oblivious to the dangers. At times I was nervous and well aware that at any moment I might be shot.

On December 1, Chainsaw Jack, who had escorted Tucker blood donors for the day to Cummins as a guard, told me that Jim Nabors wanted to talk with me urgently. I drove by Nabors' family's house in Pine Bluff, but no one was home. I left a note with the Sunday paper asking his wife to call me, so that we could arrange a "sickness" in the family which would entitle him to an emergency furlough.

I called Bob Scott, who telephoned Cummins and arranged to have Nabors furloughed because of his mother's alleged "illness." Nabors called me at 5:30 that afternoon, and we arranged to meet at 9:00 that night at the junction of Highways 15 and 76 outside of Pine Bluff.

Nabors was jumpy and nervous, his eyes constantly flicking as he told me some of the established trusties at Cummins were agitating the inmates and trying to get them to oppose me and raise all kinds of hell. One of the wardens had said that if some inmate didn't shoot me at Cummins, a warden would.

Nabors said that there was plenty of booze at Cummins and everybody there was uptight. He didn't know if there were guns inside the barracks, but there were lots of knives.

After this disturbing report I sent Nabors on to West Memphis to see his mother, to fulfill the stated purpose of his furlough. He was to return to Cummins the following day.

On December 7, Porter called me from Grady, Arkansas, to say he had just been fired from Cummins for allegedly bad-mouthing Bishop. He had been given twenty-four hours to leave the farm. This was a big blow to my plans for taking over Cummins, because Porter was the only freeman I had inside the prison who understood the guard system.

I telephoned Scott immediately and arranged for a secret rendezvous at a parking lot in Pine Bluff. Bassett and Porter arrived together from Cummins at the same time that a state police car cruised by. We all piled into Scott's car, searching for a place where we could talk unobserved, and finally stopped at a quiet place behind some new buildings. Within a few minutes of our arrival Scott saw an FBI agent he knew coming out of one of the buildings. We had inadvertently chosen the parking lot behind the local FBI office for our meeting!

Scott, who was anxious to find any excuse to get rid of Bishop, said he intended to tell him that unless he rehired Porter, the governor would fire Bishop immediately.

My alternative to this plan was to let Porter stay at Tucker and commute to Cummins. Scott said that it wouldn't be necessary for me to go to Cummins immediately even if Bishop were fired, because we could designate J.R. Price—Bishop's assistant—or warden Clay Smith as acting superintendent. Before I had a chance to react to this suggestion Bassett jumped into the conversation.

"Don't do that," he said. "Put me in charge."

As a matter of fact Bassett was totally unqualified for such a job—as were all of the other men suggested. They would have been wiped out in minutes. But I was interested in Bassett's reaction; it lent some credence to the general opinion that Bassett, too, had ambitions to become superintendent.

Bassett was not the only contender for the superintendency. As early as July, Haley had suggested that I remain at Tucker and Vic Urban should go to Cummins to head the

Accomplices to the Crime

prison system. Expectedly, Bishop's assistant, Price, applied for the position soon after Bishop announced his resignation. And late one October evening in his office, Bob Scott had told me that he would like to go to Cummins as superintendent. It was then that his actions at the prison during the prior months—"Convict X" and the rest of it— began to take on meaning.

Back at Tucker, a letter from Cummins inmate Ronnie Crabtree was smuggled out to me. It said that a car, supposedly stolen from the dairy warden a few nights earlier when three men had escaped, had actually been sold to one of the prisoners by "Captain" Deam, one of the wardens. The prisoner was charged by the prosecuting attorney with stealing the car, but actually the sale was legal—the transaction had been notarized by Charles Wimberly, assistant business manager at Cummins!

Crabtree also wrote that another man had broken out a day earlier than those three because he had lost $181 in the barracks poker game. The money belonged to the head matron at the Women's Reformatory, Mrs. Clay Smith. She had the Avon dealership for the Cummins Prison Farm, and the man who escaped was her cook as well as her agent inside the men's barracks. The money he had lost in the game had been paid to him for the sale of Avon products and rather than face up to the consequences, he had stolen Clay Smith's car and taken off. The press had a field day with stories about "the Avon man calling."

On December 8, I got a call from a Mr. McBride who said he had some information that might help me get the appointment as superintendent. We made arrangements to meet at 5 P.M. at a bus station in Pine Bluff.

I took my .38 with me and set up a portable tape recorder in the glove compartment of the car because I wasn't sure what I was getting into.

Mr. McBride and I met at the bus terminal and drove around the block. He turned out to be not some sort of decoy who was going to set me up, but a former warden at Cummins from 1948 to 1963 who now lived in Grady, Arkansas. I already knew almost everything he told me except for one item. W.C. Darby, a rank man at Cummins, was apparently taken out of the prison every Thursday by

The Eleventh Hour

one of the wardens and driven to his wife's home in Grady. Later in the afternoon, he would change into a suit and get on the bus with his family, and they would all go into Pine Bluff to shop.

Grady, with a population of about 500, is five miles northwest of Cummins along Highway 65, which we frequently had to travel. The town has one main street with brick structures, overhanging porches, three gas stations, and a town marshal who wears a badge, a gun belt, boots, and a Western hat.

Most of the people are farmers whose diet consists of cornbread, beans, and sowbelly. On the last Friday of each month, they attend the main social event—the monthly PTA meeting. This activity is surpassed for pure elegance only by the catfish fry, prepared by a detail of prisoners from Cummins, including the prison band, which plays while inmates serve hundreds of folks who make the annual pilgrimage to Grady for the event.

Many of Grady's good citizens, like those in nearby Gould, had been involved in one way or another with the penitentiary. Former superintendents and wardens tended to settle in those communities. They were hostile toward us, and were hoping our reforms would fail.

Naturally, McBride wanted something for his cooperation. His wife was a matron in the Women's Reformatory at Cummins, and he wanted her to remain there.

Later I talked with Major Kenneth McKee of the state police, who also gave me some news from Cummins. He had heard that all the wardens would resign en masse when I got there. I doubted this; no group of Arkansans ever agrees on doing anything collectively, least of all eliminating its source of income.

McKee also told me that the trusties would turn in their guns and sit down when I arrived. This wasn't a problem either, as I had already planned to lock them up in the barracks.

He confirmed what I had already heard from Nabors, that the word was out in the town of Fort Smith that one of the tower guards was supposed to shoot me as soon as possible after I arrived at the farm.

I told Major McKee about inmate Darby and his visits

to town. McKee promised that the next time the bus from Grady to Pine Bluff carried Darby aboard, a state trooper would be on hand to take him into custody.

The strategy was to continue to expose the Cummins administration in order to refute the popular belief that the prison was being run properly. This was part of my plan to define for the public what the prison was really like, and thus to gain support for the necessary changes. Such exposés would also lay a groundwork for some of the drastic actions I anticipated were going to be necessary in the immediate future.

As planned, Major McKee had a trooper meet the bus at Pine Bluff on Thursday. Darby was not on it, but the bus driver verified the fact that Darby usually made weekly trips from Grady to Pine Bluff with his family. Some days later, while I was talking with Bob Scott on the telephone about another matter, I casually mentioned that we had alerted the press to Darby's adventures and expected to expose this illegal release from Cummins at the earliest opportunity.

Scott gasped and told me that he was the one who had authorized the weekly pass for Darby.

It was this type of casual treatment of court commitments, with its attendant abuses, that had characterized the Faubus administration. The Rockefeller administration had claimed to be correcting this and similar examples of favoritism within the prison system. The actions of the governor's aides, however, made it difficult, frequently, to distinguish between the two administrations.

A scandal at Cummins was imminent, though. The inmate dental assistant, who was in prison for killing two people and brutalizing an eight year old girl in the course of raping her, had been released on furlough by Bishop. He had been due back December 15 but had just kept heading out.

On Tuesday, December 19, I met with Bishop for an hour and a half reviewing the crop situation at Cummins and the other projects he was working on. He was in a good frame of mind, doing his best to be cooperative. If he bore me any ill will, he didn't show it.

Two days later Harold Porter told me that a brawl was planned for Christmas night at Cummins when there would be open house for the wardens in the auditorium. There was talk about the inmates taking hostages. He said everybody was frightened, and a lot of booze was coming in. He said the officers were getting worried. He added, in a matter-of-fact voice, that he had been marked for assassination, and that there was a bounty on my head, too.

This was also the day of another innovation at Tucker. We held the first dance for the inmate population.

Around the middle of the month, Smitty, the band leader, and Gurvis Nichols, had sent me a note asking to see me on a personal matter. I knew the two men well enough to guess they wanted something special.

"What are you trying to con me out of now?" I had asked them.

"Well, how about having a dance here?"

I had pretended to be shocked. "How can we have a dance? Do you expect me to allow women in here with you dangerous convicts? How do you think we can handle it?"

We had talked the matter over for a while, and I'd consented to the dance.

For this evening, the inmates had moved the library material out of the auditorium into the hallway and painted the walls. They'd put crepe paper over the lights and hung streamers, to give the room a festive look.

We allowed about forty of the wives or girl friends of the inmates to attend. The women were dressed in their finest and the men wore their prison uniforms. The rank men looked good in their freshly starched whites, their carefully combed hair and their beaming faces. Some of the men from death row were there, too, in their jeans.

At first the atmosphere was like a high school social. The men stood around toeing the floor and mooning at the giggling women. Everyone was self-conscious. The Tucker Themesters played bravely and well, and soon couples began to pair off on the dance floor.

Van Winkle's twelve-year-old daughter, Dar, had come with her parents. She had the first dance of her life with Jerry Johnson, a Negro man condemned to death. Bea Crawford danced with a Negro boy, while her husband, a Kentuckian, did the Charleston with one of the Negro women.

After a while I saw there was plenty of room, so we let

more inmates into the auditorium for the fun, which also included skits. Some of them were devastating.

"One Year of Progress at Tucker" started with Larry Kelly, portraying me, addressing the inmates when I first arrived at Tucker. Larry had my mannerisms down to a T when he imitated my telling the inmates, "You guys can keep the booze and the knives for now, because there are more important things to do."

The men even put on a skit entitled "The Senile Seminar" in which Walter Brown, one of the Negroes from death row, portrayed Grady Wooley of the parole board: "You keeping your business straight, son?"

Gurvis Nichols and Larry Kelly imitated Bishop and me in a confrontation over the boiler.

The inmates had us all down pat. I was surprised and pleased to discover just how clearly they understood Arkansas justice and the power structure.

Three days later, we had open house at Tucker for the staff and the governor came by for a visit. I tried to steer him into a conversation about strategy for the Cummins takeover, which was only ten days away, but he said we ought to discuss strategy after the first of the year. In short, the responsibility for taking over Cummins was mine, and if I goofed along the way he could always say he knew nothing about it.

Just after midnight I got a telephone call from Bassett who said that two inmates had tried to cut their way out of a barracks at Cummins and were caught with a loaded .38 in their possession.

The fact that two men would cut their way out of a barracks when it was relatively easy to sneak off a work detail was an ominous sign.

On Christmas Day I went to the main building at noon to check out the inmate dinner of turkey with all the trimmings. Later, after dinner at home with my own family, I noticed Cecil Clifft, one of the off-duty officers, go by the Big House carrying a new rifle. He explained he was going into the fields to try it out. I joined him; it seemed an excellent chance for me to check my own weapons prior to going to Cummins.

I spent much of the afternoon zeroing my .30-.30 rifle, my .38 revolver, and a small .25 automatic that was my

The Eleventh Hour

secret Christmas present to myself. It was small enough to be slipped into my hip pocket. Thus I could be armed without arousing the suspicion of my antagonists or the concern of my wife.

My best gift, however, had been a simple Christmas card from the death row men:

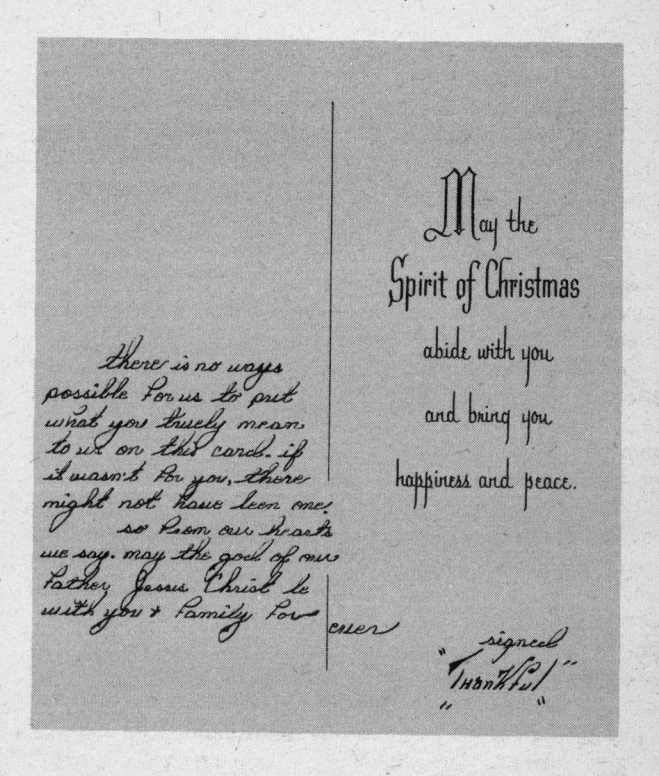

> *there is no ways possible for us to put what you truely mean to us on this card. if it wasn't for you, there might not have been one. so from our hearts we say, may the god of our father Jesus Christ be with you & family for ever*
>
> *signed*
> *"Thankful"*

> May the Spirit of Christmas abide with you and bring you happiness and peace.

For the first time in the history of the institution the men on death row considered themselves part of the community. That card was an indication of their new self-definition. For me, it made the past eleven months seem worthwhile.

The time to take over Cummins was getting near, and the situation there was still volatile, for many reasons. First,

Accomplices to the Crime

the trusties knew what had happened at Tucker: the squatter shacks had been removed, the brozene had gone, their personal empires had been destroyed, and their privileges cut out. They were stirring the men up to resist me when I arrived. Cummins was four times the size of Tucker, and this could be real opposition. A second reason was that the trusties and the freeworld wardens were keeping the inmates stirred up with lies about my intentions. Their plan was to try and create incidents that would wipe me out as soon as I arrived. Compounding all this was a third factor: the men had been kept in the barracks for three weeks because Bishop, too, was trying to create tension among the inmates for my arrival.

Early in the afternoon of the day after Christmas Bob Baty was stabbed to death at Cummins. Apparently he had lost all his money in a Christmas poker game and had strong-armed two other inmates and robbed them of their money. Baty was stabbed three times between the shoulder blades and was dead before he hit the floor.

The Cummins inmates had a sit-down strike in the mess hall at noon because there was no ice cream for Christmas dinner and because they had not received one dollar each from the Inmates' Welfare Fund, as had been done the previous years. (Tucker did not have this tradition.)

While the prisoners were having their sit-down strike, some of the Cummins wardens conducted a shakedown in two of the barracks. They found twenty-one pints of bonded whiskey and a washtub full of assorted weapons. They recovered a pistol, which had been sold by a trusty to a rank man, but they failed to find three other pistols and four rifles, which had been sneaked out of the rank barracks to the hospital on the noon food cart.

Ronnie Crabtree's familiar handwriting was on a letter in my in-basket: "Mr. Murton, you are going to be hurting if you don't bring your own men with you. All the Big Wheel Convicts and Freeworld men here are against you."

He also wrote that he had heard some of the trusties were going to move their bunks to the front of the barracks and burn the place down, and that there were reports I was to be picked off on the road to Cummins by an inmate with a high-powered rifle.

I had begun to poll the Tucker inmates I wanted with me

The Eleventh Hour

at Cummins as an advance guard. Arnold Rhodes had asked me earlier when I was going, and I'd told him I couldn't say because I didn't want anyone to know.

"All right, I understand," he'd said. "But when you go, you swing by the barracks when you're ready 'cause I'm goin' with you."

Others had said they were afraid to go, and I didn't insist because I knew they might get killed. As the tension increased and the risks grew greater, inmates lost courage, and my Cummins assault force diminished one by one.

On December 27, I learned from Bob Scott that Bishop had been offered a state job for thirteen months if he would fire me. Ironically, he still could, and the extra thirteen months would give him sufficient tenure with the state to retire.

Later that evening I got a call from a Mrs. James Kesler, who said she was angry that the inmates had not received their dollar for Christmas. She wanted to contribute a personal check to cover this. I thanked her, and promised to see that the funds were deposited to the inmate accounts. The next day a $1,500 check came; I deposited it to the Tucker Inmates' Welfare fund and credited each of my inmates with one dollar. I sent a check for the balance to Bishop—who refused to give the money to his inmates, and deposited it to the Inmates' Welfare Fund.

On December 28 Harold Porter telephoned from Cummins to say that Charlie Mann and Russell Kumpe, two of my trusted inmates, would be in danger if they went to Cummins with me.

He said that the guards in the gun cages and kitchen had been doubled, following word of a plot to throw Molotov cocktails made of lighter fluid through the guard cages.

The penitentiary board finally did approve me as acting superintendent of the prison system, but it then insisted on keeping Bishop on the payroll for another thirty days as superintendent and giving him annual leave. I opposed this because it meant I could not move up as superintendent of the prison system, which in turn precluded Van Winkle's appointment as Tucker superintendent and the employment of an associate superintendent for him.

On December 29, Bishop called suggesting I come to Cummins, talk to the auditors, and take a tour of the farm.

Accomplices to the Crime

I slipped my Browning automatic pistol into my pocket and headed out early—around noon, because I wanted to see McBride again. He had called from his home in Grady to say he had some more information for me. But when I got to Grady, the town marshal was on my tail through town and I wanted to keep the heat off McBride. So I continued on to Cummins.

Bishop took me on a tour, in the course of which he identified most of the buildings. Pointing to some barns, he said, "This is the colored mule barn here, and that's the white mule barn over there." The mules were the same color and the barns were the same color, so I asked him what he was talking about. "This here is the barn housing the mules that are harnessed and driven by white men," he said. And pointing to the other: "That's the barn housing the mules driven by colored men." I made a mental note to combine the two operations when I took over.

After our brief tour, we went back to the office and talked with the auditors, who raised the point that there could be only one disbursing agent. This would cause added difficulties if Bishop were still superintendent when I took over. Bassett, after about fifteen or twenty minutes, said he was satisfied with the audit of the books, the count on the livestock, and the equipment inventory. Then we toured the inside of the prison. There were only one or two inmates who nodded to me. We visited the kitchen, where they were feeding only twenty men at a time to prevent a riot. I saw double guards in all the cages.

That night I met with Scott, Haley, Bassett, and Van Winkle, at the Tucker Big House. We talked until midnight about the situation at Cummins, and some things that especially worried me. For one thing, Bishop had continually refused to give me a roster of the guards and had sent Lee Rogers, my former secretary who now worked for him, on furlough so I wouldn't be able to get any assistance from him.

I told them how concerned I was about the tense situation caused by the fact that the inmates had been confined to barracks for three weeks. Bishop had left fifty-five acres of cotton for me to have picked; the isolation cells had not been completed; and I was not happy about the fact that there was a price on Porter's head and mine. We all agreed

The Eleventh Hour

that one way to solve some of the problems was to appoint Bishop for thirty days to a lesser position in the prison.

The problem that was still unsolved, however, was how and when I was to take over Cummins. I wanted to go in on my own and in my own way, without advance publicity.

On December 30, I spent about an hour at a press conference at Tucker advising selected newsmen candidly of what had been going on, what the situation was, and what the odds appeared to be relative to the Cummins takeover.

I wanted to give the press some of the classified information about Cummins so they would be fully briefed in case something happened to me and I was not around later to explain what was going on.

On the same day, I met with Lieutenant Lowman, Captain Brown, and Lieutenant Evans of the state police. I asked them to keep units on call through Wednesday, at which time I expected to receive the regular appointment, and that I would go to Cummins at about 2 A.M. Thursday, January 4. But that was not my real plan. I had decided to go to Cummins without a police escort, on Monday, New Year's Day.

I made a final check at Tucker. We had just officially opened up a new cold storage unit. All the meat, milk, and eggs had been moved there from the old unit. The butcher shop was in full operation. The new smoke-house was almost ready, and the slaughterhouse was functioning.

Tucker prison was in excellent shape. We had secured the fort and our staff was now complete. Urban was in charge of probation and parole, Van Winkle was ready to take over as Tucker superintendent, and Jack Finch had reported a day earlier as "special services officer" and was going to exercise general supervision over the vocational, religious, and recreation programs. His wife, Harriette, had been appointed educational supervisor, and was to set up a full-time school program and library for the inmates. We were, finally, ready to embark on our principal goal: modifying inmate behavior with proper professional help.

I was leaving Tucker reluctantly. It still needed a couple of months to get the programs and staff members entrenched, so that no matter what happened the institution would never again be able to revert to its previous state.

Margaret had started to make a life for herself at Tucker

Accomplices to the Crime

and was gaining some degree of acceptance in the outside community. Now, she was going to have to break off these relationships and change the children's school to an area so hostile to us that some of the good citizens of Gould had signed a petition to keep us from entering that community, which bordered on the prison farm.

On New Year's Eve, Margaret and I had a long talk after the children had gone to sleep. Although I did not know it until later, she was thoroughly frightened about my going to Cummins in the morning. She knew from Porter, Bassett, and Rhodes that it was dangerous, and she was aware that the staff at Cummins was determined to wipe me out. But she communicated none of this fear to me, and I said nothing to her about my own apprehensions. We kept our talk about my going to Cummins the next day on a "business as usual" basis.

Margaret knew that the governor's office had arranged for me to have a composite group of military and civilian personnel at my disposal to maintain security and effect the transition. For weeks the governor himself, and everyone else including the adjutant general of the Arkansas National Guard, had assured me that they were prepared to cope with any situation that might arise at Cummins. They would put at my disposal, if requested, a group of sixty state troopers, a National Guard company of around two hundred soldiers, and a battalion of paratroopers from a nearby base.

But I had no intention of entering Cummins like Grant taking Richmond. I had decided to implement a plan that no one—governor's office or Cummins inmates—had anticipated. I believed there would be less public and inmate reaction if I took over quietly. Someone was bound to get hurt if there were an armed confrontation.

January 1 arrived. At 9:30 A.M., I issued Chainsaw Jack a pistol. I strapped on my own .38 and loaded my .30-.30 rifle. We got into my car and left for Cummins.

How Many Prisoners?

Chainsaw Jack and I set out alone and unheralded for Cummins on the morning of January 1, 1968. When we reached the guard shack just outside Cummins Prison, the guard was silent as he lifted the road bar and passed us through. Without turning around to look at the man, Jack said to me, "He's phoned ahead."

I accelerated though there were only a few hundred feet to go before we reached the quadrangle. I parked as near to the front entrance as possible, wondering if the tower guards might pick us off as we went from the car to the building. The gun on my hip was of little comfort. We were outnumbered and in enemy territory.

The inmate in the communications room set down his phone as we entered the superintendent's office. Either we had taken them by surprise or we were in for a surprise. It was too quiet.

My former secretary, Lee Rogers, was back from furlough and waiting in his office. He made no comment and registered no surprise at our arrival. The fact that he was waiting reassured me to some extent. If there had been trouble in the offing Rogers would have known about it and would have been some place else, not near me.

The prison was quiet. Since it was a holiday, all the inmates were flaked out in their barracks. Apparently we had surprised the trusties and hostile freeworld personnel, who had expected me to arrive at midnight.

I learned later that all of the staff had been standing by in the lobby from midnight to 2:30 P.M. to greet me. Some of the inmates had made plans, too. With the permission of farm manager Clay Smith, they had pushed their bunks and bedding up to the front of the barracks, against the grill; they were planning to set them on fire when I arrived, as a protest demonstration. The protest was called off when the inmates received word that the staff had gone to bed.

Trouble was still imminent, so even though I was in my own office I kept the .38 strapped on.

My first administrative action as head of the Arkansas State Penitentiary was to fire the state executioner. For months, I had been trying to get rid of him, because he was on the Tucker payroll drawing $1,500 a year, although there hadn't been an execution in four years

I had Rogers run off several memos which I had prepared before leaving Tucker. The first announced formally that I had taken over as superintendent of the prison system.

Another advised the inmates that we would continue use of inmate guards for at least two years and that I had no intention of demoting the trusties or putting them in the rank barracks.

I tried to set their minds at ease over rumors that I was going to take the brozene away immediately. I admitted we would take it away and replace it with a ledger system in the near future, but I promised they would have at least two weeks' notice, which would give the loan sharks time to get their money back. I ordered the money released that Mrs. Kesler had donated to the inmates for Christmas, and had it given to each inmate in brozene.

I also suggested that the inmates should not believe anything I was supposed to have said until they heard it directly from me.

My next move was calculated to put the inmates—and one freeman—completely off balance. I called in Clay Smith, the biggest troublemaker among the freeworld wardens. He came into the office with his head down, nervously fingering his hat, expecting to be fired.

As I talked with Smith about a variety of things, he became more and more uncomfortable, awaiting the inevitable.

"I have called you in because there are going to be some changes in personnel here," I said.

How Many Prisoners?

"Yes, sir, I figured that."

"You know that I am going to have to wind up some things over at Tucker, and I can't be here all the time."

"Yes, sir," repeated Smith.

"So, what I would like to do, with your agreement, is appoint you acting superintendent at Cummins."

There was silence from Smith, who was unquestionably stunned. I waited about thirty seconds and then repeated what I had said, adding that Bishop had spoken very highly of him. I said I needed someone with farm and security experience, both of which he had had over the last eight years.

"When I'm on the farm," I said, "I'll assume responsibility, but while things are as tight as they are now I can't be in both places at once, and when I'm away you'll have to make your own decisions."

Smith sat numb, with his mouth open.

"Ultimately I will assume full responsibility," I said, "but I need a man capable of making decisions at Cummins now. Are you willing to help out?"

"You want *me* to have the job?" Smith asked, his voice incredulous.

I nodded.

"Well, yeah, I'd like that," he said.

I gave Smith a letter of appointment and he started out of the office reading it, only to return in a moment and ask me if the paragraph authorizing corporal punishment meant he was allowed to beat them with the hide.

"Your methods are different from mine and it wouldn't be fair for me to put you in charge without giving you the authority you need," I said. "You know how I feel about the strap, but you are free to go ahead and use it.

"Since you run the prison with the strap now and are going to be responsible for Cummins while I'm away, I'm giving you the authority to do what you need to do to control the prison. Could you do it without the strap?"

"No, sir," he said.

That maneuver took care of Smith for a while. He couldn't understand what I was up to. Lee Rogers, who was sitting in the lobby when Smith came out of my office, later told me that Smith had his hat in one hand, the letter in the other. "I just don't get it," he said to Lee. "I went in there thinking I was going to be fired and I come out being in charge of Cummins. It don't make sense."

It made sense to me, though. Now he was responsible for keeping order through his own men, who were in charge of the prison. He had lit the fuse to explode the prison on my arrival; now he would have to put it out or be blown out of the saddle with me.

I spent only a few hours at Cummins on January 1, but the next day I returned with Jerry Johnson and Walter Brown, two of the death row Negroes at Tucker. I wanted them to serve as my entrée to the Negroes in Cummins.

When Jerry first went inside the barracks the Negro inmates looked at him in surprise.

"Man," they said to him, "what are you doing over here? Did you get your sentence commuted?"

"No," said Jerry.

"How come you are out of your cell?"

"What do you mean out of my cell? I've been playing with the band at Benton."

The inmates were incredulous. They asked how Jerry got to Cummins.

"With The Man."

"Was he armed?"

"Yeah, he was armed but it wasn't to guard me. He was armed to protect himself from you cats over here."

Jerry spent half a day inside Cummins spreading the word that if I'd done as much as I had for the men on death row, I could do much more at Cummins for men who were not under the death penalty.

In this way, I got the cooperation of the black inmates at Cummins without incident.

On my third day at Cummins, Greene, Wooley, and Wood all resigned from the penitentiary board rather than approve my appointment as superintendent of the system. Their resignations were to become effective on January 14, the same day Jeter's term expired. The governor would now have complete authority over the prisons, because the fifth member of the board, John Haley, was his appointee.

I was glad to see them go. The limitations of the system were bad enough, but when I received no confidence or support from the people to whom I was responsible, my mission seemed impossible to achieve. I had to fight both for personal and professional survival while trying to get the job done.

On the fourth day, I transferred Chainsaw Jack and Nabors to Cummins and made arrangements with Dr. Barron to house them temporarily in the hospital. I didn't dare put them in the barracks until we had better control of the prison. Meanwhile, I gave them both key positions. Jack was head yard man during the day, and Nabors was his assistant. I put Otis Standridge in charge of the night yard. Three of my men were now in control of key areas.

Chainsaw Jack started to sort out the meal situation right away. Because the men were so fearful and tense Bishop had allowed only twenty men to eat at a time, fearing that a larger number might start rioting. Jack went into the barracks and started lawyering for me, telling the men I wasn't going to take away their brozene and work them fourteen hours a day as they had heard. If they worked for me I would work with them.

Then he went into the yard and turned an entire barracks out for a meal. The freeworld yard man in the hall was in a panic. He ran for the gate, but Jack had locked it and the man was left in the middle of the yard.

"Don't let all those men out, don't let them out!" he shouted to Jack. "We only feed twenty at a time!"

"I'm in charge of the yard and I'm going to feed them when I want," Jack said.

"Orders are no more than twenty at a time!" shouted the civilian guard.

"I'm working for Murton, and he's The Man here now. I'm doing it the way he wants it," said Jack. "If you don't like it, then crawl inside one of them gun cages and wait until I'm through feeding them."

Thus was the meal schedule changed by Jack without incident, before I could even get to it.

Jack was almost beaten up, however, during that first week at Cummins. I had quartered him in the hospital with Nabors for safety's sake. I didn't know that Dr. Barron had moved an inmate from the hole into the hospital without telling me.

The inmate, a writ-writer, had been sentenced to the hole for eleven years by Bishop. After he had been in the hole only a few months, Dr. Barron decided the man needed psychiatric help so he moved him on his own authority into the hospital, where he and another inmate managed to get hold of an axe handle. They were planning to work Jack over because he was breaking up the infirmary rackets, when I heard about it and put them both back in the hole.

Dr. Barron and I then had a heated argument about who was the superintendent. Barron finally agreed that he would not take anyone else out of the hole without first consulting me.

All the inmates at Cummins, not just those in the hole, were uptight from the constant ribbing and agitation from the freeworld staff and the trusties. So I started to get rid of some of the old line head knockers. One of the first to go was warden "Big Mose" Harmon, trimmed down to a hulking three hundred pounds, slow of speech and thought, and unemotional about the whippings he had administered in the past.

When I fired him, he said, "I know your philosophy and mine don't agree, but some of the guys do need paddling. I spanked them several times but it had to be done."

After his discharge, Mose set himself up with a gas station at Grady, just a few miles away.

Another troublemaker I planned to get rid of and send over to Tucker was inmate Mose Autry, a former yard man. Unfortunately, Bishop had transferred him to the dog kennels, where it was easy for him to escape. He got the message and escaped, as might have been expected.

Officials in neighboring counties still believed Cummins was going to erupt any moment. Judge Henry Smith telephoned his nephew, Clay Smith, and told him to quit his job. He didn't want Clay in charge of Cummins when something happened. Judge Smith had obviously seen through my strategy. Clay resigned, and so did his wife.

Smith's resignation reached me just after Otis Standridge reported he had spent two hours the previous evening trying to keep James Dean Walker—who was at Cummins for killing a policeman—and some other inmates from burning their bunks. Standridge gathered the members of the Inmate Council and took them to the mess hall where, with Chainsaw Jack, he tried to sort out their grievances.

How Many Prisoners?

It turned out that although Bishop had copied our lead at Tucker by establishing an Inmate Council, he had no idea how it was supposed to operate. He allowed sixteen members of the council—two men from each barracks—to meet every two weeks to write up rules and recommendations, but their notes sat on his desk for months unopened. The council was disgusted. Now they were threatening to burn the prison down because they had received no help with their problems, and were being egged on by some of the wheels who wanted to wipe me out.

Standridge promised the council members that if they went back to the barracks and quieted down I would meet with them the next day.

Because he had promised the meeting, I had to go through with it. I met the men in the prison auditorium and took the bull by the horns.

"I've only been here a few days trying to clean this place up and you've been trying for a year, so what are your problems?" I began.

They listed their grievances, most of which were pretty minor, and I said, "Okay, you can have this," "No, you can't have that," or "I'll have to think about that one."

I told them never to threaten to start trouble again or I'd wipe them out, because I intended to run the prison.

After the meeting, four or five of the council members resigned, saying they had never been spoken to so harshly before. Meantime I sent Walker, the cop-killer, and another troublemaker, to Tucker.

By the end of my second week at Cummins, we had the inmates back at work in the fields and the prison running reasonably smoothly, with a cadre of men I could trust in charge. It was by then time to get into the kitchen situation, because the rider was refusing to feed Chainsaw Jack and Nabors, using any pretext he could find. Sometimes my men went without meals for as long as twenty-four hours.

I had a little chat with the kitchen rider and told him that if I heard any more complaints that my men weren't being fed properly I would have him catch a cotton sack and hit the field.

Then I looked into the kitchen itself and found there were about forty-five inmates working there, with as much

Accomplices to the Crime

duplication of jobs and feather-bedding as we had found at Tucker.

Meals were served around the clock, starting with the first meal at 3:30 A.M., the second at 5:30, and the third at 6:00. The first shift for the noon meal was at 10:00 and the second at 11:00. The tower guard ate the evening meal at 3:00, the short line at 4:00, and the Longline at 5:00.

The steam tables were not used because it was inconvenient, so they just slopped the food into dish pans, set it out on a table, and spooned it out.

There were two grills, and cooks who served only trusties and wardens with special meals and rations.

I started poking around the drawers and found crud everywhere. There were shoes, socks, pants, love letters, tobacco, Rice Krispies: everything imaginable was squirreled away in little nests.

From the accumulation of grease on the stoves, it was obvious that they had never been cleaned.

The refrigerator was filled with medicines and bottles of stored blood.

The bakery was almost as bad. The proof-boxes, where pans of bread dough are set to rise, were grimy—one inmate was even sleeping on one. There was a mess all over the floor, and the bread slicer hadn't been cleaned since it was installed.

I checked the boiler room and found it in fair shape, although the inmate in charge had a dog with him which he claimed belonged to one of the men in the hole.

On the loading dock, I found a bread-wrapping machine that had been there for several months. No one knew if it worked or not because it had never been used.

There were three freezers in the pantry used to store the meat for the wardens. The meat for the inmates, which consisted of two hundred pounds of ground beef with a lot of tallow in it, was sitting in a box. It had been brought in at 11 A.M., was not scheduled to be served for another twenty-four hours, and was not refrigerated.

In the back of the pantry I found the usual garbage, and four or five inmates lying around without assignments.

The kitchen was a dirty, smelly, filthy hole, and should

have been condemned.[1] If there had been any other way to feed the men I would have closed the mess hall, because it was not a fit place to prepare food for human consumption.

I abolished the separate menus, rescheduled the meal times, and set up a system to relieve the tower guards so they could eat hot food. I stopped food being carried out of the kitchen on trays to other people in the building, and ordered the sale of food from the kitchen stopped.

Following the pattern of the takeover at Tucker, I went out of the main building with Don Bassett and Arnold Rhodes on a tour of the 16,600-acre farm.

We found about twenty-two men who slept out and never came into the prison even to draw rations. The group included four men who lived at the dog kennel; one was cook for the other three. The group had two refrigerators, a range, police radios, three revolvers, a .30-.30 rifle, and a shotgun.

We found one inmate, guarding the water pump, who had been committed to the Arkansas State Penitentiary nine years previously but had never even seen the inside of the prison proper. He was living in a squatter shack a mile from the main institution. He had all the comforts of home, and each day the doby wagon drove by and left him milk or cream. Another truck brought him vegetables.

Another inmate living in a squatter shack was assigned to watching the bee house. As bees don't make the scene except when there are flowers, I brought him back into the building to await the arrival of spring.

At the seed bin, there were three men assigned to chase rats, with five guards assigned to watch them. It had never occurred to anyone that two of the guards could be reassigned, the rank men could be put in the Longline, and the three remaining guards could turn in their guns and chase the rats themselves.

Another man was guarding the mule barn. It seemed unlikely to me that the mule barn would be stolen, so I

---

[1] In fact, it had been condemned by the health department the previous fall, and criticized again on July 26, one day before the legislators "inspected" it and commended Bishop for his food-service program. The Tucker kitchen, at the same time, had been rated "superior" by the health department and condemned by the legislators.

brought him back in, along with the man guarding the cotton gin, which weighs several hundred tons and is also not likely to be stolen.

I ordered all the people sleeping out in squatter shacks to move back into the building. Coffee was the only thing authorized to be cooked outside the main building. Everything else was to be confiscated, and I told Harold Porter to bring in the squatters and all their gear.

Later in the day I asked him if he was finished with the job.

"Finished?" he asked. "I've barely started on it."

It took him three days to get the last of the squatters into the barracks and to confiscate all the equipment in the shacks.

There were four dogs chewing on a dead pig in the hog lot. Some of the hogs had pneumonia, mange, and various other ailments. They had big knots on their legs where they had fallen on the concrete and they were deformed through inbreeding. The man in charge was still using the old boars for breeding even though they had three or four new pure-bred boars. In addition, the fencing was useless and the hog lot was full of parasites. I ranked the entire nine-man crew and replaced them with four Negro inmates.

One day Frank Crawford, who had transferred to Cummins earlier in the month to assume responsibility for livestock management, told me that sixty-four of the hogs were dead or frozen to the ground alive. Others were down under the water to keep from freezing to death—and they were dying like flies.

While the men were inside cooking up a storm, the hogs were out dying because the inmates didn't get them into the shed and didn't put any hay down.

Most of the problems I inherited with Cummins were solvable, but there was one that seemed to defy solutions. Fantastic as it may seem, I was unable to find out precisely how many inmates were supposed to be at the prison.

On January 10, I sent a memo to the records supervisor, B.F. Culp, asking him how many inmates were committed to Cummins. He replied at the bottom of my memo that as of January 9, the total population was 1,318, and 35 were legally off the farm. He also noted that although there were supposedly 15 inmates in the hospital he could find only 12.

How Many Prisoners?

Culp also gave a more detailed breakdown of the population, with separate totals for separate categories. I added up his figures and got a different total. Culp tried again and came up with another estimate. Meanwhile I got the yard men to start counting prisoners. They all came up with different totals.

On January 12, I posted a memo proposing a contest among all inmates and staff to determine how many prisoners should be at Cummins. Any inmate who could come up with the correct answers to the questions, and could prove it, was to be given one week meritorious furlough, and any staff member who won would be given a week off. I gave all the figures submitted by the records office and the yard men as clues.

At the same time, I told Culp that if he didn't come up with an accurate count by January 15, I would expect his resignation.

There were lots of entries submitted in the contest but they were guesses, about as accurate as Culp's figures.

One evening after dinner my assistant, J.R. Price, got all the inmate folders out of the record drawer and set them on a desk in the yard. The inmates in each barracks lined up, and Price, who was standing behind the desk, checked each inmate's file against the name and information in the folder and the picture. Price found some inmates had two folders, each with a different spelling of their names. There were brothers who shared a single folder, and some inmates without folders. It was a chaotic mess, but Price kept at it until 3 A.M.

He finally determined that we had 1,287 inmates actually committed to Cummins. Now we had the total, but the records supervisor had resigned, becoming the sixth employee to quit or be fired since I had taken over at Cummins.

The question of how many inmates were *supposed* to be at Cummins remained unanswered, however, although as a by-product of this investigation, we learned that one of the female prisoners committed to the Women's Reformatory was actually living as a free person in El Dorado. An even more interesting piece of information was the startling fact that of those who had escaped from the prison over the last half-century, some 213 prisoners had never been heard of again.

The Four and One-Half Pound Menace

The Women's Reformatory, which forms part of Cummins State Prison Farm, is about fifty yards behind the superintendent's house and is surrounded by a high wire fence. The reformatory itself is nestled among dense hedges, its thin grass kept "mowed" by the Negro women inmates who sit cross-legged on the lawn snipping off the blades of grass with their fingernails, as they were not allowed clippers or scissors. Because of this, the women's hands were gnarled and their fingernails gone. They are scarred for life, but this was a typical work program for the Negro women, who were considered too dumb for anything else.

The women had been used in the past as slaves—and worse. There was a buzzer in the master bedroom of the superintendent's house, which a previous superintendent had ordered put in so he could summon his favored doxie from the Women's Reformatory while his wife was off visiting.

Female prisoners were even transported from the county jail to the prison in the same wagon as the men and were forced to have sexual intercourse with them if they wanted to survive the trip.

The Women's Reformatory was generally overlooked by casual visitors to Cummins, and it was undoubtedly the least discussed of the three adult penal institutions in the state.

But after a visit to the reformatory, penologist Austin MacCormick told the Penitentiary Study Commission: "If there is a more neglected institution for women in the United States, I would not know where to look for it."

The Four and One-Half Pound Menace 171

Mrs. Clay Smith quit as head matron when her husband left his Cummins job, and I sent Bea Crawford to the reformatory, which then housed fifteen whites and twenty-five Negroes. The majority of the Negro women were serving sentences for homicide and many of the white women had been sentenced for habitual alcoholism, which is a crime in Arkansas and draws an indefinite sentence, to be determined by the superintendent.

Bea reported to me that she found the women were nearly freezing to death from the cold air, sleet, and rain pouring through large cracks and holes in the walls.

The rules of the Women's Reformatory were mimeographed and hung on the wall. (See pp. 172 and 173.) They were impossibly restrictive. The women were not allowed to look at or talk to men. They could not lie on their beds or talk with other inmates. They could not smoke during the day, and they could not exercise.

There was total segregation of Negroes and whites: each group had its own dormitory or barracks, but only the white women had TV and their own dining room. The Negroes ate the scraps left over from the white women's table. The visiting rooms were segregated, and the Negroes even wore different clothing than the white women.

The Negro women, of course, had the worst of everything. They washed personal laundry for the matrons in a tub with a scrub board, even in winter, and even though there was a laundry at Cummins. A former matron had had her pedicure done by the inmates, using one of the cooking pots to soak her feet.

The women prisoners were required to make clothing for the families of matrons and wardens, in addition to making all the clothing for the male prisoners. All this cost the state $73.45 a day for everyone and everything, including salaries, food, tobacco, and other operating expenses.

Several women told Bea they had been beaten with leather straps as recently as a month previously. She heard of a woman who had died in her bed after being told by a doctor that all she needed was "more work," and a pregnant woman who went into labor in solitary confinement in a small cell behind the reformatory.

Women sentenced to the hole were fed only bread and

Accomplices to the Crime

ARKANSAS STATE PENITENTIARY
WOMEN'S REFORMATORY
RULES AND REGULATIONS

THERE WILL BE NO SITTING ON THE FLOORS

THERE IS TO BE NO BORROWING, LENDING, OR EXCHANGING OF CLOTHING AND PERSONAL ARTICLES WITHOUT PERMISSION FROM THE OFFICE.

THERE IS TO BE NO SMOKING IN YOUR BED. SIT IN YOUR CHAIR.

HAIR WASHING IS TO BE CONFINED TO FRIDAYS, SATURDAYS, AND SUNDAYS, UNLESS YOU HAVE SPECIAL PERMISSION.

ALL READING AND WRITING MATERIAL WILL BE LEFT IN THE DORMITORY OR AT YOUR BR UNTIL YOU ARE OFF DUTY.

ALL TWEEZERS, GLASSES, ECT. ARE TO BE TURNED IN BEFORE 9:00 P.M.

ALL STREET CLOTHES ARE TO BE TURNED IN BEFORE 9:00 P.M. SUNDAY

THE SEWING WILL BE LIMITED TO ARTICLES FOR YOUR OWN USE. HOME SEWING WILL NOT BE PERMITTED OR SENT OUT.

THERE IS TO BE NO EATING IN THE DORMITORY AFTER 9:00 P.M.

IF YOU ARE ON A DIET, STAY ON IT. YOU ARE NOT TO BE EATING BETWEEN MEALS, IT IS EXTRA WORK ON THE KITCHEN GIRLS TO FIX YOUR DIET PLATES.

YOU ARE TO BE OUT OF YOUR BEDS DURING WORKING HOURS, WHETHER YOU ARE WORKING OR NOT.

YOU ARE NOT TO BE SQUEEZING OR MASHING PIMPLES, OR BUMPS ON EACH OTHERS FACES OR ANY OTHER PART OF THE BODY. THERE IS TOO MUCH DANGER OF INFECTION.

THERE WILL BE NO BED CHANGING. ONLY WHEN TOLD BY THE MATRON

THERE IS TO BE NO MASSAGES OR CHIROPRACTIC TREATMENTS DONE IN THE DORMITORY. THERE IS TOO MUCH DANGER OF INFECTION OR INJURY.

THERE IS NOT TO BE TWO GIRLS FROM ANY STATION IN THE BATHROOM AT A TIME. ONLY IN TIME OF AN EMERGENCY. AND NOT OVER FIVE MINUTES. SHOWERS ARE TO BE LIMITED TO 12 MINUTES ONLY.

THERE IS TO BE NO GANGING UP AT ONE BED. VISITS TO A BED WILL BE FIVE MINUTES ONLY.. THIS IS ALSO FOR THE TRUSTIES.

THERE WILL NOT BE MORE THAN TWO GIRLS GANGING UP IN THE BUILDING.

YOU ARE TO USE ASH TRAYS AT ALL TIME WHEN SMOKING. EVERYONE IS TO IRON THEIR OWN CLOTHES. THERE WILL BE NO IRONING DURING WORKING HOURS. YOU IRON BEFORE OR AFTER WORK.

THERE WILL BE NO TALKING IN FRONT OF THE T.V.

The Four and One-Half Pound Menace

WHEN WARNING LIGHTS ARE TURNED OFF AT NIGHT AT FIVE MINUTES TILL NINE, YOU TO GO TO YOUR BED OR TAKE YOUR CHAIR AND GO WATCH T. V.

THERE IS TO BE NO LOUD TALKING, LAUGHING, OR SCREAMING IN THE DORMITORY.

WHEN YOU GO INTO THE DINING ROOM AFTER WORK HOURS YOU ARE TO WEAR SHOES AND BUTTON UP UNIFORM.

THERE IS TO BE NO FEET PROPPING ON THE FURNITURE.

WHEN YOU GET UP IN THE MORNING, OF COURSE YOU MAKE YOUR BED. THEN BE SURE YOU PUT ALL YOUR THINGS THAT YOU HAVE ON THE FLOOR AND UNDER YOUR BED ON TOP OF YOUR BED. YOU ARE NOT TO DEPEND ON SOMEONE ELSE TO DO THIS FOR YOU.

YOU ARE RESPONSIBLE FOR KEEPING UP WITH YOUR OWN CLOTHES. PUT THEM IN THEIR DIRTY CLOTHES BOXES, AND BY ALL MEANS STOP LEAVING THEM IN THE BATHROOM FOR SOMEONE ELSE TO PICK UP.

IF YOU HAVE A RADIO, YOU MUST PLAY IT SOFTLY IF YOU WANT TO KEEP IT.

WHEN A WOMAN WANTS A CONFERENCE WITH THE MATRON PERTAINING TO PERSONAL AFFAIRS, SHE WILL HAVE TO DROP A NOTE IN THE MAIL BOX, SHE WILL BE CALLED BY A MATRON WHEN SHE WANTS TO CONVERSE WITH HER.

AT ANY TIME YOU WANT TO GO TO THE OFFICE YOU MUST BE CLEARED WITH A TRUSTY.

AT ANY TIME YOU ARE IN THE OFFICE AND THE TELEPHONE RINGS, YOU ARE TO STEP OUT AND SHOW RESPECT FOR THE MATRON, SHE WILL CALL YOU WHEN THE CALL IS FINISHED.

YOU KNOW WHEN THE MAIL GOES OUT, IN CASE YOU DON'T, IT IS MONDAY AND SAT. EVENINGS. THERE WILL BE NO MAILING OF ANY LETTERS EXCEPT AT THE REGULAR TIME. SO IF YOU WANT YOUR MAIL TO GO OUT SEE THAT IT IS IN THE MAIL BOX BEFORE SEVEN O'CLOCK IN THE MORNINGS ON REGULAR MAIL DAYS.

THERE IS TO BE ABSOLUTELY NO ONE IN THE BATH ROOM WHEN THE KITCHEN GIRLS GO FOR SHOWERS IN THE EVENING. IN CASE OF EMERGENCY BE SURE TO CHECK WITH THE TRUSTY BEFORE GOING.

NO GIRL WILL GO TO ANOTHER GIRLS BED AT ANY TIME TO GET HER UP IN THE MORNING. THAT IS THE JOB OF THE TRUSTY ON DUTY.

THERE WILL BE NO EXCEPTIONS, YOU ARE TO GET YOUR SLEEPING CLOTHES ON BEFORE SIX O'CLOCK. THIS YOU MUST REMEMBER TO DO.

THE TALKING FROM BED TO BED MUST BE STOPPED. IF YOU WISH TO VISIT, GO TO THE TABLES AND DON'T CARRY ON YOUR CONVERSATION IN THE AISLE. THE TRUSTY ON DUTY IS EXPECTED TO SEE THIS ORDER IS CARRIED OUT.

THESE RULES WILL BE ENFORCED. THE TRUSTY THAT IS ON DUTY IS EXPECTED TO SEE THAT THESE RULES AND REGULATIONS ARE CARRIED OUT, WITH NO EXCEPTIONS. THE WOMAN THAT BREAKS ANY OF THESE RULES WILL BE TAKEN TO THE OFFICE. COURT WILL BE HELD BY THE MATRONS, AND THE GIRL OR GIRLS WILL BE PUNISHED.

Mrs V. Smith
MRS. V. SMITH, SUPERVISOR

Accomplices to the Crime

water and for their toilet needs had just a tin can. They could be placed in isolation for infractions of the rules, such as talking back to the head matron.

When Bea first went into the women's quarters, the inmates sat or stood like zombies, doing nothing but nod or shake their heads in answer to questions. They had been told that I was going to take away one of the few privileges they had, that of wearing freeworld clothes on Sunday.

As soon as Bea took charge of the Women's Reformatory, she began cleaning the place up and having the holes in the walls patched. She allowed the Negro women to make curtains for their dormitory and found reading lamps for them; there had been only five light bulbs in their whole barracks. She assigned Negroes to the kitchen and integrated the dining hall. She permitted all the women to have coffee breaks, and she moved the TV so that all the women could see it. She also allowed all the women to talk with one another.

Frank Crawford was the first man ever to eat a meal in the Women's Reformatory. I became the second when I visited it shortly afterward.

On January 12 we invited the press to attend open house at Cummins. Tucker Steinmetz, who was one of the first reporters to visit the Women's Reformatory, interviewed several of the inmates.

"It was a miracle and how do you describe a miracle?" a white woman told him, when asked what she thought of the changes. After a few seconds' thought, she added, "I think the improvements are here because Mrs. Crawford cares about what happens to us and I think Mr. Murton cares, too."

An elderly woman sitting by her bed spoke of the changes made since Bea's arrival. "We was so glad, we cried. That's what we did. We just cried."

"Before Mrs. Crawford came we didn't have sheets on our beds like the white girls did," said another Negro inmate. "We just got old rags and stuff like that."

Some of the mail found in a box had been postmarked six months earlier and never given out. One of the women said that she had been getting letters from her son asking why she didn't write to him. "I had been writing to him twice a week but the letters weren't being mailed," she said.

The Four and One-Half Pound Menace 175

It seemed as though Bea had, indeed, wrought a miracle. There were curtains in the freshly painted barracks. Everything was neat and clean and airy. Most important of all, the women smiled, and even laughed.

Then in mid-January, when we had an inmate dance at Tucker, I invited the women from the reformatory to attend. In the days preceding the dance, they were like schoolgirls preparing themselves and their clothes for the occasion.

Nabors and Rhodes, accompanied by the Crawfords, drove them from Cummins to Tucker in the bus and we could hear them singing and laughing as they arrived. This was the first time in the history of the Arkansas State Penitentiary that the female prisoners had been allowed to dance.

The evening started at eight and was great fun for everyone—except me: most of the thirty-one women from Cummins insisted on dancing with me. I tried my best, and one girl told me I was her first dancing partner in eight years, so judged by such standards I suppose I didn't do too badly.

Some days later I told George Douthit of the *Arkansas Democrat* about the dance in an interview. There was an immediate reaction to his article—most of it bad.

Mail started to pour in. The letter on p. 176, which was postmarked Hot Springs, was typical.

The reaction of the immediate community, and the whole state, was anger. I had committed three offenses: I had let dances occur at the prison, I had let prisoners dance, and I had allowed Negroes to dance with whites.

Although the governor's office was concerned over the publicity given the dances, the new penitentiary board members endorsed them at a meeting on January 25. This was the first time I had met the new board and they seemed to be young (average age 43), progressive, and conscientious.

The chairman was John Haley; the other board members were Marshall N. Rush, a farmer from Pine Bluff; W.L. Currie, a farmer and vocational-school teacher and the first Negro to serve on the board; Dr. Payton W. Kolb, a Little Rock psychiatrist and professor at the University of Arkansas Medical Center, and a deacon of the Baptist Church;

Well Mr Murton.

By what we see in the paper seems like you are all having a fine time at the Tucker Farm. I did not know when a person was sen t to prison he went there for a good time . if he commeted a crim he was to pay for it by being in confinement you are letting them dance and have fun leading u to no telling what.

Fine thing for a white women and a white girl dance with a stinking NEGGIR . what on earth is the world coming to I am glad that I have seen the only good times on this earch as I am now 75 years of age but I am a loo % white man and can not stand the stink of a NEGGIR. some time there will be a time when the white race will be Mollatos we will have no pure white blood .

       From a white man
       to a bunch of fools.

The Four and One-Half Pound Menace 177

and William Pierce Lytle, a Presbyterian minister and professor at the College of the Ozarks—whom I had known for almost fifteen years, since the day he married Margaret and me in New Mexico. Bill expressed his empathy, concern and support of me in a letter to us on February 21.

I convinced the board to have a look at the next dance, scheduled for Valentine's Day. That was prayer meeting night, though, and Dr. Kolb wouldn't go along with it, so we scheduled the dance for the following Saturday.

This controversy over dancing was overshadowed very quickly by a problem at the Women's Reformatory.

Bea Crawford told me that Ann Shappy, one of the women inmates, had just returned from Little Rock, where she had given birth to a baby boy. She had been kept in the hospital for two weeks but she had not been allowed to see her baby at all. She was distraught; she wanted to know what was going to happen.

Mrs. Shappy, who was thirty-eight years old, had arrived pregnant at Cummins in November from a northwest Arkansas county to serve a fifteen-year sentence on a morals charge: she allegedly aided in the rape of one of her daughters. She was half dead from a kidney ailment and was sent to the infirmary at the Little Rock State Hospital, then moved to the University Medical Center across the street when it was time to have her baby.

The baby's father was an inmate at Oklahoma State Penitentiary and Mrs. Shappy had seven other children, all girls, by another father.

I called the state hospital and asked why Mrs. Shappy had not been allowed to see her baby. The only answer I could get was that she was a convict. I went into the question with the medical center, and they didn't know why either. So I asked what the status of the baby was at the present time and was told that the welfare department was going to place it for adoption that afternoon. I checked with the mother and found she had not signed any papers. Even in Arkansas you have to go through a hearing to take a baby away from its mother, convict or not.

I went to the Women's Reformatory and found Mrs. Shappy on her bed in a state of semi-shock and depression.

"Do you want your baby?" I asked her.

"Yes," she said.

I knew that Mrs. Shappy was in prison on a serious morals charge but I also knew that she had a right to her baby unless and until a court decided otherwise. I was confronted with a problem that I would have preferred to face much later, when I had the prison settled down. But the time to deal with problems is when they arise. The woman had had her baby, and the problem existed right then.

My most basic concept of reform was at stake: that inmates have to be treated with dignity and as human beings if they are to have instilled in them some concept of human dignity, theirs and others'.

There is no way of instilling that concept in a mother more quickly than letting her have her baby. If Mrs. Shappy had been a Girl Scout or even a model prisoner, the problem would have been easier to handle, but my decision would still have been the same: she was entitled to her baby.

The other women were standing around quietly and expectantly, watching us, waiting for my decision. I went around and asked them what they thought about having a baby in the dormitory. They all thought it was great.

"Get your hat and let's go get your baby," I said to Mrs. Shappy.

She looked up at me with disbelief in her eyes, then a big smile of joy came over her face. Simultaneously, there was a shout of approval from the other women and a burst of applause.

Ruby Nichols rushed up and gave me a hearty hug and a resounding kiss on the cheek. There were tears and laughter in the dormitory as Mrs. Shappy and I packed some blankets and headed out in my car for the State Hospital with Bea Crawford.

So we took away little Woody Dwayne. He was a premature baby, and weighed only three-and-a-half pounds then, which is why the hospital kept him two weeks. En route to Cummins I stopped at a store and bought a case of Similac. By the time we got back to the farm, the other women had made little gowns, jackets, and diapers. One of the trusties had given up her bed and stretched a sheet across the corner of the room to create a nursery.

Woody Dwayne was enthusiastically welcomed and proved to be the greatest morale booster I've ever seen in any institution. Women are by nature more interested in babies than men are, and since most of these women were mothers, the baby gave them something to care for and focus their attention on.

The male inmates made little toys, a dresser, and a high chair, and one of the matrons donated a crib.

An open press policy, however, can work two ways. A newspaper man drifted into the Women's Reformatory one day early in February and said, "Hey! There's a baby here."

He took a picture, which was published with a very good but controversial article. As a result of the article, pressure was brought on the welfare department to come down and take the baby away. They sent two caseworkers to "solve" Mrs. Shappy's problems—"solve" meaning taking her baby away from her. They wanted to put Woody in a foster home for six to eight months and then put him up for adoption permanently. By their standards, Mrs. Shappy was incompetent, since not only was she a convict but four of her other seven children had been wards of the welfare department.

The welfare department assumed that there could be no change in human behavior, and the fact that both the doctor and I testified that Mrs. Shappy was functioning actively and legitimately as a mother in that setting was regarded as immaterial.

The caseworkers talked to Bea and the baby's mother for several hours, and then came back and talked to me. We had a little problem of communication, but they left to try and find a foster home; while I was to talk to the mother and see if we couldn't arrange a placement.

I wanted Woody in a foster home where he could be brought back to visit the mother occasionally, but they opposed this. Finally I negotiated a foster-home agreement between the mother and Bea Crawford, which was duly recorded. We had a crib set up in Bea's house and completed the transfer of the baby to her. I notified the front gate that if welfare department people came to the prison, the guards were to phone the reformatory and the baby would be taken over and put in Bea's house. This was all legal. The woman was the natural mother and she had the right to dispose of her child as she saw fit.

Then Mrs. Shappy had to go to the state hospital for treatment of her kidney ailment, and the baby was scheduled for a routine checkup. The welfare department had arranged to take the baby from Mrs. Shappy as soon as she arrived at the hospital. We anticipated this move, however, and did not allow the baby off the farm, thus forcing the welfare people to try another tactic. Dr. Barron performed the examination at the reformatory.

The board of welfare ordered the welfare commissioner to take whatever means he deemed necessary, including getting a court order, to take the baby off the prison grounds, which they claimed was unfit for human habitation. In their view, the prison was fit for convicts but not for free people.

The welfare commissioner was ordered to go to Cummins and take the baby away from Bea Crawford. And Bea Crawford had been ordered by me not to give him up. I issued a press release suggesting that if it was inappropriate for this six-week-old baby to live on the freeline, where there were no inmates, perhaps they should bring a bus to pick up all the other kids, because there were twenty-five other children living on the freeline. I didn't pose it as a threat, I merely tried to introduce logic into the controversy. If they were going to take one child, they might as well take all.

I also pointed out that literature on raising children is full of evidence that the first few months of an infant's life are critical and that unless a mother is mentally incapacitated, the child is probably better off with her than anyone else.

For a while, this infant—four-and-a-half pounds by then—seemed to have the entire officialdom of Arkansas in a turmoil. The governor's office was in a flap over some of the adverse reaction in the press from the electorate. They ignored the favorable reaction. Bob Scott insisted that we remove the baby.

The board of corrections vacillated. In the first of two meetings about Woody's future, the board tabled the discussion and told me that I could handle the matter as I saw fit. In a secret meeting the following day, which I was not allowed to attend, they reversed their stand and decided the baby would have to leave the farm. I learned of that decision from the newspapers.

The welfare board also met in secret session and de-

The Four and One-Half Pound Menace

livered an ultimatum to the welfare commissioner. If he did not go down and remove the baby from the prison grounds they were going to fire him for nonfeasance.

When I spoke with Mrs. Shappy about the problem, she said, "I'm not going to give up my baby no matter what, unless maybe it's going to get you fired, Mr. Murton."

"It's your decision," I told her. "But keep in mind that there's no assurance I won't be fired—even if you do give up the baby."

On February 29, I was in California attending a criminology conference. I telephoned Barbara Peterson, my secretary, on other business—and she told me that Woody Dwayne had been removed from the farm. The mother was upset, and apparently Bea Crawford had raised a lot of hell. The two women who came from the welfare department to get the baby were heartless and unbending.[1]

Mrs. Shappy had not reached her decision quickly nor without considerable thought. This was her first son; she had overcome the initial trauma of being denied the right to see him; her mental health had greatly improved; and for the first time since commitment to prison, she had hope. She had her baby with her and knew that I would not let him be removed as long as I was superintendent.

And that was the problem. She knew from press accounts that the prison board, the welfare board, and Bob Scott had ordered the baby taken from the prison grounds and that I could not long resist this pressure—and remain superintendent.

She pondered the changes that had been brought about under our administration and considered the probability of the Women's Reformatory's reverting to its former condition, after my removal. She was also aware that if she surrendered Woody Dwayne at this time she had the assurances of the welfare department that she would never see him again.

Yet this woman, deemed unfit as a mother and as an immoral person by the welfare department, chose to sacrifice her son and her feelings in an unselfish, albeit futile, effort to secure the welfare of her fellow inmates.

---

[1] They refused, incidentally, to go to the Women's Reformatory. The baby had to be brought up to the main institution. They were afraid to go and get the baby themselves.

Arkansas' "Model Prison System"

Early in January Dr. Edwin Barron, the prison physician, told me that after studying the prison death certificates through 1964, he felt there was not only a remarkably high death rate but an unusual number of young men listed as victims of organic heart disease.

Between January 4 and 8, 1959, for example, six inmates were shown as having died of "heart disease." Dr. Barron found that some other death certificates failed to list the cause of death at all, and many had the signature of the former prison physician typed in but not signed.

Dr. Barron had also talked with a Negro inmate, Reuben Johnson, who told him that he had helped bury three murdered inmates, one of whom, Jake Jackson, was listed on the records as an escapee.

Old Reuben had been in Arkansas prisons on and off for thirty-one of his fifty-eight years, ever since he was convicted in 1937 of slaying his brother. Reuben said he had seen Jake Jackson killed about 11 P.M. on Christmas Eve, 1947.

He claimed he had been working with Jake in the garage that night when the yard man came in and told him, "Captain Tom wants to see you over at the building, Jake."

Reuben said Jake and the yard man went just outside the garage and met two wardens, who asked Jake for his share of money from the sale of some scrap iron. Jake said he had lost the money gambling.

According to Reuben, the warden struck out at Jake with an old angle crowbar, Jake ducked, the bar hit the wall making a dent in the wood and Jake ran back to the shop with the warden behind him. When Jake was almost at the door of the garage he looked around to see if the warden was still chasing him. The warden was about fifty yards away; he shot Jake through the heart with his pistol.

Reuben rushed to Jake's side and brought him into the garage. The warden came up, looked at the dead inmate and told Reuben: "Bury him."

Reuben said he left the body on the garage floor until six o'clock Christmas morning. He removed the clothing and gave it to the laundry for other inmates. Then he made a rough wooden coffin out of planks, and with another inmate he toted the casket on a doby wagon to old Five Camp. The coffin was buried about five feet deep in a grave close to the fence behind a cotton gin, near a levee which kept the Arkansas River from flooding the area.

Reuben also said he had helped bury two other murdered convicts in the same place. He said one of the men, a fellow named Bradley, had had his head chopped off by a warden, and the third man had been bludgeoned to death with rifle butts by the trusties. Reuben swore he could pinpoint the exact location of the three graves.

Soon after this conversation with Reuben, Frank Crawford told me that while going over the farm he had seen some sunken holes by the levee. He had asked a Negro inmate what caused the holes and had been told that there were over one hundred murdered inmates buried in the field, and that was why the inmates nicknamed the area Bodiesburg.

The place Frank had noticed was where Reuben claimed to have buried the three murdered inmates.

I knew that since 1917 more than two hundred inmates were on the prison books as escapees who'd never been found, a far larger number than would be expected. It occurred to me that some of the men listed as escapees possibly had been killed at the prison and buried in unmarked graves.

A new "archeological project" was on my mind in mid-January when I was interviewed by Walter Rugaber of the *New York Times* about my takeover at Cummins. Rugaber asked if I had heard rumors of murdered inmates having been buried on the farm. I told him that I had heard, and

Accomplices to the Crime

I was convinced a number of inmates had been shot or beaten to death in the past and secretly buried on the grounds. I indicated we would begin digging for the bodies within ten days.

I had already told Bob Scott, the governor's aide for prison affairs, what I had in mind and he'd said, "Go ahead and dig them up." He agreed with me that the scandal would wake up the people of Arkansas.

Rugaber's story was published in the *New York Times* of January 28, 1968. The paragraph about my suspicions that bodies were buried on the farm drew attention from newsmen all over the world. The press began to hound me for a date when the digging would take place.

I had not set a definite time because I was then more concerned with the problems of the living than the dead. I couldn't spare the men while the good weather was holding, so I said that when the weather was unfavorable again I would send a detail out. I set it up with Claude Overton, who was the farm manager at Cummins now, that as soon as he had some men free on the line, Harold Porter would take them down and start digging.

On January 29, I had a call from Ed Rable of CBS News in Atlanta, Georgia. He was in Little Rock and wanted to come up with a camera crew and spend a week between both farms, doing a feature story.

Rable and his crew arrived around 9 or 10 A.M. and took extensive film shots in the barracks and mess hall. Then, at about 11:30, some men from Channel 11 in Little Rock unexpectedly came to the farm and asked if we were going to do any digging. I told them to check with Porter.

While I was inside the building talking with the postmaster from Little Rock, trying to straighten out the mail problems at Cummins, Overton decided the weather was so bad he couldn't get any work done on the crops. He told Porter he could release some men for digging. Porter picked up Reuben Johnson, who was in the hospital recovering from hepatitis, loaded fifteen of the Negro inmates into the bus, and drove out to Five Camp, followed by the newsmen and TV crew.

After lunch, Frank Crawford and I drove over to old Five Camp to see how the digging was progressing, and to check out a nearby area which he planned to turn into a new hog lot.

We had had seven inches of rain earlier in the month and our shoes sucked ooze noisily as we struggled through the muddy pasture. The air was thick with the sour smell of silage and manure and the promise of rain again by mid-afternoon.

The inmates were digging in the area posted as sites 1, 2, and 3. Trusty guards were sitting on the fences with their rifles and shotguns aside, rolling smokes.

Frank and I talked for about half an hour, discussing ways of draining the hog pasture, when an inmate came up to me and said, "We've struck a coffin." I automatically glanced at my watch. It was 2:20.

"Okay," I said. Crawford and I went over to look in the Number 2 hole, where newsmen were snapping pictures. One of the wardens was already in the five-foot hole supervising the crew and telling them to be careful as they chipped around the edges of the plank coffin.

They removed the lid and found the box filled with mud. Someone gave them some spoons and they started scooping mud out, a spoonful at a time. Then someone shouted they had struck boards in the Number 1 hole. A few minutes later the men in the Number 3 hole hit wood.

The newsmen were dancing all over the area getting in each other's way. I sent Porter up to get some sheets so we could lay out the bones, and I made notes and observations as the inmates set the skeletons out.

All the graves were perpendicular to the levee and in the precise locations that Reuben Johnson had described. The skull in the third grave was no bigger than a grapefruit, and it obviously had been crushed or shattered. The bones and skulls in the other graves were whole.

In the Number 2 grave I noticed that both of the lower leg bones had been severed from the thigh bone and stacked in beside the knees. It looked as though the legs had been cut off to get the man into the box. The skull was lying under the skeleton's right arm. The body in the first grave had been decapitated. I also made a note that the graves had never caved in.

Accomplices to the Crime

We laid the bones out onto the sheets, folded them into bags and numbered them, and then put them in the back of Porter's car for security.

By the time I returned to the office the switchboard was about to ring off the wall with calls from newsmen all over the United States. And Bob Scott had called several times in a panic, and wanted to send the state police down to make an investigation. Tom Eisele had called, on behalf of the governor, who was out of the state, advising that he was ordering Lynn Davis, former director of the state police, to come and render an "accurate and objective report" for the governor. Eisele said that the governor didn't believe he could get a valid report from me. So, later that evening, Davis and Scott arrived at the prison to assume leadership over the investigation.

Meanwhile, the inmates were in a furor. They had heard the news on the radio and they were cheering and slapping each other on the back. It was like New Year's Eve. Their story had finally hit the outside world.

I had my secretary immediately impound all the escape files; if the men in the graves had been murdered they would probably be listed as escapees.

Then I rushed off to appear in a panel discussion that had been arranged a month earlier by the Junior Chamber of Commerce. Senator Knox Nelson, attorney Lewis Ramsey, and Lloyd Henry were the other members of the panel, which was to meet at the Holiday Inn in Pine Bluff. I arrived wearing the same clothing I had worn at the grave site, including my holstered .38.

Don Bassett, who had gone on ahead with his wife and mine, was waiting for me. The place was packed with spectators and newsmen. I realized I still had my gun belt so I gave it to Van Winkle. I paused briefly to brush the mud from the murdered inmates' graves off my Levis before joining the panel on the stage.

As I settled down next to Lloyd Henry, I noticed Big Mose Harmon and former warden Cresswell standing back of the audience against the wall. Bassett armed himself and took a position where he would have them in sight. He later told me these men had a map sketched out with the location of the panel participants and an X where my name was. He had been afraid that I might be shot.

Arkansas' "Model Prison System"

After about an hour and a half of debate the discussion was opened for questions from the floor. Naturally everyone wanted to hear about the bodies we had dug up that afternoon. I explained in some detail the circumstances surrounding the exhumation.

Following forty minutes of questions Lloyd Henry said, "Well, things weren't really so bad."

That comment from the president of the Prosecuting Attorneys of Arkansas brought the house down.

A woman in the audience screamed, "How can you sit there and say the prison isn't really as bad as we've been led to believe when Mr. Murton told us he's just dug up three bodies of murdered inmates? You're doing the same thing they've been doing for years! Trying to cover up!"

I could have run for governor that night, with those people. The support of a few of the more enlightened citizens of Arkansas was not what I needed most at that moment, though. I needed the support of the governor's office and the penitentiary board—and I wasn't getting it. I had all the responsibility for running the prison system; I had only half the authority. The new prison board, under Haley's urging, had been looking for a commissioner, and this meant that while I was securing the beachhead at Cummins, steps were being taken to assure that I would no longer head up the prison system.

Since going to Cummins, I had never worked less than an eighteen-hour day. I was bone tired just trying to keep my head above water. One night later in January Margaret asked me why I didn't just say the hell with it and quit, since it was obvious both the governor's office and the board were now committed to inhibiting our reform efforts.

Rather than quit, I decided to try and make one last attempt to get support from the board. I wrote John Haley a personal note saying that unless the board would give me the authority I needed to run the prison, I saw no way for me to complete the job successfully. Lacking the board's support, I would resign in a few months, when they found someone else to take my place.

I hoped the letter would draw support from Haley, who was the real force behind the board. But the letter had the opposite effect.

The "Paupers' Graveyard"

The days following the digging up of the bodies at Cummins were hectic. The telephone rang constantly with queries from newsmen all over the world and calls and letters from inmates who wanted to give their information about other murders and unmarked graves. There were also men at Tucker and Cummins who sent notes to me saying they had information. I did not question them or reveal their names because I didn't want to put their lives in danger.

We checked out most of the information as it came in and there was reason to believe the bulk of it was accurate; the stories dovetailed remarkably.

Some of the callers and letter writers, like Pershing Mills of Fresno, California, received threats by mail or telephone after their stories were published. Mills said he received sixteen long-distance calls threatening his family.

For that reason, I will not identify the names of the men who gave me affidavits. I will quote from some of my personal interviews; I will make the documents available to any serious investigative group. Here are a few excerpts from affidavits:

- I can show you where a superintendent killed a man and buried him at Tucker. He beat the man until he couldn't get up, then he told him to get up and go to work. When the man couldn't do it, the superintendent shot him. I helped bury the man.

The "Paupers' Graveyard" 189

- Halfway between the old Seven Camp barn and the ditch is the grave where two colored men and a white man were buried after being killed.
- I witnessed a murder at Cummins on May 13, 1957.
- I saw six men shotgunned to death in the yard and taken out and buried in the field.
- The spinal meningitis epidemic of 1952 was a fraud. The prisoners were killed in hospital and the prison doctor wrote it up as meningitis.
- I saw an inmate killed when barbed wire was wrapped around his neck and he was dragged across a field by a horse.
- In 1943 I was chopping cotton when I saw a twenty-one-year-old inmate beaten to death.
- I saw a man shot behind the loading dock of the mess hall in March, 1964. It was claimed he was escaping, which was not true. The trusty who did the killing was given a two-week furlough.
- I saw three men beaten to death with bats.

Reuben Johnson was the real hero, because he knew from first-hand experience that men could be murdered and did not hesitate to tell it. I feared for his safety. When I heard that some of the old pecks at Cummins were threatening to kill him, I arranged for Van Winkle to take Reuben over to Tucker for safekeeping. Reuben became the only Negro not under a sentence of death at Tucker.

I received a few threatening letters myself, mostly from cranks, and we had some minor, even ridiculous harrassment. A man in Gould, Arkansas, circulated a petition to the health department requesting that the inmates and staff of Cummins Prison Farm be quarantined on the basis that the unearthing of bodies constituted a health hazard and might cause a typhoid epidemic. One writer even seriously suggested that we make a special divining rod to help locate the graves and thereby, unintentionally, broke the tension which had been building since the first spadeful of dirt was turned.

Most of the comment was not so light. I was criticized by Bob Scott of the governor's office for not letting the CID handle the digging up of the bodies. However, the procedure we followed was exactly as agreed upon initially with Major McKee. He had contended that it would be a waste of manpower to station a trooper at the prison each time we dug exploratory holes.

Although the CID came in the next day to investigate, it was apparent from the start that they were not planning to do anything but put a lid on the publicity with a whitewash investigation. Major Bill Streubing, who was in charge of the CID investigation, told the press in Little Rock before coming to Cummins that he was certain we had come upon a paupers' graveyard. He repeated his statements at Cummins and again during a press conference in the prison.

One of the state police troopers sent to investigate was Buck Hawsel, who had formerly been stationed at the penitentiary. He had been noted for his cruel treatment of prisoners, especially during interrogations, when he reportedly had handcuffed them to a chair and beaten them with a blackjack.

I met with Governor Rockefeller myself on February 1 and explained the circumstances leading up to the excavations of the grave site, as well as the events which prompted me to write the letter announcing my intention to resign. I recommended that the penitentiary board take the initiative—announce that we would relocate all the bodies in a proper cemetery, which would give us an excuse to dig them all up and stop the rumors.

The governor, Tom Eisele, and Marshall Rush, vice chairman of the board, who was also present at the meeting, agreed that this would be good strategy. At the press conference later in the day, the governor announced that all the bodies would be exhumed and "an investigation would be pushed fearlessly but in an orderly manner—and let the chips fall where they may."

He also said, "We could be on the brink of uncovering a scandal of untold proportions," and promised a full and complete report after the investigation was finished.

Within a week, however, the governor did a complete about-face. Despite the fact that I had had the concurrence of Bob Scott, his aide on prison affairs, on digging up the bodies, the governor claimed he first learned of the ex-

The "Paupers' Graveyard"

humations in the *New York Times*. He told a press conference that he had halted all further digging and had concluded that in his opinion I was not the man to head the department of corrections.

The governor was obviously reacting to pressure. He was doing what was politically expedient. I had been taken to task in both the state house of representatives and the state senate for "destroying the image of the State of Arkansas"—which would be like murdering a corpse. Virgil Fletcher, a state senator, sponsored a resolution censuring me for removing the bodies.

A packed audience in the state senate listened for an hour and forty minutes as Charles Clark, a former convict and right-wing political organizer, described the Arkansas penitentiary as "the finest atmosphere for rehabilitation of asocial inmates that has ever been developed in the world." He said he had been whipped with a strap at Cummins but he'd deserved it.

Mr. Clark, a service-station operator, member of the Minuteman political organization, and self-described "hustler," received two standing ovations. Individual senators rose to praise and thank him.

I then became a political liability to the governor because he had appointed and sponsored me. His opponents in the Democratic Party tried to make the digging a political issue, but they would not encourage an investigation.

The impaneling of the grand jury was a perfect example of how the Arkansas kinship system functions to preserve and perpetuate itself. The sheriff of Lincoln County, where Cummins was located, was the son of a former warden who had worked at the prison when inmate abuses and corruption were common. He got in touch with Circuit Court Judge Henry W. Smith, suggesting it was probably illegal to dig up bodies. Judge Smith was the uncle of Clay Smith, who had worked at the prison for years and had resigned soon after I went to Cummins. He had boarded his horses at the prison for years before this had been stopped by board action.

Judge Smith appointed the three jury commissioners, who in turn selected members of a grand jury. The grand jury was to investigate the grave digging at Cummins. Traditionally in Arkansas the commissioners pick juries to fit the case, and the foreman of this grand jury was the brother of a man who had worked at Cummins and the nephew of "Captain" Deam (see page 54). Another brother was an ex-Cummins warden who had had his house built at Gould by prison labor.

The Lincoln County Grand Jury met on February 12 in a little room on the second floor of the courthouse in Star City. In his instructions to the jury, Judge Smith asked them to determine if any laws had been violated in digging up the bodies, pointing out that Arkansas law makes it a felony to take a body from a grave, to steal or dissect it, or to act out of "mere wantonness."

The grand jury was also charged to look into the physical quarters of the superintendent, the records office, the free-line housing, and the Women's Reformatory.

The system of interviewing witnesses was interesting. The witness sat at the end of a table facing the jury but his questioner was behind him. The questions seemed to be designed to entrap rather than enlighten. During my own interrogation, on the first day of the hearings, February 13, it became clear that the jury was not interested in why the bodies were buried—only why they were dug up.

The jury subpoenaed the telephone records of both Cummins and Tucker. They wanted to find out who I'd called and whether I had tipped off the New York newspapers or any other news media in advance of the digging.

Although more than fifty witnesses were eventually subpoenaed, most of the former Arkansas prison inmates who claimed to have first-hand knowledge of murders were not asked to testify.

The deputy state medical examiner told the grand jury that he doubted that any of the three men whose skeletons had been unearthed had died violently. He said that the men had probably died of natural causes, and this seemed to satisfy the grand jury.

The grand jury also claimed to have a map, purportedly made by the U.S. Army Corps of Engineers, which showed a church and graveyard on the location of the site where the bodies had been discovered—in the face of the facts: the graves were unmarked; nothing showed there was a graveyard in the field; nor did the prison records mention any such burial ground. Local newspapers refused to give the story much credence, since they were unable to verify it, and no such map was ever produced.

I had expected support from the board, but I got none. At a regular board meeting on February 7, I asked Haley if the board had acted on my letter of intent to resign. He pulled it out of his pocket and said No. I said I would like to ask officially for permission to withdraw the letter because, although nothing had basically changed, I felt I had a commitment to the prisoners and the institution needed to be settled down before I left.

Although I didn't mention it, the real reason I wanted to withdraw the letter was that I realized that if I were to quit, the Ford Foundation might withdraw its funds, and this might be a crucial factor for the men on death row, whose cases were being investigated through a legal-aid grant. I had to stay and fight it through, but I didn't want to state this publicly—I could not count on the public's sympathy for black men who wanted justice from the judicial system.

Haley seemed taken aback that I did not intend to resign, but he said that the letter did not require board action and that I could withdraw it. He also said that he had several appointments, however, to meet with people who had applied for the job of commissioner of corrections. He had started recruiting after receiving my letter. Haley said he could not consider me for the job now because I was a transient and had no permanent roots in Arkansas.

I polled the other members of the board individually, asking for their responses to his statement. They sat like knots on a log, looking to Haley for guidance. It was obvious he was running the show.

Three days after this board meeting, we held the next dance at Tucker. The press was to cover the dance. Just before it began John Haley arrived and got Van Winkle and me to one side.

"These dances are about to blow us out of the saddle," he said. "Let's not have any pictures of whites and Negroes dancing together. It's not that I personally object to it—and I know what you're trying to do—but you don't understand

Accomplices to the Crime

the cultural habits of the South and you don't know what kind of impact such pictures will have. All you're doing is thwarting true reform."

"The hell with it," said Van Winkle, who was in charge at Tucker. "Why hide it? Let's just do it and not play the hypocrisy game with the inmates."

I realized we were going to have to make a concession to Haley, so I suggested I head off the bus that was bringing the women from the reformatory, take them over to the Big House, and have them stand by.

"We'll set aside the first thirty minutes for the newsmen to get their pictures," I said. "Then, when they leave, we can continue as scheduled."

Haley agreed to the plan. I told the desk to let me know when the women from Cummins cleared the front gate, and left instructions that the bus was to go to the Big House before coming to the auditorium.

The bus cleared the gate but the guard forgot to send it to the Big House and the women were heading directly toward the main building. I jumped into my car, and with red light flashing, headed the bus off in front of the flagpole. Nabors was driving the bus, and he followed me to the Big House.

I told the women that we were going to have to play a game and they understood. They were grateful for the chance to go to the dance and didn't want to make trouble.

The dance went off without incident. No "offensive" pictures were taken, and everyone, including Haley, seemed to have an enjoyable time. He even danced with some of the female inmates himself.

The next day at the first of two secret, and therefore illegal, board meetings in Haley's Little Rock office, the board began to tighten its control over me as superintendent of the prison. They ruled that:

1. I would no longer be allowed to undertake any basic innovations at Cummins or Tucker without prior board approval.

2. State purchasing was not to receive any purchase orders from the penitentiary until Haley had approved them.

3. We would grow cucumbers and okra again at Cum-

mins this year despite the fact that we had somewhere around four hundred inmates fewer than last year and could have made more money growing sweet potatoes.

4. Inmates at the Women's Reformatory were forbidden to attend any more dances at Tucker.

Haley had convinced the other board members that the prison was facing a crisis in administration and at his urging, the board moved to assume direct prison management under the guise of "providing leadership." The board's insistence on unilaterally developing a prison philosophy, reviewing all my actions, and depriving me of the authority to remain in control of the prison, led us to only one conclusion— we would soon have to abandon any hope of achieving true prison reform. It was apparent that we "couldn't get there from here."

The Wipe Out

Looking back, I can see a pattern to the events that came after the grey January day we had uncovered the bodies.

The random pattern of harassment was suddenly focalized, and the point of focus was me, my administration, and the inmates on my staff. There was a concerted effort to remove me from the prison system because I was making too many waves in a stagnant—and very foul—pond.

Although we had made good headway in some areas of reform, my demands for an in-depth audit of penitentiary records for the previous two years were constantly frustrated. Many people in Arkansas had made large amounts of money on the slave-labor prison system; they did not want an audit. Such an investigation would result in great embarrassment to the State of Arkansas, as well as many of its citizens who had profited from the prison system.

Even the legislature's joint auditing committee refused to pursue the obvious avenues of investigation which would have exposed prison corruption:

February 8, 1968

Mr. T. O. Murton, Superintendent
Arkansas State Penitentiary
Varner, Arkansas

Re: "Search Audit"

Dear Mr. Murton:

I just want to officially report to you that I attempted, unsuccessfully, to get the "Search Auditors"

The Wipe Out

to check into such areas as commodity contracts and livestock being sold or traded, and other areas too numerous to mention here.

In my opinion, it was definitely a "White Wash" of the former regime and a slight attempt to undermine us.

For example, they checked our personnel classification and questioned the fact that we currently employ female secretaries in warden positions and a lab technician as a pharmacist.

In a nutshell, nothing of past records, contracts or alleged transactions were investigated. Their prime concern, apparently, was what we are doing as of now.

                  Sincerely,

                  Don R. Bassett
DRB/adc   Business Manager

Citizens such as state senator Knox Nelson, who had men furloughed to do work on his farm, people in the communities near the prison who had their cotton picked by inmates, penitentiary board member Grady Wooley, whose insurance company carried a policy with the prisons which brought in $50,000 a year in premiums, legislators who had prisoners work for them in deer camps, manufacturers of farm machinery sold to the penitentiary, members of the police in the habit of picking up free meat at the prison, doctors in the medical association who went dove hunting on prison property, farmers such as Ronnie Bruton who made it a regular habit to run cattle on the prison, superintendents who permitted the murder of inmates, high-placed people and just plain citizens who knew what was going on but, like the three wise monkeys, preferred not to see, hear, or speak of evil—all of these were guilty.

Reforming the prisons in Arkansas meant shaking up the whole rotten system, from the governor to the judiciary to the Arkansas housewife.

Arkansas was not yet ready for reforms on even a minor scale, let alone a vast one, as the tenor of the newspaper editorials showed. The discovery of the graves had cast another shadow on the image of the state and a scapegoat was needed. I was the logical choice. It soon became obvious that I would be fired in the near future.

The state legislature convened in special session in February, and passed a bill establishing a department of corrections, on March 1. Now it was possible for the Rockefeller administration to move into the final phase of prison reform by appointing me commissioner. I would then be able to complete the reorganization of the prison and create the correctional system that I had come to Arkansas to build.

On March 2, the board held a secret and then an open meeting, at Cummins, which I attended. Most of the time was taken up by John Haley, and two things were apparent: I was not going to get the position of commissioner of corrections; and I would probably soon be out as superintendent of the prison. I reminded Haley that the governor had said that if I succeeded at Tucker, and a department of corrections were established, I would not be scuttled for any political expediency.

Haley said, "If you are scuttled, I assure you it will not be for political expediency."

"Well, let's include competency then," I said. "Will I be scuttled for competency?"

Haley answered, "I think that's the only question."

He went on: "In my opinion, you have demonstrated near-genius in doing what you have been able to do at Tucker. You have made drastic reforms, you have completely turned over an inmate society in a period of a year, done it more effectively than anybody else could. . . . As concerns the relationships with the inmates, as concerns with dealing with an inmate population and inmate society I cannot conceive . . . any substantial quarrel with what you have done. Insofar as your administrative capabilities are concerned with the running of a huge institution, 20,000-acre farming operation, a state institution which out of necessity must deal with other agencies and institutions and a penitentiary which a large part of the operation is operated for profit, why I think that all too often if there is a hard way of doing something and an easy way of doing something, sometimes you approach things the hard way, which is a way calculated to very

The Wipe Out

likely ruffle feathers and result in disgruntlement and this is somewhat of a problem. I am not particularly happy over some of the fiscal affairs in the institution. That's my personal opinion. When it comes to operating all of the facilities and operations of this penitentiary, very likely some man with greater administrative abilities in this area would be better suited."

On the evening of March 5, I opened the *Pine Bluff Commercial* and read: GOVERNOR ABANDONS MURTON. "Governor Rockefeller said yesterday that he never promised the job of Commissioner of Corrections to Thomas O. Murton." He added, the article went on, in a letter to members of the board of corrections:

" '. . . Not only are you under no commitment to appoint Mr. Murton to this position, but you are under no commitment to retain him in any position whatsoever in the Arkansas Prison system.'

"Rockefeller said Murton had demonstrated 'competency as a penologist' but that he is totally incapable of and insensitive to the requirements of operating in harmony with his associates in a governmental structure.

" 'The loyalty of his subordinates is impressive but his callous disregard for the problems of his equals and superiors has created a totally untenable situation.'

"The Governor took credit for initiating prison reform in the state and said it would continue 'whether Mr. Murton remains or not. No individual is indispensable.' "

I received a copy of the governor's letter on March 6, at about the same time that John Haley arrived at Cummins with Bill Leeke, Deputy Director of the South Carolina Department of Corrections. Apparently Mr. Leeke was a candidate for the job of commissioner of corrections. Haley asked me to take him on a tour of the farm.

When I returned to the office, Haley told me quite bluntly that as far as he was concerned I was out of the running for the commissioner's job, and I could not continue as superintendent of Cummins.

Obviously Haley had made up his mind.

He spoke now as if all this had been decided, but when I asked if it was the consensus of the board as a whole he said No, adding that the question would be brought up that afternoon, when the board met at Cummins. I attended this meeting for an hour and a half, while Haley attempted to construct a case against me.

The inmates at Cummins were, of course, aware of what was going on. Every five or ten minutes the desk officer got telephone calls from the inmate on the desk in the yard asking if I had been fired. When I was excluded from the board meeting, I found Ronnie Crabtree waiting by the door to tell me that the inmates had pushed their bunks up to the bars in the barracks and hung their sheets and blankets on the bars; they were all set to burn the place down if I were fired. These were the same inmates who nine weeks earlier were planning to burn the prison down in opposition to my coming to Cummins.

I went into the barracks with newsman Tucker Steinmetz to talk with the Negro inmates, who were most upset. After I quieted them down by saying I hadn't yet been fired, I went back to the board.

I tried not to alarm the board, but I had to ask them what they intended to do after they removed me. I had removed Price as associate superintendent that very day because of his incompetence and deceit and there was, in my opinion, no one available to handle the job. The board was thinking that over when Charlie Mann knocked on the door and barged in with inmate petitions from each of the barracks asking the board not to fire me. It was his second such visit; in the space of twenty minutes the inmates had managed to get the signatures of 1,084 inmates out of a total population of about 1,250. Considering that fifty of the inmates were unavailable in the Women's Reformatory and another fifty were on duty, this was a sizable response.

Haley scoffed; he threw the petition on the table, saying he didn't consider it meaningful. Obviously he did not intend to let anything steer him from his plan to fire me.

Van Winkle and Finch—the Tucker superintendent and the special services officer—asked for permission to talk with the board and were promised that at the next official meeting, to be held one week later, they would be heard.

Immediately after the open session, Haley went into Bassett's office to make a telephone call. One of the inmates dutifully put his ear to the heat duct and overheard Haley calling Bob Scott to tell him, "We didn't get as far as we planned, because of the possibility of difficulty here at the institution, so we'll have to finish this later."

I didn't approve of the inmate's methods, but I must admit I was interested in his report. It fitted my own feeling that the afternoon's charade was part of a plan between Scott and Haley to fire me on behalf of the governor.

Until I was actually fired I was responsible for running the prison. So the next morning, March 7, I put up a memo explaining that brozene would cease to be legal tender at Cummins after March 31.

I also took steps in anticipation of being fired. I had my secretary, Barbara, prepare a memo transferring all of the parolees I'd hired as officers from Cummins to Tucker.

The parolees would need that protection. My primary concern, however, was the group of inmates who had put their lives in danger to support me at Cummins. Another memo Barbara typed was entitled "Emergency Transfer," and listed twenty-three inmates who were to be transported to Tucker immediately if I were removed from duty.

I told Barbara to have the bus filled with gas and to give the keys to Nabors. In the event an officer were not available to accompany the men, I assigned Chainsaw Jack or Charlie Mann as sheriff in charge of the transfer.

It was essential to get those men out of Cummins, because without me around it would take only minutes to reshuffle them into different positions and expose them to violence.

I spent the afternoon roaming through the state-purchasing surplus warehouse at Little Rock, where I selected many useful items for transfer to the prison. I also arranged with Major Bob Goss of the National Guard for the loan of a ditch digging machine so we could dig out about fifteen miles of trenches to improve the security around Cummins.

On the way back to the prison, in the late afternoon, I was thinking how ironic it was that the board said I was unable to get along with other agencies when an officer of the National Guard was willing to stick his neck out and provide us with army equipment and an operator on an unauthorized project, just because I had asked him for it.

I tuned in on the 5:30 news broadcast and heard there would be a board meeting at Cummins at 6:30. This was typical of how I got my information—though the governor's office had criticized me because they said they got their information about the prison from the press.

I stopped the car and telephoned Tucker to tell Van Winkle and Finch to drive on to Cummins as soon as possible so they could talk with the board.

As I sped on to Cummins myself, I noticed state troopers parked beside the road. There were more law-enforcement cars cruising. The closer I got to Cummins, the more vehicles I saw. It was obvious that something unusual was in the wind.

I arrived at the prison about 7 P.M., stopped at the superintendent's quarters briefly, then headed directly for my office. Newsmen stopped me to ask where I had been and what I was doing and to tell me that the board had been in executive session about forty-five minutes. No one was with the board except Vic Urban, which seemed odd to me. The newsmen had been informed of the meeting at 4 P.M.

Van Winkle and Finch had arrived immediately before me but said they had not yet had a chance to talk with the board. I pushed my way through the newsmen, but before I got to my office Haley came out of the board meeting and accompanied me into my office.

"Tom," he said, "the board has decided to dismiss you forthwith and relieve you of your duties as superintendent effective immediately."

He handed me two letters prepared on penitentiary stationery, in separate envelopes. One letter terminated my employment and advised me that Victor Urban had been appointed acting superintendent of the Arkansas State Penitentiary.

The second asked me to clear my desk and office of personal possessions and deliver my keys to Urban immediately. I was given until noon the following day, sixteen hours from then, to vacate the premises. "Assistance in moving your family and household furnishings from the farm will be provided by Penitentiary personnel," the letter said.

The Wipe Out

Both letters were signed by John Haley.

My initial reaction to the letters was total disbelief. I was stunned and shocked, even though I had anticipated this; the fact that it had come so soon made no sense at all. The state had nothing to gain from such an action. They allowed no time for transition; they had no regular superintendent in mind. Moreover, there had been no incident which had precipitated my dismissal. They had reneged on their promise to listen to Finch and Van Winkle, as well as their promise to give me notice. And no reasons were given for my dismissal.

My first comment to Haley was, "You've got to be kidding."

"I am dead serious in this matter and this is a firm action of the board," he said.

Within the hour, I had asked for and received from the board seventy-two hours' extension on the moving time, but I was placed under house arrest until then, presumably so I could not foment disorder.

I told Barbara that I had been fired, and to institute the emergency plans.

The bus had been gassed and moved to the west end of the building, but Nabors, who was at a meeting of the trusties called by Urban, had the key in his pocket. Porter tried to get Nabors' attention but Urban spotted him and asked why Nabors was needed. Porter said it was to drive a bus to Tucker.

Urban ordered the bus stopped. I went back to the open session of the board immediately and demanded attention. I told Haley that a group of inmates who had put their lives on the line to work with me at Cummins in an effort to change the prison were on a bus waiting to go to Tucker. I had promised them that I would not leave them at Cummins because of the serious threat to their lives and welfare.

I said that Urban had canceled my order of transfer and the blood of those men would be on the hands of the board if my order was countermanded. The board said they would leave the matter up to Urban and let him decide what was best to be done.

I left the meeting sick at heart, and weak with frustration and anger.

The press then asked me to give an interview—during it, the Crawfords came in and resigned. It was a pretty solemn occasion, more of a funeral or a wake than a regular news conference. I summed up the situation as best I could and concluded that it was up to the press to keep the new administration honest, which was the best we could hope for.

I stepped out into the hall; Ronnie Crabtree was standing in the door: good old cruddy convict Crabtree, always there when you needed him. He was all shook up when he grabbed my hand and said that even though things worked out wrong, I still had his support.

Suddenly it came over me that I had really let these people down: Chainsaw Jack, Crabtree, Rhodes, Kumpe, Nabors, all of them standing in the hallway looking at me. I had not even been able to get them transferred back to Tucker.

And then the strain I had been going through got to me. I lost my composure and started to cry like a baby. Crabtree started to cry, too, and we collapsed in one another's arms in a sobbing, body-wracking embrace that seemed to last for hours. I tried to apologize for having failed him and the others and Rhodes, who had joined us, said, "No you haven't, Mr. Murton, no, you haven't. You've given us something we will never forget."

One of the last inmates I saw at Cummins was a Negro who had brought us some boxes to pack our things in. As he set them down he had tears streaming down his face. He said, "I've been a slave for twenty-five years and now I'm gonna be one for the rest of my life."

At 6:50 P.M. on March 10, 1968, I loaded my four children and our two St. Bernard dogs into the van, slipped my .38 into my belt, and drove through the main gate for the last time. I waved to the inmate guard, who had replaced the freeman I had assigned as gate guard.

I left the Arkansas prison system as I had come: I had a gun in my belt; I passed an armed inmate at the gate; and I did not know what to anticipate.

Epilogue

Politics

Bodies

It was only later that we learned the extent of Winthrop Rockefeller's vindictiveness and the power he brought into play to repress the true Arkansas story.

Ralph D. Scott, a former FBI agent, and director of the Arkansas State Police, submitted to the governor and the state prosecutor an eighty-page report of the CID investigation of my allegation that prisoners had been murdered in the Arkansas prisons.

Colonel Scott said he had written the report because he wanted "to be personally informed on the scope and thoroughness of it." He had been appointed by Rockefeller on February 29, 1968, and he'd submitted the report March 21.

Governor Rockefeller's response to the report was: "I must admit that I'm not sitting here terribly excited." He suppressed the report as former Governor Faubus had suppressed the August, 1966, CID report of prison abuses. John Haley advised the press that while the police report was secret, he was convinced it definitely proved that inmates had been abused and murdered and that there was enough evidence "to put several people in the electric chair."

Governor Rockefeller, in a typical response, said that he would "have been happier if he [Haley] had not said it."

Finally bowing to demands of the press, Rockefeller released a condensed sixty-eight-page unsigned report on May 11, the day before the special session of the legislature was to convene. John Haley told the press that the timing of the release of the police report was an "effort by Governor Rockefeller to influence the legislature to implement prison-reform legislation."

The Associated Press said that the "conclusions" of the police were that "two of the three [skeletons] were not murdered inmates which a convict claimed to have helped bury"—by implication, *one* of the skeletons *was* that of a murdered inmate.

On June 8, at a press conference in Little Rock, I made an evaluation of the state police report concerning the grave diggings. As a police document, this report is particularly distinguished by the lack of professional and competent preparation or construction: There is no indication of what period of time the report covered, who the investigators were, who was interrogated, the purpose of the investigation, or other essential information usually included in a standard police report format.

It is readily apparent that the report has been censored. The original text of eighty pages has been pared to sixty-eight; three different typewriters were used to prepare the report.

Though the FBI had been asked to join in the investigation, there is no indication which portion of the report was prepared by the FBI.

There was no attempt made to group all the allegations pertaining to a single incident in one section.

The report is so obscure that one of the incidents is listed as "an alleged death of an unidentified victim by an unknown subject."

There was no effort made to question relatives of men known to have died at the prison, or listed as "escaped."

There were no signed statements. All testimony was summarized by the investigators and was therefore subject to prejudicial reporting.

Several statements made by the investigators are contrary to the facts. Frequently, following a charge by an informant, the investigator avoided reconciling the allegation by stating "penitentiary unable to locate jacket [file]." Yet, official records which did sustain the allegations of brutality and murder were in the inmate files and seen personally by both the *New York Times* reporter Walter

Rugaber and me *one month after* the state police commenced their investigation.

No effort was made to examine Reuben Johnson on the polygraph to determine whether or not he was telling the truth about inmates' being murdered.

The report includes a reference to the pathologist's findings—Dr. Rodney F. Carlton's—and thus perpetuates his erroneous contentions. On February 13, Dr. Carlton, who had examined the three skeletons, concluded that they "do not show any evidence of trauma or a violent death. There are fractures that are older and make one suspicious that this was due to blunt trauma to the side of the skull; however, this must be tempered with the knowledge that the fractures could have occurred several years after death due to a 'cave in' of the grave."

They could have, but they didn't. It apparently never occurred to the investigators that primary evidence is the best evidence. Dr. Carlton's statement could easily have been refuted by taking testimony from the twenty witnesses to the excavations or by looking at the film taken at the site by CBS News camera crews, or those of Channel 11 in Little Rock. This evidence would have substantiated my statement that the skeletons of two of the victims were decapitated and the skull of the third was crushed to the size of a grapefruit—and it would have shown there were no "cave ins" of the graves.

Although I had stated the obvious—that a murdered inmate most likely would be listed as an "escapee"—it was ten days after the investigation began before the investigators bothered to ask for these files. They had been available since the day of the digging, when I had impounded them in my office to prevent possible tampering.

It was almost three weeks before the investigators thought to take a statement from me as the primary-source official and the complaining witness. They never did ask me to report on the condition of the skeletons at the time of excavation.

Again, the state police ignored primary evidence by not excavating the other graves. This would have been one way to confirm or refute Reuben Johnson's contention that at least two hundred murdered inmates were buried in this pasture. Or perhaps the investigators were fearful that they

would find a corpse with a bullet hole through the skull—
which could not be explained as appropriate for an "indigent inmate buried in the prison paupers' graveyard."

On this point, in fairness to the investigators, it should
be noted that Major Bill Streubing, who was in charge of
the investigation, informed me that he had orders from the
director of the Arkansas State Police not to exhume any
bodies, and furthermore to leave the farm immediately if I
should do any more digging.

There was no summary, no conclusion reached anywhere in the document. No attempt was made to evaluate
the recorded information. No recommendations were made
that the investigation be suspended, continued or halted.
No suggestion was made that evidence of brutality and
murder should be referred to the district attorney for prosecution.

Winthrop Rockefeller termed the report a "mishmash."
He was correct. Yet it was his appointee who had prepared
the original document, and his office had released the
doctored version. Rockefeller must be assigned the responsibility.

In my opinion, the public statements made by Major
Streubing and Dr. Carlton, the quality of the investigators
assigned, the method of conducting the investigation, and
the final preparation of Colonel Scott's report, lead ultimately and inevitably to only one conclusion: the investigation was a deliberate fraud, perpetrated upon the
people of Arkansas and the inmates of the Arkansas State
Penitentiary in order to suppress the truth about atrocities
within the prison.

The Conspiracy

An Arkansas statute (46–158) grants to the prison board
the power to "prescribe the mode and extent of punishments to be inflicted on convicts for the violations of the
prison rules." Judge Henry W. Smith ruled on May 13
that the statute "is completely void of guidelines" and that
"the legislature exceeded its authority in surrendering to
the board its duties."

Consequently, he dismissed the charges of excessive

punishment and brutality against former Tucker superintendent Jim Bruton and two of his wardens, Jess Wilson and E.L. Fletcher. No one connected with the prison system ever expected them to be convicted by an Arkansas jury of their peers. But most believed the charade would proceed to a court hearing, set up to imply that the agencies of criminal justice were indeed functioning properly.

There was, and is, a conspiracy to suppress the truth in Arkansas. Other participants are the Arkansas Peace Officers, the Lincoln County Grand Jury, the legislative council, the legislature, the prosecuting attorney, the circuit court judge, the old penitentiary board, former wardens of the prison, and both inmates and freemen who have a vested interest in continuation of the punishment-for-profit philosophy of the prison system.

Winthrop Rockefeller, his office, and the new board of corrections, must now be added to this list. Prior administrations were guilty of knowing and not caring. The current administration is guilty of knowing, pledging reform—and recanting for the sake of political expediency. It shares the greater burden of responsibility for what ultimately happens to the prisoners of Arkansas. It is ironical that all the reform measures were implemented under the Faubus-appointed penitentiary board. It was only after a department of corrections was created, with Rockefeller's "progressive" board of corrections, that prison reforms were stopped.

On March 21, 1968, Bob Scott, the governor's aide on prison affairs, spoke before the Young Republicans Club in Fayetteville and vowed that "all bodies at Cummins State Prison Farm will be exhumed this year, before the election." They were not. Neither have they been exhumed since the election.

Since the grave-digging episode and the investigative conspiracy that followed, I have received more than two hundred letters from Arkansas and around the world. With two or three exceptions, they all urged us to complete reform of the prison and expressed great concern for the fate of the Arkansas prisoners (see p. 215, for example).

To have knowledge that a murder has been committed and not report it to the proper authorities for prosecution, subjects the individual to criminal sanctions, in Arkansas and most other states. By failing to press for the truth, for the prosecution of those who brutalized and murdered, the board of corrections and the governor of Arkansas in effect become co-conspirators and, as such, accessories after-the-fact to the crime of murder.

The Corruption

The prospect of an audit in depth, which would reveal the extent of prison corruption and exploitation, panicked my opponents in Arkansas.

As a minority member of the penitentiary board, John Haley had been quite courageous and vociferous in his demands for an audit. At one time, in July of 1967, he convinced the board to authorize such an audit; pressure from Grady Wooley caused the board to reverse its position.

The state auditor declared that he did not even know what a search audit was and he could find no deficiencies in accounting for prison property.

The prison study commission agreed to an audit in the *future,* but refused to conduct or suggest an audit of the past operations of the prison.

The Lincoln County Grand Jury was ordered to make an extensive inquiry into the operations of the prisons in November, 1967, and again in February, 1968. They directed their investigation toward my management and carefully avoided any inquiry which might reflect on prior administrations.

The Committee on Penal, Charitable and Correctional Institutions "studied" the prisons, but did not direct their attention toward past practices.

The Legislative Council made a routine inquiry but addressed itself only to my administration.

With the resignation of the Faubus members of the penitentiary board in January, 1968, Rockefeller was able to make his own appointments and thus control the board for the first time since he entered office; no longer would the prison board be an obstacle to his reforms.

At one time, Rockefeller had even offered to pay for an audit from his personal funds. He agreed with me—

Politics

then—that this was the only way to demonstrate to a large segment of the public the need for reform of the prisons. Now he was able to order an audit and finally expose the old prison system as it was.

But John Haley and the governor suddenly grew strangely silent on the matter and there has been no public discussion of the elusive audit since Haley became chairman of the board of corrections. Because of the secrecy clamped on the prison since my dismissal, the press, and consequently the people of Arkansas, are unaware that an audit was actually initiated during my brief tenure at Cummins.

The board entered into a contractual relationship with E.L. Gaunt and Associates of Little Rock on February 14, 1968, to conduct the long-promised audit. John Haley and I discussed the nature of the investigation. Don Bassett and I compiled information to demonstrate incidents of corruption under prior administrations. According to the auditors, we had enough evidence to "hang" a former business manager and a warden.

At the time of my dismissal, the auditors were reviewing the amazing prison contracts; tracing missing equipment and livestock; examining board member Grady Wooley's interest in an insurance company that insured nonexistent prison farm machinery; and attempting to document, to Haley's satisfaction, "discrepancies" in the inmate commissary.

I had reported in January to the board that the officer in charge of the inmate commissary had resigned unexpectedly, leaving a shortage of $2,308.97. Haley remained unimpressed by the official report of the Legislative Joint Audit Committee that sustained our contention, and required further proof. He suggested a variety of explanations for the deficiency other than embezzlement, and instructed me to investigate further. We verified the previous audit and the current inventory; the result was the same. The money had disappeared from the inmate funds during a three-month period.

The Gaunt audit of the entire prison system was finally completed by mid-summer of 1968 and delivered to John Haley. Neither the report nor the fact that it had been completed was made public until I advised the press. John Haley then admitted the audit had been made; he said it was not released in order to avoid charges that it was "politically motivated."

The board of corrections referred the audit report to prosecutor Joe Holmes, who, on December 4, 1968, said he was "considering" it but doubted if there were sufficient grounds for prosecution. Haley agreed with Holmes. The report has not been released to the press. No criminal charge has been filed. The audit has been buried, along with other relics of prison reform.

Governor Rockefeller has chosen not to ferret out the root of the problems at the prison and solve them. Instead, he has imitated the tactics of prior administrations: he has suppressed the truth, and tried to lend credence to the fiction that reform has really taken place without the agony of revolution. It can't be done. The reformist administration has become indistinguishable from the decadent one it replaced. The methods are the same. The content is the same. Only the mask of respectability remains to confuse the uninformed.

February 4, 1968

Governor Winthrop Rockefeller
STATE HOUSE
LITTLE ROCK, ARKANSAS

Dear Governor Rockefeller:

Your personal honor as a man, the honor of your family which your grandfather so carefully presented to us as a monolithic unit, and therefore, the honor of your brother, Nelson Rockefeller, for whom I would like one day to vote as president of this country, is at stake in your suspension of further disclosures in your infamous prison farm operation. No white-wash, no cover-up, no soft-pedalling at this point can stop the indignation of the American people over the Nazi methods of extermination practiced by a state agency over which you have been presiding and, therefore, can be held accountable before the world.

Any hesitation, any equivocation now about proceeding to clean up the torture chamber that is your state and you are lost. And we as Americans are lost as a decent people. You are lost as a person and as a politician—as well as your brother—because you and your brother cannot any more be separated in the public view than the Kennedy brothers can be separated. And we as Americans are lost because we will have had destroyed for us the belief in our heritage of law and justice and our ideal of democracy—no matter how badly they all seem to be challenged at this point.

The world is beginning to think of us as murderers of innocent peoples abroad as in Vietnam, the CIA-inspired carnage in Indonesia and the Dominican Republic; and now with the disclosures of your extermination camps in Arkansas, we are to be branded as murderers of our fellow citizens at home. If you do nothing else as Governor of Arkansas—and what is more important than to reaffirm the right of due process of law, see justice done, and redeem the trust a democracy places upon an elected official—you must bring to justice those who are guilty of such heinous crimes and immediately put a stop to a system of barbarity that is continuing at this moment. Otherwise, you become—if indeed, you have not already—a participant in the same crimes.

The damage has already been done to your state. No matter what further disclosures, they could not do more damage than is already done. The damage was done to your state by Arkansans and by Arkansans who represented the state in an official capacity. The damage was not done by the press which reports what has and is happening. I wouldn't drive through this State of Arkansas until you assure the world that those conditions no longer exist or could exist in a state ruled by law. I might get arrested for speeding, be thrown into a farm camp and be murdered. The only thing that can correct that image is a full disclosure of all the facts and a swift indictment of all public and private officials involved for murder.

I congratulate you that you picked a man like Thomas O. Murton to try to clean up the mess. He seems to be the only man in Arkansas at this point who has a democratic and American conscience. He also seems to be the only one who has the guts to face up to the events as they happen. I hope he does resign and carry the fight to the American people if you permit political considerations to frustrate his investigations. I have not heard any statements from you except those that might hint at your trying to scuttle the investigation. The damage is done. You can only undo it.

The greatest dilemma of this decade is the one of the citizen's trust in the veracity of his government—federal and state—and their elected officials. The Bobby Baker case which threw a shadow on the activities of Senator Kerr of Oklahoma and others, the Senator Dodd disclosures, the exposure of bribe-taking and corruption in Washington and state Capitols, all have begun to erode the base of our confidence in government itself. These events in Arkansas put a further strain on that crisis of trust. If you fail to move swiftly and dramatically, you will betray further our trust in our elected officials and the governments they preside over.

Sincerely yours,
/s/ Paton Price

Murton's Failings: Fictions and Facts

No reason for my dismissal was ever given to me by John Haley, the board of corrections, or Governor Rockefeller. In response to pressure from newsmen, Rockefeller and Haley hastily called a press conference in Little Rock the day following my termination.

This conference proved to be the longest and most caustic in Rockefeller's administration. He opened his remarks by admitting that he had been avoiding the press for over a week while Haley "solved the prison mess." Then he sat passively as Haley read a "statement of charges" alleging a variety of misdeeds committed by me. After Haley's twenty-minute recital, the newsmen attacked him and Rockefeller for the ludicrous reasons given for firing me.

For the next one and a half hours, the administration tried unsuccessfully to justify my firing. Rockefeller later observed that the news conference was "like being confronted by a group of prosecutors" and Bill Conley, his press secretary, told newsmen that he would stop future press conferences if they again became "shrill and emotional."

This press conference was but a forerunner of Governor Rockefeller's attempts to rewrite prison history. To justify my dismissal, he found it necessary to discredit my administration, blame me for all deficiencies thereafter, and claim credit for the remnants of reform which had popular acceptance.

The following "charges" are from Haley's notes to himself for his press conference, at which he discussed my actions and character and the reasons for dismissing me, and subsequent reports of this press conference in the newspapers. My replies had to come later—at a press conference a week after—since I was not invited to hear the charges.

"Insubordination"

a. *Charge:* Murton failed to provide the personnel division with a list of prison job descriptions.

Response: I prepared the material in August and Urban personally carried the descriptions to the personnel division and discussed it with them in September. By order of Governor Rockefeller, I was not allowed by the personnel division to see the descriptions for Cummins because they had been sent to Bishop nor was I allowed to even see the ones I had previously submitted for Tucker.

b. *Charge:* Murton wrote a letter to the governor in an effort to be sarcastic.

Response: When the board expressed reluctance to appoint me as commissioner of corrections as planned, I wrote the governor a personal and proper letter reminding him of his original commitment to prison reform and my appointment.[1]

c. *Charge:* Great policy changes such as hiring ex-inmates as guards, holding dances and applying for grants were made by Murton without prior approval of the board of corrections.

Response: The governor's office and/or John Haley were informed of all innovations in advance; all were done *prior* to creation of the board of corrections; there was

---

[1] "Dear Governor Rockefeller:

"This is to refresh your memory concerning a commitment made to me one year ago as one of the terms and conditions of my employment. I agreed to place my professional reputation and life on the line to bring about needed prison reforms. In return Tom Eisele, John Haley and yourself agreed to appoint me as Commissioner of Corrections at such time as the department would be created. Such appointment is essential to completion of basic reforms thus far initiated. I have fulfilled my portion of this agreement.

"I ask that you urge the Board of Corrections to fulfill your commitment to me by appointing me as Commissioner of Corrections, with the same vigor and dispatch focused upon the continuing employment of O.E. Bishop.

Sincerely yours,
Tom Murton"

nothing to be gained by discussion of reform measures with the hostile penitentiary board; and the new board was informed of all these practices and asked for approval at the first meeting which I was allowed to attend.

d. *Charge:* Murton unilaterally canceled the cucumber contract for 1968 with an anticipated loss of $100,000.

Response: Cucumbers are a critical crop; Bishop had to plant cucumbers twice the previous year because inmates sabotaged the vines; the projected inmate population for the summer of 1968 was four hundred less than the previous year, which would result in a reduced labor force; a study established that a less critical crop, sweet potatoes, could be machine harvested—requiring less manpower and producing an income which would *exceed* that anticipated for the usual cucumber crop. Furthermore, I informed John Haley in advance that I planned to cancel the cucumber contract for the stated reasons and he agreed. Subsequently, he admitted in a secret board meeting that he was reversing his position because of the strong lobby by Atkins Pickle Company.[1]

e. *Charge:* Murton refused the board's order to retain Bishop on the payroll for two months beyond January 1.

Response: The old penitentiary board requested that Bishop be retained for *one* month to help him while he was looking for a job; I appointed him for one month; the new board of corrections suggested his salary be extended one month to honor a "deal" made by Bob Scott; Bishop was appointed by me for the additional month as requested.

"Fiscal Irresponsibility"

a. *Charge:* Murton intentionally circumvented the state purchasing law.

Response: Eventually it became necessary for me to devise a method to overcome slow-playing by the purchasing department in order to run the prison; that Sidney Kegeles was eventually fired as director substantiated my claims. However, the basic problems with purchasing were never resolved and in the interim I had to make a choice between allowing an agency to stop penal reform and developing a

---

[1] "Well, rest assured it [the planting of cucumbers] is a political decision. There's no question about it." — Statement of John Haley in board meeting at Cummins Prison Farm on March 2, 1968.

method of overcoming the interference. I chose the latter.

b. *Charge:* Murton did not exercise budget supervision until ordered to do so by the board and then instructed the dieticians to order "anything short of caviar."

Response: O.E. Bishop was the penitentiary fiscal officer for six months of the fiscal year prior to my appointment; funds were expended during my brief sixty-seven-day tenure as penitentiary superintendent primarily to meet obligations he had made; I never issued orders to buy anything short or long of caviar.

c. *Charge:* Murton has no conception of how to run an institution on limited funds.

Response: I ran Tucker for ten months in spite of O.E. Bishop, Eugene P. Nunn, Sidney Kegeles, and the governor's aides. I did so well at Tucker on limited funds that I was given Cummins to run as well!

"Intention to Leave"

a. *Charge:* Murton corresponded with Alaska concerning job opportunities.

Response: As it became apparent that I was no longer being backed by Rockefeller, it was obviously only a matter of time until my employment in Arkansas would be terminated.[1]

"Penal Reform"

a. *Charge:* Murton played no part in the preparation of the 1967 prison budget.

Response: Bishop was the fiscal officer for the penitentiary at the time; Governor Rockefeller had stated that I was not a consultant to his office on prison affairs; and Haley refused to allow me to appear before the legislative committees, choosing instead to do so himself.

---

[1] "Governor Rockefeller disclosed Wednesday that he had discouraged the appointment of Thomas O. Murton to a position in Alaska before Murton was fired as superintendent of the state penitentiary. He said he had learned that Murton had applied for a job in Alaska before Murton submitted a letter of resignation to John H. Haley, chairman of the State Penitentiary Board, in January. Mr. Rockefeller said he had talked with the governor of Alaska about Murton. He said he felt that Murton was an 'extraordinary penologist' but because of other shortcomings 'I could not in good conscience recommend him.'" — *Arkansas Gazette*, Little Rock, Arkansas, March 14, 1968, p. 1.

Accomplices to the Crime

b. *Charge:* Murton played no part in preparation of the prison industries act.

Response: Haley never let me see the bill; he did not discuss it with me; and did not allow me to testify in support of it before the legislature.

c. *Charge:* Except for a few comments, Murton played no part in drafting or planning the department of corrections bill.

Response: I submitted a 108-page proposal for creation of a department of corrections to Governor Rockefeller in August of 1967. The proposal was drafted in John Haley's cabin, made available to me for this specific purpose; Haley and I discussed the model corrections code on several occasions and I made suggestions, most of which were incorporated in the final report; I wrote the "good time" provisions of the bill; but Haley ultimately chose to have Vic Urban revise the final draft in February of 1968.

d. *Charge:* Murton failed to make suggestions on the Juvenile Training School Act as requested by Haley.

Response: I provided Haley with my verbal evaluation, which he said would be sufficient; I included written recommendations for care of juveniles in my master proposal; yet, Haley ignored my suggestions because Austin MacCormick contended it was "immoral" to care for adults and juveniles within the same department and the governor's office wished to make concessions to the legislators to ensure passage of the major bills.

"Reasons for Resigning"

a. *Charge:* Murton refused to honor the board's agreement to retain Bishop on the payroll for two months.

Response: (Duplication; see earlier comment "e" under "Insubordination.") The prison vouchers show that Bishop received a full paycheck for the months of January and February of 1968.

b. *Charge:* Murton says MacCormick has archaic ideas and it is not in the best interests of the system that he be a consultant to the legislature and the commission.

Response: This is true.

c. *Charge:* Murton accused Kegeles of state purchasing of slow-playing him.

Response: Governor Rockefeller eventually fired Kegeles for slow-playing me.

"Inability to Cope with Other Individuals"

a. *Charge:* Murton never held a staff meeting at Cummins.

Response: In combat situations, formal staff meetings are customarily dispensed with while attention is focused on the exigencies of the moment. Nevertheless, I met regularly with my personal inmate and freeworld staff, and had daily meetings with individual staff members; I held a staff meeting with all the field wardens but I did avoid congregating the hostile wardens who were dedicated to effecting my removal.

b. *Charge:* Murton seems to bend over backward to inspire irritation in others.

Response: True reform is an intolerable irritant to the Establishment.

c. *Charge:* Murton claimed the board could not fire him because he and prison reform are one and the same in Arkansas.

Response: I said that the board could fire me but if they did so they could not maintain a commitment to true penal reform.

"Grave Digging"

a. *Charge:* Murton stated that people generally will never be convinced that the graves constitute a "potters' field" and that this will be a great impetus to reform.

Response: True.

"Abrasive Personality"

a. *Charge:* Murton uses descriptive adjectives such as "you can't get there from here."

Response: True. And you can't!

In the discussion that followed the formal charges, Haley listed additional deficiencies for the newsmen who rejected those given as the real reasons for my firing.

Charge: Murton bought Log Cabin Syrup, individual

packages of Krispie Krunchies, shelled pecans, shelled walnuts, and asparagus tips.

Response: Log Cabin Syrup was bought to thicken existing watery syrup; individual packages of breakfast cereal were acquired because they proved more economical due to better portion control; I never ordered shelled pecans or walnuts. No asparagus tips or asparagus were ever ordered or served in the prison to freeworld staff or inmates during my tenure, although 137 cases were bought for other state institutions by the state purchasing department.

Charge: Murton barred the state police officers from Cummins prison farm.

Response: I restricted access of peace officers in general to the prison unless they had some legitimate business on the farm; I prohibited officers from getting haircuts, shoe shines, meat, meals and other "fringe benefits" from the prison. I never denied access to the prison of any officer having business to transact nor did I at any time bar the state police. Captain Gene Donham unilaterally ordered his officers to stay away from the prison during the transition period in order to prevent their precipitating any incident.

Charge: Murton barred the school bus driver from coming on the prison grounds to pick up the school children.

Response: The bus driver, a school teacher in Gould, was disgruntled because I had refused to sell pecans to his wife, who had been buying them from the prison for years at 10 per cent of their value. Our children were abused on the bus and some were assaulted on the school grounds; he attacked me in a public forum without reason and circulated petitions to obtain my removal. He constantly sought to foment disorder in the community and on the prison grounds, so I barred him from the farm.

The Spiral of Reform

Arnold Rhodes refused to work for Urban. He returned to Tucker the night I was fired, and worked there as gate guard and sheriff until one day in May, 1968, when he got drunk during a manhunt and took off for the Missouri border. After serving some time in the hole, he was assigned to the kitchen and is now a tower guard.

Jim Nabors, who was yard man when I left Cummins, was put in the hole for thirty days, presumably because he was one of my supporters and refused to work for Urban. He was released on a furlough in December but got drunk, thus eliminating any chance this year for parole.

Gurvis Nichols made it: his sentence was commuted in August, 1968, and he was paroled. He enrolled as a student at the College of the Ozarks, where he had a 3.3 average last September. Although studying a general curriculum, he is preparing himself to be a social worker.

Reuben Johnson was paroled late in September, but because of threats made on his life by Arkansas law enforcement officers, he applied for a permit to visit Alaska. He has since worked there at a variety of jobs. He acquired an apartment and brought his wife to live with him. Reuben is somewhat handicapped in his readjustment in view of the fact that all he learned from thirty-one years in the Arkansas prison was how to drive a doby wagon, and there is not much demand for that skill. But, he is alive and outside of Arkansas, and keeping his business straight. I am his unofficial parole officer.

Ronald Crabtree was paroled, but he couldn't make it

under the Arkansas parole setup. His parole was revoked and he is now back at Tucker as yard man. He is still loyal to the principles of reform, and still believes in the Good Fairy, the Great Pumpkin, and Tom Murton.

Chainsaw Jack Bell returned to Tucker soon after I was fired and continued on as the inmate sheriff. One day, while making a routine check of the hen house, he found that Jimmy Wayne Cox, the inmate in charge, had disappeared. Chainsaw reported Cox's absence and the dogs were turned out. The inmate posse found Cox by the bayou, ostensibly fishing.

A few days later, Jack returned to the hen house to make another routine check. This time Cox was lying in wait, a trace chain in his hands. When Chainsaw stepped through the door, Cox attacked him viciously. Chainsaw pulled back, blood streaming down his face. Although nearly blinded, he managed to draw his gun and force Cox and another man into a corner while he staggered out to his truck and radioed for help.

Chainsaw was taken to the state hospital. He lost one eye; he is nearly blind in the other. He has spent the last few months attempting to adjust to a glass eye. The authorities have decided to "compensate" Jack by paroling him to a home for the blind.

Cox has never been prosecuted.

Cummins

Victor C. Urban achieved one of his goals when he was appointed superintendent of Cummins and simultaneously acting commissioner of corrections on a "temporary basis," on the evening of March 7, 1968. It was eight months before the commissionership was filled, and one year until Urban was relieved as superintendent. What took place during his tenure indicates the direction of prison reform in Arkansas.

Promising to "continue Murton's reforms," prison authorities have succeeded only in creating the myth of reform while the prison has systematically regressed. Tucker resisted reversion a little longer than Cummins, because of the momentum of reform, and Van Winkle's tenure.

At Cummins, many of the old head knockers and wheels

The Spiral of Reform

that I had removed were immediately placed back in power. The freeworld desk officers and gate guards were replaced by inmates; officers I had hired were either fired or transferred; my inmate staff was eliminated; Price was reinstated as associate superintendent; the incompetent food supervisor was promptly returned to the kitchen.

Female staff were not allowed to eat in the prison dining hall; a freeworld kitchen operation was reinstituted to provide a special meal for the male staff; the board ate only at the superintendent's quarters; and both male and female inmates were assigned as servants to the freeworld staff.

The freeworld barbershop was reopened; mail processing was turned over to the inmates; record keeping again is done by inmates; and inmates still operate eight commissaries in the barracks.

By early summer the prison population had declined by several hundred inmates from the previous summer's average. The decrease in the work force, coupled with the deliberate planting of hand-harvested crops, created a predictable crisis.

Because of a $1,500 daily loss of revenue from unharvested cucumbers, all services not directly engaged in crop production were either eliminated or curtailed.

For the first time in prison history do-pops and trusties were ordered into the fields to do the manual labor of harvesting. Urban made a deal with the trusties not to remove the brozene in return for getting the crops out. Not only has the brozene stayed, but freeworld money is prevalent again throughout the institution. Because the economy was not destroyed, it is not possible, now, to attack the inmate power structure. The result has been buying and selling of jobs, buying good time, laundry and food rackets, renewed trade in freeworld alcohol, and gambling. The latter two activities have caused several fights and deaths.

It has now been twelve years since the trusty barracks was last shaken down.

The humiliation ceremony I had abolished—shaving an inmate's head upon arrival—has been re-instituted.

Urban's recreation program for the inmates was abruptly interrupted when he ordered the gymnasium used to store hay in. The hay surplus was a result of a decreased milking herd when the prison sold some fifty cows in June to make payroll that month. Urban's plan to upgrade the dairy suffered a setback when the state police arrested his "professional dairyman" at the front gate one night, for stealing a 250-pound heifer he had in the trunk of his car. At Haley's request milk is sold to other state agencies for "public relations" and to obtain much needed revenue. Consequently milk has disappeared from the inmates' ration and for a time even the freeworld staff were not allowed milk.

The Inmate Council was never reactivated, although such was the order of the board. Cummins has not been racially integrated, although so ordered by the board and the federal court. No educational or vocational training programs have been initiated—other than "leathercraft": Urban ordered nine straps made "for souvenirs."

Dr. Barron resigned in May of 1968, but no doctor has been found to accept the appointment as prison physician. Inmates are once again dispensing medications through the reinstituted position of "convict doctor." Rebellion against this procedure precipitated a serious incident at Cummins the following October.

The press is no longer allowed open access to the prison farms but occasionally, as in mid-October, 1968, stories of problems and atrocities leak out to the public.

During the crop season the inmates at Cummins had conducted one sit-down strike after another in protest against the working conditions, the food, and the medical treatment. Then on October 14 there was an incident that again catapulted the Arkansas prison system into the international news.

On that Monday morning 120 men refused to report for work. Urban, who had been advised of the disturbance in advance, had chosen not to seek out the cause of the problem and settle the issue before it escalated into disorder. His solution was to meet peaceful protest with force. Officers who had worked the night shift Sunday were kept over on the day shift, issued shotguns with No. 8 birdshot, and stationed outside the building. Ten freemen were positioned outside the security fence surrounding the main building, and five inside. In addition, twelve inmate riflemen were armed with carbines and mounted on horses, with the usual complement of eight shotgun men, armed with twelve-gauge shotguns loaded with double-O buckshot. Riflemen were posted in three towers near the portion of the building where the sit-down occurred.

Little wonder that associate superintendent Gary Haydis could not accomplish much during a three-hour conversation with the inmates who were enclosed inside the security fence.

The inmates presented a list of grievances: the convict doctor was inhibiting medical services and charging exorbitant prices for medications that should have been provided free; the Longline rider threatened them with his gun; and the work hours were excessive. (Haley later conceded that the men were working in the fields twelve hours a day, compared with eight the previous summer; and Urban admitted they had been working from sunup to sundown.)

After the conference, Haydis promised correction of the medical problems; but the inmates wanted more than promises. Twenty-two of them agreed to go to work, but the remainder refused to go to the cucumber fields until they had evidence that issues were being resolved to their satisfaction.

Haydis pumped a shell into the chamber of his shotgun and fired from short range into the group of huddled inmates. The remainder of the guard force followed his example and cut loose from all sides. Twenty-four wounded inmates were taken to the hospital. One subsequently lost his eye.

While Urban and Haydis conducted a press conference explaining that "tear gas would have been ineffective in the open"—a statement refuted by empirical evidence—the board of corrections went into emergency session and the governor dispatched Bob Scott to Cummins to make a report for him. The FBI began an investigation to determine if the civil rights of the inmates had been violated.

Meanwhile, Urban stated, "If we had a closed prison with walls, there would have been no hesitation to shooting into the group for this kind of act. I will not permit any inmate body to take over and rule, which is what this one would probably have wanted to do." The irony is that the central issue of the inmates' protest was that the privileged inmates were running the prison.

Nearly two weeks later, the board of corrections ruled that the shooting was "altogether unnecessary to restore order." Haydis was immediately placed on special assignment and sent to California, which removed him from the probing questions of the press. Governor Rockefeller said, "perhaps that [Haydis] is the type of person we don't need in our prison system." The FBI's report went to the U.S. Attorney, who presented the evidence to a federal grand jury. The jury returned forty-six indictments against fifteen persons on July 11, 1969, at Little Rock, charging that the defendants had deprived inmates of their constitutional rights.

On an earlier occasion, in June, 1968, Haydis had scuffled with an inmate in the superintendent's office, Urban reported to newsmen (some months after); Haydis grabbed the inmate "in the neck area, but not for the purpose of stopping his breathing."

Haydis eventually resigned and returned to his former position as training officer for the California department of corrections. Urban commented, "there was no pressure and he was not asked to resign. It was nothing of that nature . . . the whole damn thing is unfortunate."

Two weeks after the shooting incident, the inmates of Cummins filed a petition against Urban in federal court in Pine Bluff, alleging mistreatment which constituted "cruel and unusual punishment" as prohibited by the U.S. Constitution. A photograph of inmates chained to a fence was smuggled out of prison and circulated to the press.

The petition stated that the inmates were chained to a fence in what they called the "dog pen" by leg irons and handcuffs for several days at a time. They also protested the lack of bedding, jackets, and toilet facilities; being forced to sleep on the ground; receiving bread twice a day for meals and no water "except from rain falling on the ground"; as well as being fired at by shotgun guards.

At least one man was treated at the prison hospital for gunshot wounds resulting from a guard shooting at him while he was confined to the dog pen. Another inmate

The Spiral of Reform

claimed to have contracted pneumonia from sleeping on the ground in the rain. But to most, the worst was the humiliation—having to squat in the open compound in sight of visitors to defecate while chained to the fence.

Urban admitted that he had initiated this new "disciplinary stockade" in June to quell a sit-down strike at the cucumber patch. He said, "the stockade is one of the punishment devices used to replace corporal punishment abolished at the prison farm last January. Its continued use was by my authority. You might compare it to shock therapy, hoping it would snap the guy out of his problems."

Governor Rockefeller stated that he had been kept advised of the chaining of inmates and endorsed such practice. He contended that under the circumstances, it was necessary.

As a result of petitions from inmates, a hearing concerning conditions at the prison was held before federal judge J. Smith Henley. On June 20, 1969, Judge Henley ruled that conditions at the isolation unit at Cummins amounted to cruel and unusual punishment; he said that prison officials "failed to discharge a federal constitutional duty to use ordinary care to protect inmates . . . from violent assaults, injuries and death at the hands of other inmates." Commissioner Sarver, ordered to report to the court within thirty days what measures he planned to take to improve prison conditions, admitted there had been seventeen stabbings at the prison in the past few months, and four deaths.

The women, who had been traditionally mistreated in Arkansas, had worse conditions now. For the first time in prison history, women were sent to work in the fields. Some of the women sewed prison garments all day—until 4 P.M.—and then worked with a hoe until sunset.

Religious services were discontinued; food service declined notably; the facilities were not improved; dancing was prohibited; and a wedding that had been planned was cancelled. A tentative agreement I had made with Tennessee prison authorities for care of our female prisoners under the Interstate Compact for Prisoners was never consummated. Conditions became so bad that one woman escaped from the institution during the summer—an unheard-of event. No woman had escaped before:[1] the women were more passive than the men, and as well, they were under constant armed guard inside the security fence surrounding the Women's Reformatory. Men had more opportunities, too, because they were occasionally sent to town, or to work in areas where escape was more easily possible.

The women inmates say they are no longer allowed to listen to the prison band. On June 29, 1969, inmates of the Women's Reformatory complained to newsmen that they are again being confined in solitary for "talking back"; are fed one spoonful of food; and bathroom facilities consist of a tin can. They report they are once again not receiving proper medical attention.

Tucker

Tucker remained a satellite institution of Cummins, and it would be unreasonable to expect that the reforms I'd initiated there would remain in force. Regression did not take place so rapidly at Tucker, however, because Robert Van Winkle was able to exercise some internal control and resist interference from Cummins as long as he was in charge.

Van Winkle was unable to hold out for long, however. He was doomed to be fired as "Murton's man." Three months after I was discharged, John Haley and Victor Urban came to the prison with the express intent of removing Van Winkle, who resigned seconds before they had the opportunity.

On the day of Van Winkle's resignation, William Barker toured the farm with him and Barker was unable to tell the difference between a pasture and a rice paddy. Barker was then appointed acting superintendent at Tucker.

Van Winkle had complained that Bassett had slow-played his requisitions, denied orders for construction materials, refused to purchase clothing for inmates, curtailed food orders unnecessarily, and even confiscated, for

---

[1] The woman inmate we found living in town when I took over Cummins had not, actually, escaped—she'd been "misplaced" in the inefficiency of moving her to medical facilities outside the prison.

The Spiral of Reform

his own use, a four-wheel-drive vehicle, which arrived at Tucker one year after it had been ordered.

Without conferring with Urban or Bassett, the board of corrections hired Bob Goss as prison business manager in September of 1968, a position which he held for seven months before being dismissed for incompetence. Goss' appointment forced Bassett out of a job. Urban then assigned him as Tucker superintendent, forcing Barker to step down to associate, thus requiring reassignment of his former assistant to Cummins as a parole officer which in turn made it necessary to transfer the former Cummins parole officer to Tucker in that same capacity. They ran out of positions. The Tucker parole officer, Jack Finch, had to accept the directorship of pardons and paroles in Little Rock—a position that had been vacant since Urban's prison appointment seven months previously.

Since Van Winkle's removal, most of the death row inmates have been removed from their job assignments; additional gun cages have been established; there has been an excessive problem with liquor; assaults, deaths, blindings, and escapes have increased significantly; the quality and quantity of food have almost returned to the previous level; and most programs have deteriorated.

Tucker did not have an adequate labor force, so "okra therapy" replaced education once more. Those inmates who had been working half time in the field and half time in the classroom were ordered full time in the fields, despite Governor Rockefeller's original promise that education would take priority over crop production. The department of education threatened to discontinue support of the school unless more students participated.

One inmate chosen as librarian by Bassett could neither read nor write. The band was not allowed to leave the farm and has been disbanded; the inmate panel was discontinued and the inmate newspaper ceased publication.

As part of the purge following my dismissal, the garage foreman, livestock foreman, farm manager, rice foreman, business manager, construction foreman, and prison chaplain have all been removed. One officer resigned after the trusty guards forced him to lie down in the field while they shot over his head. There was such staff unrest that eight employees resigned in January of 1969.

It is no longer safe for the mailman to go inside to distribute the mail until the inmates are locked up.

The religious program died with the departure of Jon Kimbrell, Tucker's "Swinging Preacher." The religious intern program I had planned with Bill Lytle never materialized. Individual religious counseling was replaced by guided tours for religious groups to gain support for the new chapel.

The new chapel, which is to house all inmate services, has been located outside the perimeter of the institution adjacent to the visitors' parking lot where its presence will prove that the inmates' needs are being met. Its location precludes its use except by the minimum custody prisoners. Hence, the remainder will be required to forgo church services, counseling, school, visiting, use of the library, or access to the parole officer.

At the ground-breaking ceremonies, Governor Rockefeller donated $5,000 to this monument to the myth of reform.

The predictable decay of the operation at Tucker is attributable to the purge of dedicated officers I had hired; emphasis on crops instead of vocational training; administrative incompetence; and re-emergence of the inmate power structure.

Arkansas Penology

On November 15, 1968, Charles Robert Sarver was appointed as commissioner of corrections. Sarver, who has a law degree, had served in West Virginia as assistant prosecuting attorney, director of motor carriers, assistant attorney general, and deputy director of corrections until he was fired for insubordination. Then he became campaign manager for West Virginia gubernatorial candidate James M. Sprouse. He was thus engaged when he was approached for the Arkansas position. The low salary, and the uncertainties of the elections in West Virginia and Arkansas, caused him to defer judgment until November 8. Rockefeller was successful; Sarver's candidate was not.

The legislature was relieved to hear Sarver proclaim: "I don't care at this point what went on before. I don't intend to waste my time pulling skeletons out of closets." Or, he might have added, out of a mule pasture.

The Spiral of Reform

State representative John Miller summarized the opinion of his colleagues when he commented that Sarver "impressed me good. He's a good salesman. I don't know what kind of man he is at running the penitentiary, but he is a good salesman."

Sarver's personnel management can be said to be, at best, interesting. On the anniversary of my dismissal, he reorganized the top prison management. Bassett was asked to resign because he lacked the experience needed for superintendent. In a perplexing statement, Sarver mused that "the worst place in the world to get experience as a superintendent is in the job of superintendent."

Barker again became acting superintendent of Tucker while Urban was relieved of the Cummins superintendency, appointed as director of pardons and paroles and promoted to deputy commissioner.

This appointment once again forced Jack Finch to scurry for a position while the board of corrections played musical chairs. He accepted the Tucker superintendency on the condition that it would become an academic and vocational school. For the third time, Barker resumed his role as associate superintendent at Tucker—until the next crisis.[1]

Administration of the Arkansas prisons under the guidance of the board of corrections has been somewhat less than productive. It took eight months to entice a commissioner to the state; 72 of 97 prison employees have left within one year; and there was a decline in total number of employees.

Prison industries, authorized in the spring of 1967 and promised by Haley in April, 1968, still do not exist. Haley also periodically has predicted the prison system would soon be awarded federal funds in varying amounts from $300,000 to $750,000 under grants pursuant to the Manpower Development Training Act or the Crime Control and Safe Streets Act of 1968. Although we had a tentative commitment for one such grant effective in July of 1968 (for which I was chastised), none of these funds has been awarded as yet.

---

[1] Because promises to make Tucker a vocational and educational unit were not kept, Jack Finch resigned in disgust on July 3, 1969. J. R. Price was named superintendent at Tucker.

Too late, Haley conceded the error of separating juvenile and adult corrections departments. In September, 1968, he urged the merging of the two departments. But two separate bureaucracies are now firmly entrenched and a merger is not likely.

In the fall of 1967, I taught the first course in criminology at Little Rock University. This was part of an effort to train potential officers for the prison or parole services. Two courses were planned for the spring; eventually the curriculum was to lead to an Associate of Arts degree. With my departure, the board failed to continue the program and there is no such training now available in Arkansas.

Board member Marshall Rush, in an official board meeting in July of 1968, protested to Haley that the prison had been unable to acquire desperately needed farm machinery for the current farming operations. He charged the state purchasing division, interestingly enough, with "slow-playing the prison."

The legislature refused to provide funds for operation of the prison. The board decided to sell cattle and milk and cut down on the number of prison staff in order to reduce expenses. Trying to be helpful, state senator Olen Hendrix suggested the prison could reduce costs by abandoning the farming operations because the inmates "wouldn't eat as much if they didn't do nothing."[1]

Governor Rockefeller was forced to call a special session for the purpose of funding prison operations. Toward the end of the two-week session, representative Ivan Rose, observing that none of the legislation was likely to pass, reminded his colleagues: "We got rid of Murton for you so give us a good vote on it."[2]

They didn't. The legislators adjourned without providing funds for operation of the prison, in spite of the enormous campaign to "improve public relations at the prison."

The 1969 "corrections conscious" legislature, as Sarver termed it, provided little more. An intermediate reformatory was authorized, but this could not be implemented until the maximum-custody facility was built. In its wisdom,

---

[1] *Arkansas Democrat*, Little Rock, Ark., November 26, 1968, p. 2.
[2] *Pine Bluff Commercial*, Pine Bluff, Ark., May 30, 1968, p. 3.

The Spiral of Reform

the legislators authorized this facility too, but did not immediately fund the proposal.

They refused to authorize employment of additional parole officers; refused to fund the probation system, authorized in 1968; revised the liberal parole law of 1968 to the former one-third-of-the-sentence requirement for parole eligibility; and passed a sterilization law.

At the prison, our classification system was abolished, and the result was incidents both inside and outside the prison, because those selected for furloughs were not screened. Faced with public criticism, the corrections administration chose to abolish the furlough system rather than find out what was wrong with it.

Similarly, when problems arose over visiting procedures, they were tightened up; when embarrassing mail was sent out of the prison, the board chose to make the mail rules harsher; when liquor control seemed impossible inside the prison, Urban authorized the freeworld staff to bring it on the farm (in violation of Arkansas' felony statutes), and even suggested that there might be some merit in authorizing drinking of alcoholic beverages by inmates as a reward for good conduct in the prison.

A frightened and incompetent prison administration, not knowing what to do, frequently chooses the easy way and does nothing. When pressure from the inmate population inevitably requires some action, such administrations invariably deal solely with the surface symptom, and do little or nothing to correct the basic problem.

When, for one brief moment in the sordid history of the Arkansas penitentiary, attention was focused by my administration on the fundamental deficiencies of that system, the proponents of the "status ante" sought to divert attention from the basic issues by attacking me. I was accused of publicity-seeking when I exposed systematized homosexuality, official corruption, subversion of criminal justice, brutality, torture, and murder of inmates.

But then, perhaps I was unduly concerned about the treatment afforded those "dirty old convicts" down in Arkansas. In March of 1969, Arkansas Commissioner of Corrections Robert Sarver testified before the United States Senate that "When I read of an exposé of homosexualities, bribings, escapes [and] political corruption in prisons, I think most knowledgable correction administrators think: 'So what else is new?'"

In Conclusion

There is no question in my mind that Governor Rockefeller was committed to prison reform during his campaign of 1966 and even after his inauguration in 1967. Initially, he seemed dedicated to clearing up the "prison mess," but the fact is that power structures can tolerate only a limited amount of integrity. There comes a time in a reform movement when the new administration discovers that its goals and objectives are radically threatened by the very reforms that have been initiated to correct the deficiencies of the former system.

Purism has no place in politics. The candidate's first thesis is that everything, including integrity, must be subordinate to his election. He claims that some reform is better than none—which would be the result if he were not elected—thus justifying the compromise of basic reform measures. The reasoning is fallacious: the compromise of *any* principle could lead ultimately to the forfeiture of all principles.

Rockefeller lacked the courage to be great. And, as a result, the prison system reverted, in essence, to the low established during the Faubus era. Arkansas could have had the most advanced correctional system in the United States. For a fleeting moment, the inmates knew the dignity of man. The memory of this experience is an important part of my legacy.

The model of reform viewed from the perspective of time can be represented as a spiral. At the low point there is a scandal which sparks a demand for drastic reform measures. The reforms are implemented. The curve of progress arcs upward toward the apex of achievement.

But the prison does not remain static. The reformer must race the clock to complete the maximum number of innovations before the apex is reached because reform consists of two facets: achievements within the dimension of time.

Just short of consolidating the gains, the reformer is removed. The process is reversed and the arc curves downward until it approaches the point of origin.

The lineal difference between the beginning point of the spiral and the new low indicates the net gain (or loss) that has been accomplished. The reformer must be willing to scale a mountain of obstacles and fall short of the pinnacle of "success" to attain the foothills of reform.

As the hiker climbs the mountain "because it is there," the reformer must seek the impossible "because it needs to be done."